Working Hours

Working Hours

An Economic Analysis

John D. Owen

Wayne State University

Lexington Books

D.C. Heath and Company
Lexington, Massachusetts
Toronto

Library of Congress Cataloging in Publication Data

Owen, John D
  Working hours.

  Bibliography: p.
  1. Hours of labor. I. Title.
HD5106.93   331.2'57   78-22287
ISBN 0-669-02740-5

Published simultaneously in Canada

Printed in the United States of America

International Standard Book Number: 0-669-02740-5

Library of Congress Catalog Card Number: 78-22287

Contents

List of Figures

List of Tables

Preface

Many observers believe that we are now ready for a change in standard hours scheduling practices. The standard workweek has shown little or no change over the past several decades. The very duration of the 40-hour standard is in sharp contrast with the earlier tradition of gradual reduction in hours. Moreover, the rapid growth of a parallel, part-time job market can also be cited as evidence that we may be due for a change in the standard schedule. This view gains support from the special appeal of the part-time market to those groups in the labor force which are growing most rapidly: women, students, and older workers.

The ferment caused by the introduction of the 4-day, 40-hour work-week by a number of firms in the early 1970s and the more recent introduction of the flexitime system in a wide variety of establishments may also be symptomatic. Finally national opinion polls showing increased dissatisfaction with work schedules, the new movement to share the work to reduce unemployment or to conserve scarce materials and energy, and the demands by some minorities (especially feminists) for a workweek that is not geared so closely to the needs of male heads of households all point to some widespread doubts about the utility of standard schedules. In fact even among those who reject the idea of a general reduction in the standard workweek, many now believe that a much wider variety of individual schedules will provide the most practical alternative.

The manuscript reflects my long-standing interest in hours of work and leisure.[1] An earlier effort, *The Price of Leisure,* was focused on the determination of hours of work in the 1900–61 period, though it did describe in some detail complementary relationships between working hours and the demand for commercial recreation. Several years ago, the National Science Foundation sponsored a study, under my direction, which considered the likely future direction of working schedules and their effects on all aspects of society.[2] After the completion of that study in early 1975, I began a more detailed investigation of working schedules, especially flexitime, part-time employment, and the standard workweek. This effort has had a much narrower focus—the economic and leisure-time aspects of work schedules. The present work reflects my attempt to synthesize this more recent research.

The text of the book is divided into two principal parts: standard schedules and leisure, and alternative work schedules and leisure. Several technical papers are presented in a third section. The text itself is written without the use of mathematics. However, the professional economist will probably wish to read the appendixes as well, since these endeavor to provide less informal support for a number of the arguments advanced in the first part of the text.

Financial assistance for this project was received from the Employment and Training Administration of the U.S. Department of Labor and from the General Electric Foundation. Helpful comments on earlier drafts of this manuscript were received from Greg Ballentine, Daniel Hamermesh, James Heckman, Janice Hedges, Jacob Mincer, A.K. Sen, Alan Sorkin, Miron Stano, and Daniel Taylor.

Notes

1. Parts of the manuscript draw upon Owen (1975, 1976*a*, 1976*b*, 1976*c*, 1977*a*, 1977*b*, 1977*c*, 1978). The larger portion was written as original material for this book.
2. See Owen, Haldi, and Vietorisz.

Part I
Standard Work Schedules
and Leisure

1 Introduction

An Overview

Social critics have come to regard Americans of working age as rushed, busy, harried. We are seen as being in a "time bind"; as having insufficient free time to pursue the good life. One reason many Americans feel pressured for time is simply that we still put in surprisingly large amounts of time at work or quasi-work activities. (Both time on the job and time spent in work about the house and in other off-the-job locales can be included under these broad headings.) A second dimension to the problem of the time bind relates to the quality of much of the time available to the individual: conditions which make it difficult for him to use his time to pursue his ends effectively, both in housework and leisure-time pursuits.

It is obvious that a higher material living standard in the United States has not brought with it a concomitant increase in free time. Per capita consumption of goods and services (deflated for price inflation) is now 2.33 times the 1940 level and has more than quintupled since the turn of the century. The gain in free time since 1900 has been much more modest, and there apparently has been relatively little gain for prime-aged adults since the 1930s and 1940s.

A good argument can be made that the busyness of the average citizen is in fact an inevitable price which we have had to pay for our high living standard: the fairly long hours of work and the large proportion of the population employed in the labor market appear to be necessary inputs in our economy if the flow of material goods and services is to be maintained (a view discussed in chapters 3 and 12).

It is somewhat less well known but nonetheless true that our high level of consumer goods and services purchases have done little to liberate American men and women from the time required for work (or quasi-work) activities outside the marketplace—what economists call household production—despite the predictions of a number of optimists. The total time spent in commuting, shopping, housework, child care, and the like has not been reduced by very much in some decades. In analyzing these data, some observers now actually argue that the higher material living standard has so complicated the life-style of the average American as to require more time for these household production activities.

The relative scarcity of free time will be treated at some length in the first part of the book. Succeeding chapters will describe this problem, analyze its constituents (the leveling off in average weekly hours, the higher proportion of women working, and the persistently high amount of time spent in commuting, housework, and other household production activities) and will consider underlying causes.

These chapters will also develop further the argument that the small growth in leisure time can be best understood as resulting from the fact that the amount of time spent at work or quasi-work activities is determined in a trade-off situation—we obtain a higher material living standard than we could otherwise by putting in long hours of work for hire and spending much of our so-called nonwork time in commuting, household chores, and the like. This may yield a package of goods and leisure time that is more attractive to the average American than a combination of shorter hours of work and a lower material living standard.

However, the scarcity of time is only one part of the difficulty which we have dubbed the time bind. The quality of time now available to the individual is regarded by some observers as not very satisfactory, especially when account is taken of the considerable increase that has occurred in the amount of consumer goods the individual can utilize per hour of his time.

It will be argued that a principal cause of the relatively poor quality of time is the maintenance of rigid schedules by employers, schools, and many other commercial and governmental institutions with which the individual must deal. Since the usefulness of an hour of time depends upon when it is available, limitations due to rigid scheduling practices can have serious effects on the productivity or quality of time (see chapter 5).

The negative impact of these scheduling practices raises a question as to whether or not they are socially desirable. A discussion (in chapter 6) considers whether rigid work scheduling practices are inevitable at present, analyzes underlying trends now tending to undermine the rationale for schedule rigidity, and arrives at a guardedly optimistic forecast of change.

The second part of the book considers the possibilities of alternative work schedules as a means of improving leisure time. In fact many millions of Americans already work at some alternative to the standard workweek. The most important of these alternatives is voluntary part-time employment, which now accounts for about one in five jobs in the country. These jobs allow more time for leisure and are often scheduled so as to fit in well with the personal requirements of employees. However, part-time work is usually poorly paid and confined to low-status jobs. Americans generally cannot move from full-time to part-time status at the same hourly wage, so that the consequent decline in their living standard is more than in proportion to the reduction in their working hours. This is not simply due to employer prejudice against part-timers (though that is said to be a contributing factor); a shift to part-time workers typically imposes real economic costs upon employers. However, under some circumstances employers do find it worthwhile to use part-time labor. (The part-time labor market is analyzed in some detail in chapters 7 and 8.)

Another major type of alternative to the standard work schedule permits the employee to vary the timing of his hours of work, without changing the total number of hours. These flexitime practices have been widely accepted in some parts of Europe. They have only recently been introduced into this country, but could revolutionize work scheduling practices here. A good argument can be made that flexible work schedules can be introduced with little or no sacrifice in productivity in many job situations where part-time work is impractical or costly. At the present time, management inertia, legal obstacles, and union opposition are slowing the pace at which the system is being adopted here. But if flexible-hours scheduling of some sort is widely accepted and a majority of employees have at least some say in the design of their individual schedules, some of the time pressures of modern living could indeed be relieved: at least if workers do not instead choose to use this freedom to adopt still more complicated life-styles, raising further time allocation problems. (These issues are discussed in chapters 9, 10, and 11.)

Finally the most obvious way to relieve time pressures is simply to reduce the standard workweek. This alternative would impose very serious economic costs but might be regarded as a reasonable choice in the years ahead, especially if advances in technology lead to substantial gains in labor productivity (work-week reduction is discussed in chapter 12).

How Much Free Time Do We Have?

Any objective discussion of the time pressures on the average American must include a consideration of the number of hours of free time that he has at his disposal. The data indicate that he has much less than is popularly supposed, especially by those convinced that there has been a "leisure revolution" in the country since the end of World War II. There is one group of people that does have an abundance of leisure—retired and semiretired workers. But a rather different picture emerges if we examine workers in their prime, say, 25 to 54 years of age.

In the first place, the workweek of the average male in this group is much longer than many believe. Though the standard workweek is at most 40 hours, and some have a 35-hour workweek, the average married American male works 45 or more hours a week, unless he is unemployed or sick.[1] The discrepancy between the standard workweek and the actual average arises because of the number on nonstandard hours. About 8 percent own their own business and another 5 percent are in agriculture. About 6 percent of all male wage and salary workers in nonagricultural industries moonlight at a second job. Of those in this group who do not moonlight, over a third of the married males are working overtime in a given week.[2]

Moreover, in addition to this commitment to market employment, the average married male must put in extra hours in commuting and household chores,

Table 1-1
Work and Leisure Patterns[a]

	Married Men Employed	Married Women Employed	Married Women Other
Paid work time	44	33	*
Household production (including commuting, house-work, child care, shopping)	22	39	55
Recreation	29	24	35
Other (including sleeping, eating, organizational activity, personal care)	73	72	78

Source: Adapted from J.P. Robinson and P.E. Converse, *66 Basic Tables of Time Budget Research Data for the U.S.,* University of Michigan, Survey Research Center, 1967, p. 11.
[a]Hours spent per week.   *Less than one hour.

ranging from helping with the shopping on Saturdays to building an extension to his house. The most recent national study of time use for which detailed data are available was carried out in 1965. Such studies are based upon much smaller samples than those used to estimate hours of paid work and are subject to a number of measurement problems. Nevertheless they provide the best available estimates. These data[3] indicate that married males put in about 22 hours per week at these household production activities, in addition to their paid work time (see table 1-1).

The time pressure on women is almost as severe. However, there is apparently more diversity in the work loads of women. The average nonemployed housewife puts in about 55 hours a week (see table 1-1). But over half of all women 20 to 64 years of age now work, and these average a total of 72 hours of work per week, including 33 hours at paid work. The data on time use cited above are based upon a national sample. But a more detailed study of a sample of Syracuse residents in 1968 shows still more diversity among women.[4] In this study, people were tracked for an entire year, so that the effect of holidays and vacations was included. Still, wives average 63 hours of work a week, and husbands 64. In the Syracuse study, the average nonemployed housewife put in a total of 57 hours a week (divided among 16 hours for activities connected with food, 11 hours for cleaning the home, 9 hours for clothes maintenance, 13 hours to child care, and 7 hours to marketing and record keeping). When these housewives are divided into subgroups, still more diversity is found. Total time spent on housework ranged from 40 hours a week for full-time housewives without children to 66 hours a week for those with seven to nine children.

Preliminary results from a still more recent study indicate that there may have been some decrease in time spent in housework since the 1960s, partly because of the smaller size of families, which reduces the time needed for housework and child care.[5]

Leisure or Consumption Time

The various national studies of time use cited above showed that much of the remaining time of the average American is spent sleeping and eating, leaving relatively little free time (see table 1-1). About half of this time is spent watching television.

On weekdays, television watching uses more leisure than all other activities (excluding sleeping and eating) combined. Given the data on total hours worked, it is perhaps not too surprising that the small remaining amount of time is largely given over to such a passive, nondemanding activity. When the worker has a full day off from paid employment, as on a weekend or holiday, television watching is not very much increased over its weekday level, allowing more time for diversified activities. Much of this time, it is true, is taken up with more ambitious household work activities, which cannot easily be done after a day's work. But it is also in these comparatively narrow time intervals that one finds much of the expensive recreational activity—from boating to skiing—described by those who claim that there has been a leisure revolution in the United States.

Notes

1. Average weekly hours of married males in nonagricultural employment were 45 in May 1977, despite less than full employment conditions. Hours were longer in agriculture than in nonagriculture. *Employment and Earnings,* June 1977.

2. *Employment and Earnings,* various issues; Brown; and *Special Labor Force Report* no. 196, 1977.

3. Robinson and Converse, national urban sample, table 1, p. 11.

4. Walker and Woods, pp. 44, 50, and 62.

5. J.P. Robinson.

2 Changes Over Time in Paid Work Time

Contrary to popular opinion, the number of hours supplied to the market by American families—at least by members in the 20–55 year age group—appears to have increased, not decreased, in the past 40 years, considerably exacerbating the problem of the time bind.[1]

One factor contributing to this startling result has been the increasing level of female labor force participation. The proportion of women working has always been high, if we include work in the home. But the past century, or century and a half, has seen a long-term upward trend in the proportion working outside the home (or family farm or business) for hire in the labor market. More recently the female labor force participation rate has risen from 31 percent in 1940 to 56 percent in 1977.[2] This upward trend has been attributed to the higher wages paid females in the market (both as a result of higher wages in general, and of the relatively higher wages earned by females as new technologies were introduced which put less stress on physical strength) as well as to noneconomic reasons. It has also been argued that females have been liberated from some of their housework by timesaving technological advances in the home. (We will return for a critical discussion of this point in chapter 4.)

However, the upward movement in female labor force participation since the 1930s or 1940s is, as noted, actually part of a much longer-term trend. A new element which has sharply exacerbated the time bind in recent decades is the seeming termination of another time trend, the downward movement in average hours worked per adult male. These hours have not changed since the end of World War II, and in fact are not any lower than they were 40 years ago.

There was a rather modest decline in measured average weekly hours. Thus average hours of nonagricultural employees went from 40.9 in 1948 to 38.5 in 1977. However, this drop appears to reflect changes in the composition of the labor force rather than a reduction in the hours of work of the individuals or groups that compose the work force. As a result of postwar trends, a larger proportion of the work force are women and students: female nonagricultural employees made up less than 29 percent of the work force in 1940 and are over 41 percent of it today; students made up 1 percent or less in 1940 and 2.5 percent after World War II, but now are over 6 percent. In the same period, the proportion of nonstudent males in the nonagricultural work force dropped to under 57 percent.[3] Because of group differences in hours worked—women average 34 hours, male students 23 hours, and nonstudent males about 43 hours per week—the declining proportion of nonstudent males in the labor force has produced a

9

statistical decline in average weekly hours. However, these compositional shifts do not necessarily reflect a real reduction in working times.

Hours of Nonstudent Males

Hours data for the majority group, men not in school, are probably the most reliable indicators of average work input, partly because this group has changed relatively little in composition, partly because the work effort of this group has been measured more carefully over the years than the input of what were once considered marginal workers. Table 2-1 shows hours of work of nonstudent men employed as wage and salary workers in nonagricultural industries. This tabulation actually shows a slight increase in hours from 1948 to 1969 (two years of relatively full employment) and a slight decline in 1969-77 resulting from persistently high unemployment. Over the whole period, there was no net change.

In 1948-75 the hours of male students, however, increased by about 4 hours per week. Those of women declined somewhat, and the difference between the weekly hours of men and women roughly doubled. However, these changes reflect changes in the composition of the women and student groups rather than any change in the hours of work of individuals. For example, there was a steady increase in the average age of male student workers in nonagricultural industries; the proportion under 18 years of age fell from 62 percent in 1947 to 38 percent in 1972 and has continued to decline since. (This decrease in very young male workers reflects the increased proportion of young people finishing high school and going on to college in more recent years.) Since older students generally

Table 2-1
Weekly Hours of Nonstudent Males Employed in
Nonagricultural Industries

Year	Unadjusted	Adjusted for Growth in Vacations and Holidays
1948	42.7	41.6
1950	42.2	41.0
1953	42.5	41.4
1956	43.0	41.8
1959	42.0	40.7
1962	43.1	41.7
1966	43.5	42.1
1969	43.5	42.0
1972	42.9	41.4
1975	42.4	40.8
1976	42.4	40.9
1977	42.8	41.3

work much longer hours than younger students—those 20-24 years of age average about 28 hours per week, while those age 14-15 average only 10 hours and those age 16-17 average about 18 hours—the increasing average age of students has produced an increase in their average hours of work. Within age categories, however, there has been no significant change in students' weekly hours of work.

Similarly the decline in hours of working women is largely the result of changes in the composition of the female labor force. Among employed women, the proportion who are married with husband present increased from 30 percent in 1940 to 56 percent in 1977. The proportion of working mothers with children under 18 years of age rose sharply to 39 percent in 1976. The rising proportion of wives, and especially of mothers, tends to reduce average hours for women, since wives and mothers generally put in fewer hours of work than other women of comparable age. On the average, employed wives work about 1.4 fewer hours a week for every child under age 15 at home.[4]

Changes in the statistical procedure used by the U.S. government have also altered the measurement of hours of women and students and helped to generate the statistical trends described above. The measurement of part-time work has been improved in the postwar period in an effort to eliminate the undercounting of part-time workers that had once been common. This has tended to reduce the average hours of women workers, many of whom are part-time. On the other hand, the decision in 1967 to exclude those ages 14 and 15 from the labor force base used to calculate average hours has increased the reported average age of the labor force somewhat and the average hours of student workers in the current population survey.

In summary, a decomposition of the measured statistical decline in average working hours does not indicate that any significant reduction in paid work actually took place in the total work force. Further, and perhaps more important, the various compositional shifts in the labor force responsible for this apparent decline in hours of work may not have yielded any net gain in leisure time. Indeed one could more reasonably interpret the increased employment of groups with extensive nonmarket work responsibilities as tending to reduce free time. Students must go to school, attend classes, and prepare assignments; the additional time many of them now spend at part-time work leaves the conscientious student, who is also employed, with very little leisure available (though some would argue that study time is more pleasant than work for pay and should not be treated as a subtraction from leisure).

Similarly the rising proportion of females who work obviously does not reflect a gain in leisure time. As we have seen, employed women have less leisure time than do employed men (the larger amounts of time they put in at housework more than offsets the gap in male-female hours schedules) and much less free time than full-time housewives (even if we treat all their housework activity as a subtraction from their leisure time). The shift from full-time housewife to employed wife which so many women have made probably yielded a decline, not an increase, in their available free time. (This interpretation gains support from a study of changes in housework over time discussed in chapter 4.)

For these reasons, the hours of work series for nonstudent men probably provides us with a better indicator of net changes over time in the leisure of the working population than could be constructed from available data on women and students. Yet this measure is still flawed in two respects. First, as an indicator of leisure time it may be biased upward, insofar as the rise in female labor force participation over the past 30 years has been accompanied by an increase in the amount of housework done by men. A comparison of a nationwide statistical study of time use in 1965 with earlier studies suggests that there have been only minor changes in this area since the 1930s.[5] However, scattered reports indicate that in the last 10 years men's contribution to household tasks may have increased more significantly.[6]

The second flaw in the series is that it is in fact biased downward as an indicator of changes in leisure over time because it omits the effects of increases in holidays and vacations. On the basis of available data on vacations and holidays, the weekly hours series can be adjusted to reflect this growth, as has been done in table 2-1. When this adjustment is made, no significant change is found in hours in the 1948-69 period, though a slight decline is observed in the next few years as unemployment levels increased.

The data on vacations and holidays may not be as accurate as are those on weekly hours.[7] But even if this estimate understates the growth of vacations and holidays by as much as one week, this would only require an additional adjustment of .8 in the hours series—hardly enough to demonstrate a downward trend.

Longer-term Trend in Hours

This recent movement (or rather lack of movement) contrasts with earlier years, when there was a true downward trend in hours. Hours of employees in the nonagricultural sector declined from 58 a week in 1901 to 42 in 1948 (see figure 2-1).

Progress toward shorter hours characterized the entire period, though it was more rapid in some decades. The 1900-14 period saw vigorous pressure to reduce hours in a number of industries. Government controls over hours during World War I, and the favorable consideration given to union demands during this period, led to further reductions. After the war, unions were greatly weakened in some industries which had earlier obtained the 8-hour day; in many of these industries hours were actually increased somewhat in the 1920s, though generally not to pre-World War I levels. However, the 1920s saw continued progress toward hours reduction in other industries; the greatest progress was made in the iron and steel and canning and preserving industries, which were nonunionized and where hours had been very long.

Hours in the 1930s followed a somewhat different pattern. There was a

Average weekly hours

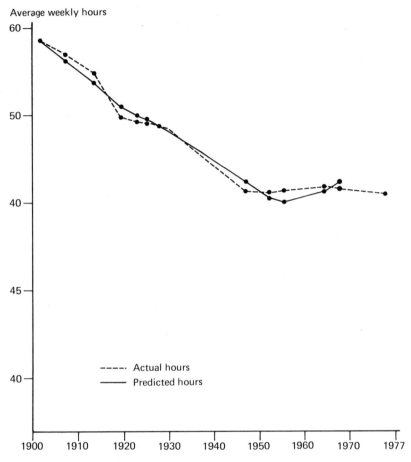

Figure 2-1. Long-term Movements in Hours of Work

virtual collapse of hours schedules from 1929 to 1934 as a result of the Great Depression. Hours recovered moderately in the late 1930s, then rose to a rather high level in the overtime economy of World War II. But when they returned to a more normal level in 1948, they simply appeared to be continuing a long-term downward trend.[8] Thus there seems to be little basis in the earlier history of hours for predicting the postwar leveling off.

Moreover, the record of the 1900-48 period appears to have been a continuation of a much longer-term trend. Data for the nineteenth century are not as good as the more recent numbers, but the trend does appear to go back to the early decades of that century when hours were very much longer than in 1900.

In this period also, overall trends for the entire industrial work force of the United States, or of England, conceal a great deal of diversity. Thus at least one writer, M.A. Bienefeld, argues (using British data) that the hours of work in a number of the more traditional crafts never were much above 10 per day, or 60 per week. even during the period of the industrial revolution. But the hours of others were much higher, often determined only by the limits of human endurance. For example, bakers (a relatively light occupation) are reported as sometimes working over 100 hours a week. In some of the new occupations created by the industrial revolution—in the new textile mills, for example—workdays of 12 to 14 or more hours were not uncommon. These new industries typically employed a work force with a high proportion of women and children, recent immigrants from the countryside, who were less bound by the traditional upper limits on hours found in other older industries or trades and less well able to bargain over hours and working conditions. More generally, one finds an important distinction in this period between the hours of the skilled and unskilled worker, with the poorly paid, unskilled workers usually putting in much longer hours. Some of the longest hours were apparently worked by those on the domestic system (the majority of the manufacturing work force in the early part of the nineteenth century), who were paid by the piece and could set their own schedules.

Though considerable dispersion in hours is found in the nineteenth century and different groups in the labor force progressed at different speeds (so that the gap between unskilled and skilled workers was narrowed), there does appear to be a definite overall tendency for hours to be reduced in the nineteenth century, as in the first half of the twentieth.

Conclusions

The abrupt leveling off in hours of work after World War II, in combination with the continued upward trend in female labor force participation, have contributed to a leveling off or possibly an increase in the number of hours supplied to the labor market by the average married couple in their prime years. This appears to be in sharp contrast to trends toward reduction in working times that extend back as far as the early nineteenth century.

Notes

1. Since the elderly in this country now generally live separately from their children, the undoubted increase in leisure time resulting from earlier retirements has had little spillover effect on the time problems of the rest of the population.

2. *Employment and Earnings,* January 1978 and *Current Population Reports,* Series P-50, 1947.

3. Unless otherwise noted, data on hours of work and employment are

derived from two publications of the Bureau of Labor Statistics, *Employment and Earnings* and *Special Labor Force Reports,* and from the U.S. Bureau of the Census, *Current Population Reports,* Series P-50, 1947.

4. Calculated from a multiple regression using the matched March–May 1973, U.S. Bureau of Labor Statistics, Current Population Survey data tape. The other independent variables in the regression were race, schooling, age, and other family income.

5. See Robinson and Converse; Komarovsky, Lunderg, and McInerny; and Campbell and Converse. See the discussion in chapter 4.

6. See, for example, J.P. Robinson.

7. See Henle.

8. See Owen (1970).

3 Why Did Hours of Work Level Off?

An explanation of this important new element in the dynamics of labor supply—the leveling off in hours of work—is essential for an understanding of current time pressures. Economists generally reject the popular view that hours are primarily determined by laws and trade unions, and instead argue that long-term trends in hours of work are more importantly influenced by underlying forces on employer and employee preferences, which in turn determine the labor market results. (Short-term movements in hours are largely determined by fluctuations in the level of business activity which produce temporarily reduced workweeks as well as unemployment.)

This emphasis on market forces as a long-term explanation is partly due to the fact that most of the decline in hours of work took place under very competitive labor market conditions in the nineteenth and early twentieth centuries, before there was an effective national law controlling hours and before more than a very small minority was enrolled in trade unions. In a competitive market it appears reasonable to assume—as a simplifying approximation—that entrepreneurs will tend to try to minimize their labor costs by seeking out the hours schedule which will enable them to hire the best labor at the cheapest unit cost.[1] The discussion of past movements in hours of work here will begin by following this tradition (though some necessary qualifications will also be discussed).

One corollary of the assumption that employers are simply interested in minimizing their labor costs is that they will be willing to pay the same price or efficiency wage for each unit of effective labor input supplied regardless of the number of minutes or hours needed to produce it. An effective labor input is defined as an hour of work, standardized for differences in the quality of work performed; the term "efficiency wage" is used to describe the price the employer pays per unit of effective labor input.

If the employer is only concerned with obtaining effective labor inputs at the lowest possible efficiency wage, but his employees for one reason or another desire a change to a shorter workweek, he will be willing to accommodate them as long as they are willing to take a cut in weekly earnings at least sufficient to keep the efficiency wage at the old level. If employees generally prefer a shorter workweek on these terms then, it has been argued by advocates of this competitive theory, those employers who are perspicacious enough to perceive this shift in preferences and accordingly reduce hours (without changing the efficiency wage paid) will attract labor from the holdouts, who do not reduce hours. Only if the latter are willing to pay a higher efficiency wage could they hope to keep their work force intact at the old work schedule. But since payment of a higher wage would raise costs with no apparent compensating advantage for the employer, this would not be a likely outcome in a competitive market.

In a sense, this theory argues that changes in the preferences of employees will induce employers to lower hours of work, all in the interest of minimizing the employer's labor cost. A moment's reflection indicates that this theory abstracts from much of the reality of the day-to-day determination of hours of work and wages. It is most readily applied in those situations where the individual worker is allowed to choose both the intensity and duration of his hours of work, as in the common nineteenth century arrangements in which workers were paid by the piece, setting their own hours, often taking the work home. Where hours are set by the employer, the strength of the theory depends upon the degree to which competitive forces (or simply the employer's desire for higher profits) push him to discover the income-leisure preferences of his workers so as to obtain the most work for the least dollar outlay.

The theory also implicitly assumes that the worker's hourly rate is proportionate to the intensity of his work (since we assume that the worker is paid for his effective labor input, not just the number of hours he works). This condition is obviously met in the domestic system or where a fairly designed piece rate system is installed. But it also has at least some application in the very general case of industries in which some employers pay a premium wage, and in return expect better quality work. For example, in the nineteenth century labor market, robust workers in good health could command much better hourly wages at the heavy work which they could do than could those less able workers who—whether weakened by malnutrition and the diseases of poverty or simply by reason of inheriting an inferior constitution—were confined to ligher tasks. Today physical strength is less important in most lines of work and the work force is somewhat healthier, but employers still choose and reward employees on the basis of their qualifications—education, training, aptitude, and attitude as well as physical capacity—and those employers who pay a better wage are generally still able to attract a better quality, more productive work force.

The most obvious shortcoming of this simple competitive theory is that where employers have standard hours and hourly rates, the theory at best holds for the employer's work force as a group—not for each individual employee in it. This point will be taken up in some detail in the second part of the book, when we consider the problem of the individual worker who needs a schedule different from that appropriate for the majority of the firm's work force. More generally, this competitive, employee-oriented theory has only a limited use in analyzing differences among individual employers in a given period. However, despite the definite shortcomings of this simple approach for such cross-sectional analyses, it has proven its value in interpreting broad movements in hours of work over long periods of time. For this purpose, the major assumption made is that employers are concerned only with the efficiency wage paid, not with the number of hours worked as such. (This hypothesis is modified in the discussion on pp. 25–26.)

Changes in the Absolute Return to Effort:
Wage Rates and Hours of Work

In applying the competitive model, economists have treated the steady growth in the wage rate (the price the workers receive per unit of effective labor input) as the principal factor which has acted to change employee preferences for work schedules and hence, in this theory, to change hours of work.

The crux of the argument is that the higher wage increases the money income of the worker and hence his purchases of consumer goods and services, enabling him to satisfy his more pressing wants for food, clothing, housing, and so on. But the worker also has a demand for time off from work and, as he satisfies his more urgent wants in other areas, he will, it is reasoned, seek to fulfill his demand for time off by opting for a somewhat shorter workweek. This will reduce his weekly income though not of course to the extent that his weekly earnings would be brought down to the level prevailing before the wage increase. It would then follow that the rational employer will more or less gradually reduce work schedules as the hourly wage is increased. (As we have seen, the competitive theory would predict that those who reduce hours first could have a competitive edge over other employers in obtaining labor on more advantageous terms.)

However, the analysis here is complicated somewhat by the fact that a wage hike not only raises the income of the worker (producing a positive "income" effect on the demand for time off), it also increases the opportunity cost or price of an hour of time off: since each hour of work is better paid, each hour of time off has a larger implicit cost in terms of foregone goods and services. Economic theory predicts that an increase in the price of time would, other things being equal, encourage workers to substitute goods and services for time off, and so reduce the demand for it (just as an increase in the price of butter relative to oleomargarine would, ceteris paribus, be expected to reduce the consumption of butter relative to that of oleo). In principle, this "substitution" effect, resulting from the price-increasing impact of a rise in the wage rate, could be just as strong as or even stronger than the income effect, so that a rise in wages would have no effect on hours worked or would actually produce an increase in hours.

But in practice, the long period in which hours of work declined as hourly wage rates increased convinced many observers that the income effect was indeed the greater. Still the role of the substitution effect of higher wages is thought to be important, inasmuch as it is used to explain the fact that only a small portion of gains in real hourly wages has been absorbed by leisure. (It has been estimated that in the late nineteenth and early twentieth centuries, a period of rapid decline in hours of work, a quarter or less of the potential growth in consumption went to reduced hours, the remainder to consumer goods and services.) If the national gain in productivity had been distributed to the individual in a different manner—for example, if each person received an annual dividend from the state whether he worked or not and if this dividend (but not the wage rate) rose as national productivity gained, economic development would have brought only income gains to the individual—there would have been no increase in the price of his time. Under these circumstances, economic theory predicts that a higher proportion of potential economic growth would have been taken in the form of reduced work time[2] (a view that is supported by the fragmentary statistical data on the relative strength of these income and substitution effects).[3]

Changes in the Relative Return to Effort:
An Alternative Explanation

While this traditional analysis appeared to fit the facts well enough in the period in which hours were declining, it failed to predict the leveling off of hours over the past several decades, and does not now provide a satisfactory explanation of this stability in hours.

One reason for this failure is the implicit assumption that the worker's effective labor input (and hence, by the traditional theory, his wage income) will increase in strict proportion to his hours of work. This assumption is not essential to the competitive view of hours determination and is generally not valid; even if the employee is paid in accordance with his effective labor input, the latter will generally not vary in strict proportion with the number of hours worked. The most obvious example of this point is fatigue: if the workday of the employee is sufficiently extended and the worker is fatigued, additional hours per day will make little or no contribution to his daily input.

As another example, critics of the progressive income tax and the present system of welfare subsidies argue that both these institutions reduce the ratio of the marginal to the average return to effort, the relative return to effort, and hence probably tend to discourage work by the groups affected by these programs (examples would include highly paid movie stars and, in the second group, poorly skilled female heads of households).

Even more relevant to this discussion of historical changes in hours of work, is how the extent to which an extra hour of effort yields a proportionate or disproportionate increase in wage income (so the worker's income rises by more or less than 1 percent, with a 1 percent increase in hours worked) has changed over the long course of economic development. This further complicates the analysis, since changes in this relative payoff to work (what economists have called the elasticity of income with respect to effort) can have as much or more effect on the worker's supply of effort as changes in the absolute level of the payoff itself—the wage rate. For example, a wage rate increase may raise both income and the price of time in the same proportion, and so yield income and substitution effects on hours of work which partially offset each other, producing only a small reduction in hours; but if, for some reason, income rises sharply with only a small increase in the price of time, a much more significant decline in hours is likely.

For example, suppose a factory worker has been paid a low straight-time wage, but offered unlimited overtime at time and a half pay. A new management policy raises straight-time wages by 51 percent, but eliminates premium pay for overtime. Under these circumstances, economic theory would predict that a decline in overtime hours would be likely (or at least more likely than if the overtime premium had been retained); the worker's income has risen sharply, but the marginal price of his time is little changed, making a decline in hours a probable result.

Though consideration of variations over time in the relative return to effort does complicate the analysis, it does not render it intractable; in periods in which the relative return to effort is declining, one would expect more progress to be made in hours reduction than in periods in which it were stable or increasing.

In fact there is some historical evidence that seems to support the importance of this theory for explaining long-term changes in hours of work.

Productive Consumption: Declines in the Relative Return to Effort

At the beginning of the long downward movement in hours of work in the early nineteenth century, many workers were at true subsistence levels, and the relative return to long hours of work was very high indeed as a consequence: in fact the worker at the margin of subsistence had little or no choice but to put in long hours so as to earn as much as possible. If he worked less and earned less, he would likely die of malnutrition or one of the diseases of poverty. As the wage of labor increased, these pressures were reduced—it was no longer necessary to work very long hours to survive—permitting some reduction in work schedules. However, the worker was still under pressure to work long hours: in effect, he had an extra incentive to put in additional time because of what economists call the "productive consumption" effect of higher consumption levels on his productivity. When considering the gain from working an extra hour per day, employees under semisubsistence conditions had to take into account not only the direct benefit from the wage paid for this extra hour but also the indirect gain from the expected improvement in their future health and productivity—and hence in their hourly earnings in every hour of the workdays ahead—resulting from a higher-income level today, with greater current consumption of foods and other goods necessary to good health. In terms of the theory used here we would say that as a result, the marginal return to effort was raised relative to the average, increasing the relative return to effort and encouraging long hours of work. We should also note that these long hours were scheduled despite the strength of the countervailing force of fatigue, which would tend by itself to reduce the contribution of the final hours of work.

But as the efficiency wage rate gradually rose over the course of economic development, the productive consumption factor slowly lost its force. As the worker's income rose, further gains in income would yield only diminishing returns in terms of gains in worker productivity. The gradual diminution and eventual disappearance of this extra incentive to work long hours (along with the persistence of the problem of physical fatigue) helps to explain the reduction in working schedules in this period of industrial development.

However, the worker eventually reached a level of affluence at which his health was no longer dependent upon marginal gains in his wage; as a result, he no longer received a positive feedback of this type from an extra hour of work. From this point, then, additional increases in the worker's income did not further reduce the relative return to effort (since the feedback effort is already posited to have reached the zero level), and so no additional downward pressure was exercised on hours of work on these grounds.

One can only date the ending of the productive consumption effect on hours of work in this country in very approximate terms. We do know that as late as 1915, an extensive study of all the then extant surveys of living conditions of the American working class[4] concluded that a large majority of the industrial work force was still in the range where significant gains in productivity would result from further increases in their consumption. But in succeeding decades this majority was reduced to a minority, a diminishing minority in the years following World War II. Hence the timing of the cessation of the productive consumption effect as an important factor appears to be roughly consistent with the leveling off in hours since the 1930s and 1940s.[5] As supporting evidence, one can also note that the first half of the twentieth century saw the diminution of economic class differences in morbidity and mortality rates in the United States (at least among the white population).

Because of the strong effect of this argument on the present problem of the time bind—by explaining much of the reduction in hours by a factor that is no longer operative, it indirectly helps to explain the present leveling off in hours—the analysis of this point is given in somewhat greater detail in appendix A.

Affluence: Increases in the Relative Return to Effort

Education

The relative return to effort theory also provides a more positive explanation of the recent leveling off in hours of work. There are factors at work in our affluent society that now act to increase the marginal above the average return to effort, and hence raise the relative return. Society, and individuals, now make an enormous fixed investment in the education of the average young American. Many years of earnings are foregone, as are the direct costs of schooling (books, tuition, school taxes, and so on). One can think of these outlays as a reduction in the average family's income—an investment made to increase the marginal return to effort, or hourly wage rate, of the graduate. Since the marginal return to effort is increased by education, while the average return (i.e., lifetime money earnings minus education costs, divided by lifetime hours of work) is not increased in the same proportion, the net effect is to raise the ratio of the marginal to the average return, and so increase the relative return to effort. (In practice, this basic argument holds whether the student borrows funds for his education or, as is more often the case, receives them from his family, then commits himself to making the same provision for the education of his children.) Putting the point somewhat less abstractly, it can be shown that only if the graduate puts in relatively long hours can he economically justify the financial investment his family, and society, have made in his schooling—by spreading this fixed cost over a larger number of lifetime hours of paid employment.

These arguments predict that better-educated employees will work longer hours. And indeed cross-sectional data usually do show better-educated workers, other things being equal, putting in longer hours.

Moreover, the argument also predicts that in periods in which education outlays are increasing rapidly—and hence the ratio of the marginal to the average return to effort is rising—hours will tend to stabilize (or possibly even increase). In other periods, when schooling outlays were growing more slowly, hours would be more likely to decline. (The influence of schooling investment on hours of work is discussed at greater length in appendix B).

Table 3-1 shows the results of an attempt to determine the relative importance of hourly earnings and education outlays in determining weekly hours in the 1900-75 period. The results were determined by the technique of multiple regression, which measures the partial influence of an independent variable on a dependent variable, adjusting for the influence of other independent variables. The table presents regression estimates of ceteris paribus effects on hours of work of a 1 percent change in the real hourly wage rate and an index of educa-

Table 3-1
The Determination of Working Hours

	Change in Hours
Hourly earnings	-.20
Education costs	+.10

tion costs per worker. The wage rate was measured as compensation per hour in nonagricultural employment, divided by the consumer price index. Education costs are measured by educational outlays per member of the work force (also adjusted for price changes). This measure reflects trends in two major factors: the number of children per adult, and the number of years in which the child is supported before entering the labor force.[6] As expected, education costs have a positive association and the hourly wage rate a negative association with hours of work.[7]

This statistical relationship can now be used to help us understand the leveling off in hours of work in the years since World War II. The post-World War II years followed upon a decade and a half of depression and war. Consumption needs of all sorts had gone unmet in those years of unemployment and shortages; in the first few years after the war, workers tried to catch up on purchases of clothing, household appliances, and other consumer goods. There was very little demand for a reduction in work times.

But there were also somewhat longer lasting effects of the catching-up process. Birthrates were at a very low level in the 1930s, then rose sharply with the return of better times in the war and postwar periods. This type of catching up had long-term effects on American work and consumption patterns because (unlike a purchase of a refrigerator or a car) a decision to have a child imposes costs that extend for two decades.[8]

The effects of this sudden increase in child rearing was further exacerbated by another postwar development—the education revolution—which increased the average years of schooling by about three years and increased the proportion of high school graduates going on to college to a near majority. This vast increase in education investment is believed by some obervers to be a reaction to labor-market conditions, which generated a higher level of demand for college-trained labor and an increasing level of unemployment for those with below-average schooling. In any event, the extension of schooling greatly increased the average cost of raising a child.

As the combination of the baby boom and the education revolution increased total education costs very considerably in the postwar period, the enormous outlays required diverted resources from other consumption and savings in the average household and made a shortening of the working hours of adults—with the loss of earnings that such a reduction would entail—less attractive.[9]

Figure 2-1 shows hours of work of adult males in nonagricultural wage and salary employment (adjusted for vacations and holidays) for full-employment peak years. The dashed line gives the level of actual hours. The solid line in the chart shows the level of hours that would have been predicted in each full-employment peak year from this statistical analysis. In the post-World War II period, rapid rises in the real hourly wage rate and soaring child rearing costs have tended to offset each other, and a leveling off in hours over the past 25 years is correctly predicted. Comparison of actual hours worked over the past 75 years with the levels predicted by this analysis also shows a rather close correspondence, increasing confidence in this interpretation of the post-World War II experience.

Moreover, when the role of variations in education outlays is ignored in the statistical analysis and hours are predicted without this variable, a decline of one-half day in working time is incorrectly forecast for the post-World War II period: these results underline the importance of considering changes in the relative return to effort, in this case, the increasing level of education required to earn the average wage in our affluent society.

Training and Experience

The relative return to effort, and hence hours of work, has also been influenced by other types of investment in "human capital." After he has completed his formal education, the typical American youth today receives substantial amounts of on-the-job training and experience, which further enhances his earnings capacity. One widely respected estimate puts the value of these postschool investments at about four-fifths of the cost of formal education itself.[10] This investment provides another incentive to increase hours of work, so that the fixed cost of acquiring these skills can be spread over a larger number of work hours. The argument here is almost identical to that advanced in support of the view that higher levels of formal education encourage longer hours of work.

One important difference, though, is that employers frequently underwrite much of the cost of postschool training. This provides the employer with a special incentive to set longer hours of work, so that he can recoup his share of the investment cost. (This employer interest in longer hours of work—a modification of the simple competitive assumption about employer behavior—is discussed in chapters 7, 8, and 12 and in appendix G.) In a sense, then, the employer's interest is complementary to that of the employee, who has a large fixed investment in himself.

Some economists believe that the aggregate level of training investment per member of the work force has increased over the past several decades. If this view is correct, it would afford a supplementary explanation of the leveling off in hours offered above in terms of increased investment in formal education.

The Graying of America

The fact that Americans can now look forward to a longer period of retirement (because they both retire earlier and live longer) may also contribute to stabilizing hours of work. One would expect that the relatively low market value of time later in life compared with its relatively high value in the prime years would be expected to lead to a rearrangement of working time, with longer hours in the earlier years, as well as retirement later on, to provide for the years of low earnings potential.

Social security and private pension schemes both reflect and reinforce this pattern by reducing take-home income during working years (and so encouraging work) and by both increasing income during retirement and, in the case of many pension plans, discouraging work by specifying a lower pension for those who continue to have earnings.

For all these reasons, if the proportion of the aged in the population and the cost of supporting retired workers continue to rise in the years ahead, hours reduction for prime-aged workers will, other things being equal, be expected to be more difficult[11] (see chapter 12 for a discussion of factors which may work to facilitate future reductions in hours).

Other Explanations

A number of other explanations can be and have been offered for the leveling off in hours of work. Some argue simply that the achievement of an 8-hour day has so reduced the marginal gain from additional leisure as to make future reductions in hours unlikely. This view has some merit in a discussion of daily hours, but does not afford an explanation of the present interest in reducing hours by obtaining more days off per year (see the discussion in chapter 12).

Others believe that while the number of hours worked has shown little change, there has been a reduction in the intensity of work and an improvement in working conditions, reducing the demand for further cuts in hours schedules. It is extremely difficult to make meaningful comparisons over time of the intensity of work, partly because the necessary data are not collected, partly because the nature of work demands has itself been influenced by technological change, so that less emphasis is now placed on the intensity of physical effort and more on responsible, dependable behavior. On the other hand, there is little doubt that there has been an improvement in working conditions, and that this has been an additional factor influencing the level of working hours. (This point is discussed at greater length in the next chapter.)

Summary and Conclusions

1. The recent leveling off in hours cannot be explained in an institutional analysis. The major institutions affecting hours of work, unions and legal regulations, are believed to act to reduce them. Yet these only became effective at the beginning of the period in which hours reduction ends.

2. The traditional economists' explanation is that rising hourly wage rates have a greater income than substitution effect on leisure demand, and so reduce hours of work. This is a valid argument as far as it goes, but does not explain why hours leveled off in a period in which the wage rate was rising at a rate much in excess of its long-term historical trend.

3. A modification of this traditional explanation, which stresses changes in the relative return to effort, appears to be more promising. In the years in which hours were declining, rising wages were reducing the material incentive to work long hours by reducing the importance of the productive consumption effect of such long hours (or more properly, of the resulting higher income) on hourly productivity. This acted to reduce the relative return to effort, and hence hours of work. In recent years this has ceased to be an important factor.

Moreover, in this more recent period, the fixed costs of education, by reducing income available for other purposes (while increasing, not reducing, the marginal return to effort), had been increasing the relative return to effort, thus tending to act to level off hours of work. Increases in the fixed costs of post-school training have probably had the same effect. In other words the leveling off in hours might be thought of as being due both to the cessation of factors which had been reducing the relative return to effort and to the introduction of factors tending to increase this relative return to work.

4. This principle of emphasizing changes in the relative as well as the absolute return to effort has other applications, depending upon forces operating on the relative return in a particular period. For example, the widely discussed graying of America as well as other factors—for example, a possible future trend toward a welfare state in this country—may have very important effects on the relative return to effort, and hence on hours of work, in the years ahead (see chapter 12).

Notes

1. See especially p. 25–26. Chapter 7 considers several other factors that may also influence the employer's decision on the number of weekly hours per

worker. Chapter 6 considers factors that influence the employer's decision on the timing of weekly hours. Institutional factors will be given more weight in discussing possible future hours reductions in chapter 12.

2. Indeed it is for this reason that some advocates of shorter-hours schedules have favored this method of distributing national producti rity dividends over the conventional practice of raising hourly wages.

3. See Owen (1970) for a discussion of this point.

4. See Lauck and Sydenstricker.

5. Though hours continued to decline in the 1920s, indicating that other factors were at work in addition to the productive consumption effect. See Owen (1970).

6. R^2 = .98, Durbin-Watson = 1.94. The predictive ability of the measure here indicates that it can be a useful long-run index of child-rearing costs.

The relative price of recreation goods and services was also included as an independent variable in the regression. Since these prices have not changed much since 1920, they do not help us to understand the more recent movement in hours. However, the breakthroughs in recreation technology in the first two decades of the century led to a sharp decline in the relative price of recreation in the 1900-20 period that does help to explain the drop in hours of work in those early years. For more discussion of the use of multiple regression in the long-term analysis of changes in hours of work, see Owen (1970).

7. The dependent variable in the regression in the text was hours worked per week by nonstudent male wage and salary earners in nonagricultural employment, adjusted for vacations and holidays. The three independent variables were average compensation per hour worked, educational outlays per member of the work force, and the relative price of recreation goods and services. The sources for these variables were the following: hours of work data for 1941 and later are obtained from various issues of two publications of the Bureau of Labor Statistics, *Employment and Earnings* and *Special Labor Force Reports,* as described in the text. Data for 1900-41 are based on manhours and employment data for nonagricultural employees developed by John W. Kendrick for the National Bureau of Economic Research (see Kendrick). Real hourly wages data for 1961 and later are employee compensation in nonagricultural employment, divided by manhours worked. These data are derived from the U.S. Department of Commerce, *Statistical Abstract of the United States,* various issues, and *Survey of Current Business,* various issues. Data for 1929-60 are U.S. Department of Commerce estimates of compensation divided by manhours estimates developed by John Kendrick for the National Bureau of Economic Research (Worksheets for Kendrick, 1957). Data for 1919-29 are Kendrick data on manhours used in conjunction with compensation estimates from Simon Kuznets, *National Income and Its Composition, 1919-38* (New York, National Bureau of Economic Research, 1942). Data for 1900-19 are Kendrick estimates of compensation per manhour in nonmanufacturing employment combined with compensation per

manhour in manufacturing estimates from Albert Rees, *New Measures of Wage Earner Compensation in Manufacturing, 1914-57* (New York, National Bureau of Economic Research, 1960). Compensation data in each time period are divided by the consumer price index to obtain estimates of real earnings. Real educational outlays per member of the labor force data for 1900 and later are educational expenditures at all levels of education (elementary, secondary, and higher) divided by the labor force and the consumer price index. Data are from *Statistical Abstract of the United States, 1972, Historical Statistics of the United States,* and U.S. Office of Education, *Digest of Educational Statistics, 1972.* Relative price of recreation goods and services data for 1948 and later are the recreation component of the consumer price index divided by the consumer price index. Data for 1900–48 are recreation price series extended back to earlier years through the use of advertisements in catalogs and newspapers (Owen, 1970 and 1964). See Owen (1976*b*) for further discussion on these results.

8. See Easterlin.

9. For statements about the expected positive relationship between hours of work and investment in children, see Finegan, Owen (1970), Lindsay, and Barzel.

10. Mincer (1962).

11. See appendix D. Compare the discussion in Burkhauser and Turner.

4

Work and Leisure Activities

No Change in Leisure Time?

The study of leisure time requires that we also examine the allocation of time not spent in paid employment between leisure and household production—the hours spent in commuting, housework, shopping, and so on. The analysis of these patterns in chapter 1 indicated that almost as much time was spent in such household production activities as in paid employment, in fact was a more important use of time for many women employees. A study of changes over the years in the allocation to this household production time also reveals some interesting results. A recent analysis—the widely quoted study of time allocation by Joann Vanek—indicates that there had been no decline at all in the amount of time spent at housework by full-time housewives over a period of more than 40 years (though preliminary results from a new study suggest that the smaller families of the past several years may finally be reducing the burden of housework somewhat). Fragmentary data available on males are difficult to analyze but suggest that their household production time has actually been increased. When such data are juxtaposed with the available information on total hours supplied to paid employment, the series on hours of work and on labor force participation, a rather negative picture is obtained of the growth of leisure.[1] The millions of women who have moved from housewife status to that of working wife have presumably suffered a loss in leisure time. At the same time, there is only limited evidence of offsetting gains in the leisure of full-time housewives or working husbands.

Of course it would be a mistake to place too much reliance on these scattered estimates of time use; nevertheless they do appear to indicate relative long-term stability in the leisure time of the average prime-aged couple.

Explanations

These comparisons over time of household production and leisure time contradict the earlier thinking of a number of writers. For years, most economists in this area believed that the development and widespread use of a number of time-savers in household production had caused a sharp reduction in the need for housework. A leading spokesman for this viewpoint, C.L. Long, argued in *The Labor Force under Changing Income and Employment* (some 20 years ago) that the development of three types of timesavers—packaged food and other products that required little further work by the housewife; commercially available services, such as drycleaners, to replace the housewife's time; and household appliances—had enabled female labor force participation to rise without any net sacrifice in leisure. As we now know, the data do not appear to support this analysis.

However, the reason for this error was not that the technical improvements mentioned by Long were not developed and widely used or that they were not potentially effective timesavers. The problem was rather that the earlier predictions of economists about the effect of such innovations on actual time use patterns were based upon primitive, unsophisticated theories. Economists had limited their theoretical analyses in this area almost exclusively to considerations of the so-called work-leisure choice—that is, the division of time between paid employment and all other uses. There was little or no theory available to deal with such questions as the likely effects of timesavers on leisure time. (In fact most economists regarded such questions as well beyond the proper scope of their discipline.)

However, an important step toward such a theory of nonwork time was made by G.S. Becker in his 1965 article, "A Theory of the Allocation of Time." Becker challenged the standard doctrine that the labor-leisure choice could best be studied by positing a worker who simply wanted more leisure (and so less work) because of his preference for leisure over work, and who balanced off this desire against wants for more consumption goods, obtainable through work. Instead, Becker extended conventional economic theory to include what he called "consumption activities," essentially activities carried on for their own sake in nonmarket work times. Examples would include going to the movies or preparing a homecooked meal and enjoying it with friends. Becker argues that such activities should be the basic unit of analysis since, he believes, the worker-consumer is essentially interested in maximizing the number and quality of such satisfying activities. In Becker's view, both nonwork time and the goods purchased on the market should be regarded as necessary inputs for activities—mere means to an end.

In this path-breaking effort, Becker treats various possibilities for substituting goods and time in the production of activities: for example, a cheap double feature of two B-grade movies might be as satisfying to a consumer as an expensive A-grade movie. In a discussion that is most relevant for our purposes. Becker shows that as the wage rate increases, then, unless hours of work decline very rapidly, the ratio of goods input to consumption time input must necessarily rise, forcing the consumer to find ways of substituting goods for time.

Becker's paper, in other ways so useful to the present discussion, does not make a clear-cut distinction between household production and leisure or consumption time (leisure and consumption time will be used interchangeably in the remainder of this discussion). However, this distinction is given a strong emphasis by S.B. Linder. Writing in a popular style, Linder argues in *The Harried Leisure*

Class that as the real wage rises, workers purchase more and more consumer goods. But these goods—automobiles, suburban residences, washing machines, and the like—all require time for servicing and repair. (Linder points out that even those determined to avoid the do-it-yourself pattern must still spend time taking an appliance in for repair.) Hence as the living standard increases and appliance ownership multiplies, household production time must rise also. In consequence, unless hours of work fall very quickly, true leisure time is reduced for the harried leisure class.

The contributions of Long, Becker, and Linder shed some light on the problem of the leveling off of leisure time, but leave a number of questions to be answered. For example, the Linder theory predicts an increase in consumer maintenance time; but the hours of household production time of the full-time housewife have not increased, and the millions of women who have moved to employee status do much less housework as a result. Increases in housework time of males have been observed, but these appear to be quite modest in comparison with the observed decline among women. Hence while accurate data are lacking, it would be more reasonable to characterize the last several decades as seeing some minor reduction in household production time. It certainly would be difficult to find evidence of a sharp increase as the Linder model would predict.

However, the question of the division of nonwork time between leisure and household production can be discussed in a rather straightforward fashion if we use a model of worker-consumer choice which builds upon the Becker-Linder contributions, but directly poses this time allocation problem. A model of this type is depicted in figure 4-1.

Here the individual divides his total time K (a constant) among three types of activities: market employment time M, household production time H, and consumption of leisure time L (so that $K = M + H + L$). His hourly wage is w, yielding an income of $X = wM$, which he uses to buy consumer goods and services. These goods and services, when combined with time in household production H and skill level S_H, produce a level of goods and services P. This household production output is then combined with consumption time L at a given level of skill in consumption S_L to produce satisfying consumption experiences A.

This choice framework highlights some similarities between the household production sector and the market employment sector. In each sector, labor input is combined with material inputs at a given level of skill or technology to produce an output. Moreover, in a somewhat less obvious way, the consumption sector also has this characteristic of combining goods (the output of household production) and time to produce an output: satisfying consumption experiences. The symmetry among the three sectors in this model offers the important advantage that the various theoretical tools used by economists to analyze choice in the market employment sector can be applied to the consideration of questions of choice in household production and consumption (see appendix E).

This facilitates the discussion of the principal question posed here: how to

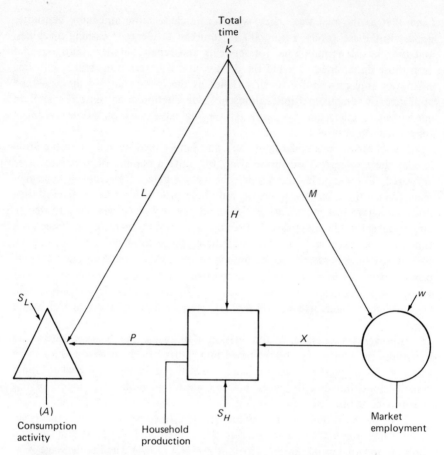

Figure 4-1. The Allocation of Time and Money to Maximize Consumption

predict the division of time other than paid work time between household production time and leisure or consumption time, when paid work time is unchanged, while the wage rate, and hence the flow of consumer goods and services, is steadily increased?

One can start with the assumption that the individual makes this allocation in a way that maximizes the amount of satisfaction he gets from consumption (i.e., that he maximizes A). It follows from this assumption that the rational worker-consumer will allocate his time in such a way that, on the margin, an hour spent in one sector will yield as great a gain in consumer satisfaction as would an hour in another sector. In this sense, the marginal hour spent in each sector is equally productive. One can next ask how an increase in the wage rate would affect the optimizing allocation of time (holding hours of paid work constant)? It follows that this will in turn depend upon whether an hour spent in household production will become relatively more productive in yielding net consumer satisfaction than would a marginal hour in consumption time, thus stimulating a reduction in leisure time and an increase in household production time, or whether the reverse would hold, leading to an increase in leisure time?

One can begin to consider this question by returning to the lower level of abstraction in Linder's book, and restating his theory in a more positive fashion. Linder's theory implies that an increase in consumer goods X raises the productivity of time spent in household production: with more consumer goods and services available to work with, an extra hour of household production time will yield a greater gain in consumer satisfaction. Linder puts the point rather negatively, arguing that the modern worker who neglects the maintenance of the large number of appliances and other property he owns will find that he indeed pays an imposing economic price; in terms of our theory, the productivity of the time spent in this type of household production has been increased by affluence.

Going beyond the Linder framework, more positive examples of affluence increasing productivity in household production can also be developed. For example, the more affluent worker can afford to pay more for personal transportation, enabling him to travel further on his daily commuting trip and while shopping. His incentive to increase the length of these trips is also enhanced by a larger economic reward for doing so: a longer commute will probably enable the consumer to buy residential land more cheaply. But the more he can budget for land and housing, the greater the total payoff will be for him for a given decline in land prices. Hence his return from additional commuting time will increase with income. Similarly a consumer in a position to purchase a more expensive bundle of goods has a greater incentive to spend time shopping for bargains. Similar arguments could be adduced for most areas of household production.

However, the increases in productivity resulting from a rise in the wage rate are not confined to household production time; the productivity of consumption time is also increased. Consumption time is productive because a satisfying consumption experience requires time to enjoy consumer goods. Hence as consumer goods are increased in number and complexity, it is reasonable to predict that more time will be required for their enjoyment. For example, we have argued that higher income permits the worker to pay for a longer commute and buy a home in the suburbs (thus tying up much of his time in commuting, home repairs, and suburban shopping centers). But his higher income and affluent lifestyle also generate a demand for time to enjoy his expanded level of consumption goods—to invite the neighbors over for a backyard cookout or to go for a Sunday drive with the family in his new automobile. In this sense, the productivity of consumption time is increased.

The notion that increasing levels of consumer goods in the hands of the working population requires more time for their enjoyment is hardly a new one. Trade union advocates of the 8-hour day in the 1870s, and later, used this as one of their principal arguments for hours reduction. Similarly Henry Ford employed this argument as a major justification for pioneering with the five-day workweek in the 1920s.[2] And spending and leisure time continue to be linked in much of the popular discussion of further workweek reduction in business and labor magazines today. Much of this discussion has been exaggerated (a typical argument, made over and over again in the past 100 years, is that unless hours are reduced and workers have the leisure to enjoy the products they make, they will not buy them and a depression will ensue). Nevertheless the discussion has served to develop the point that higher incomes tend to create a demand for more consumption time.

But we now have a surplus of predictions: the Linder argument that affluence will yield a shift from leisure to household production time, and what might be called the Ford argument, that leisure time will have to be increased. The relative strength of the two arguments must still be resolved. The model in figure 4-1 indicates that this should depend upon relative substitution possibilities. As the level of market goods and services X increases (holding work time, and hence the sum of leisure and household production time, constant), either much more X has to be used per unit of time in household production H, or much more household production output P has to be used per hour of consumption time L, or some combination of the two possibilities must be employed. In other words the net effect upon leisure time would depend upon the feasibility of increasing the ratio of goods to time in household production X/H, relative to the possibilities for raising the ratio of P/L in producing satisfying consumption experiences. The fact that there has been so little net change in the ratio of leisure to household production time may indicate that the two types of substitution possibilities are roughly equal—that the Ford and Linder effects are roughly similar in magnitude. (This question is discussed more rigorously in appendix E.)

The Role of Timesavers

In practice, the analysis of the division of time between leisure and household production is further complicated by the fact that economic development has not just brought higher wages, and hence more consumer goods in general, but has been embodied in a number of technical developments, improving almost every area of daily life. Many of these technical developments have served to improve the productivity of household production time by reducing the amount of time needed to carry out a given task. (In figure 4-2, these advances can be treated as improvements in S_H.)[3]

While timesavers—especially in commuter transportation and in housework—have greatly reduced the time needed to carry out a variety of tasks, we find that paradoxically the long-term result of these improvements does not appear to be any saving in time. Instead the timesaver is more typically used to facilitate an expansion of the activity, with little net change in the amount of time devoted to it.

Commuter time provides a good example; in the past century and a half, technical advances have made it possible to commute at speeds that were inconceivable when most people walked to work. "Shank's mare" has been successively replaced by the horse trolley, the electric trolley, the gasoline-powered bus, and the automobile. But students of our cities tell us that the principal long-term result appears to have been an outward expansion of cities and metropolitan areas as individuals took advantage of the opportunities opened up by the new modes of transport to live ever further from their jobs. There is no evidence of a net decline in commuter time.

Personal cleanliness provides another example. One might not think of the technology of personal cleanliness as having undergone changes comparable to the increase in speed in personal travel. But in fact timesavers have been made available which have made a significant difference. Suppose Americans had maintained the sensible tradition of the Saturday night bath: central heating and control of hot water, development of the stall shower, better commercially available soaps and shampoos would all now permit that ritual to be conducted in a few minutes, allowing more time for Saturday night leisure. Instead, Americans have made a daily bath the national standard.

Moreover, many Americans (men as well as women) now indulge in bath salts, shampoos, hair conditioners, hair setters, deodorant sprays, colognes, and so on, which increase the time requirement of a bath (while presumably improving the quality of the result). In consequence, the data show no net decline in time allocated to personal cleanliness.

Not ever form of household production activity has had constant time input. There has been an important net reduction in time spent in food preparation. A number of technical improvements, both in the kitchen and in the commercial preparation of foods, have greatly reduced time requirements. Equally important, there has not been a sufficiently strong offsetting tendency to improve the quality of food consumption. In fact the trend toward fast foods has been deplored by gourmets, nutritionists, and home economists as tending to deteriorate quality. This trend might be explained as resulting from the scarcity of time and the apparent indifference of many Americans to high-quality cooking. On the other hand, time spent shopping has increased, despite the proliferation of shopping centers with adjacent parking lots, computerized cash registers, packaged foods, and so on.

Thus no overall pattern is revealed when we examine individual categories of household production. In each case, timesavers initially appear to do just that, reducing household production time and increasing leisure time. But in the longer run, consumers adjust to their new opportunities—living further from their place of work, developing new rituals of personal cleanliness, and so on. More household production output is obtained, reducing or eliminating any saving in household production time. It is argued in appendix E that here too the long-run net effect on leisure time will depend upon the substitutability of goods for time in household production, and of household production output for time in consumption activity. If both these substitution possibilities are relatively good (i.e., if both X/H and P/L can readily be increased), there will not be a reduction in household production time, or a gain in leisure, as the result of the introduction of new timesavers; rather there will simply be a higher level of household production activity per unit of consumption time, presumably increasing the quality, not the quantity, of this time. The relative stability of leisure and household production time, despite the radical improvements in household production technology, would be consistent with this assessment of the substitution possibilities in both consumption and household production.

The Quality of Work and Consumption Time

The Quality of Work Time

The analysis to this point indicates that there may have been little progress in increasing leisure time in the past 40 years; that despite the very considerable increase in consumer goods that has occurred, relatively little net change in either household or paid work time appears to have occurred. However, it would be inaccurate to conclude that we have been sacrificing the quality of most of our waking existence (the hours we spend each day at one type of work or another) simply to improve the quality of the few hours of consumption time remaining to us. There have been striking gains in the quality of life on the job and in household activities, as any unbiased comparison of 1979 conditions with those of 1779 or 1879 would demonstrate. There is little doubt that work today is on the average much cleaner, safer, and less demanding physically than it was just 50, or even 30, years ago. One way of dramatizing the change is to note that many workers, perhaps a majority, can now work in their street clothes.

The improvement in the quality of household production time has been less widely remarked as such. One reason for this neglect is that the improvements in household production working conditions have usually been treated as consumption gains, as part of the overall upgrading of the American standard of living. But the improvement in these conditions has been almost as dramatic as that in conditions of market employment. For example, personal transportation today is typically in a smooth-riding automobile, perhaps with air conditioning and stereo radio; in sharp contrast to the recent past, when the daily trip to work was in an overcrowded, steaming subway or trolley, often redolent of human odors.[4] In still earlier decades, the commuter made do with the horse car or walked (which probably had much less appeal to our nineteenth century great grandfathers, on their way to a 12-hour day of heavy manual labor, than it would to today's generation of overfed, underexercised clerks).

Striking improvements have also taken place in working conditions in the home: we can compare the washing machine of today with yesterday's scrubbing board or contrast a modern kitchen with its nineteenth century counterpart. More generally, working conditions, in the conventional sense of temperature control, adequate lighting, and the quality of work clothes, have all been vastly improved for the average American wife.

These developments are quite consistent with the economic analysis of time introduced in the preceding section, though they do raise some further complexities. A model of choice suitable for studying improvements in working conditions—on the job and at home—can easily be developed from the schema in figure 4-2, which builds upon the presentation in figure 4-1.[5]

The worker's potential market wage here is w, but w^* of this is used to improve working conditions (i.e., to provide the pleasant working environment in figure 4-2), so that the worker actually receives $M(w - w^*) = X$ to spend on goods and services (where M continues to denote time spent in market employment). These goods and services are all used in the household production sector. But of the total X, Z is used to improve working conditions in the household production sector (the pleasant homeworking environment in figure 4-2), and Y is used as raw material input into household production ($Y + Z = X$).

The input Y is then combined with H hours of household production time (and a level of household production skills and technology S_H) to produce consumer goods and services P. As in figure 4-1, P is then combined with hours of consumption or leisure time L (and with skills and technology in consumption S_L) to produce consumption activities A.

As in the earlier model, the worker should be regarded as allocating his resources—time and money—so as to maximize his overall satisfaction. But now satisfaction comes from three experiences: paid work, household production, and leisure-consumption activity. The satisfaction of these experiences is in turn a function of six classes of inputs: the duration and quality of his market employment and household production experiences, and the duration of consumption activities and the level of household production output applied to improve their quality.

In this expanded model of choice, workers can utilize the potential benefits of an increase in the market wage (the basic factor initiating change here) to improve their lives in at least six different ways: (1) work fewer hours in the market, (2) improve conditions of work at paid employment, (3) work fewer hours at household production, (4) improve conditions of work in household production, (5) spend more hours in consumption activity, and (6) increase the amount of goods and services used in consumption activity.

The traditional income-leisure analysis (see chapter 3) considers only the

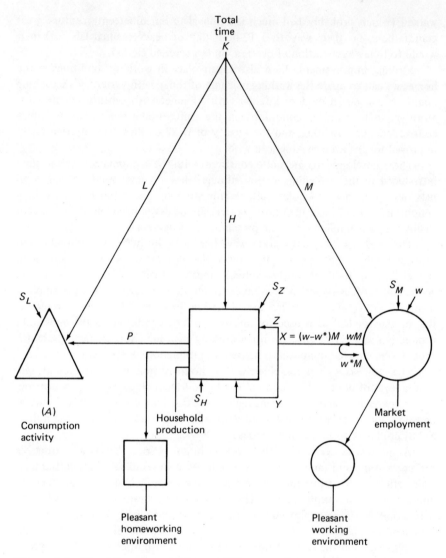

Figure 4-2. The Allocation of Time and Money to Improve Working Conditions and Consumption Activity

first and sixth choices. The analysis in the preceding section examined four choices: the first, third, fifth, and sixth. Now the reader is asked to consider the second and fourth choices, in addition to the others. Actually, the possible choices are even more complicated, in the sense that a wage increase may be divided among all six uses in almost any algebraically possible combination.

In practice, economic theory narrows the range of likely outcomes, predicting that choices among these alternatives would actually depend upon (1) the satisfaction gained from improvements in one activity (leisure, household work, or market work) relative to that obtained from improving another; (2) the productivity of one input (duration or quality) relative to another in improving each of the three activities; and (3) the relative cost of increasing any of the six inputs. These three factors are all influenced by long-term changes in wages; together they provide three types of reasons for expecting that higher wages would be correlated with improvements in working conditions (see appendix F).

In the first place, increases in goods consumption has brought important gains in the quality of consumption time. Consumption theory would predict that this would reduce the satisfaction from providing yet an additional improvement in the quality of consumption time relative to that obtained by improving working conditions (if the ratio of the satisfaction obtained from additional units of one good to that obtained from additional units of the second declines as the ratio of the consumption level of the first good to that of the second increases). To see the logic of this diminishing returns principle, the reader should ask himself would it not be highly incongruous for an American skilled worker to leave his air-conditioned home, his color television set and backyard swimming pool, drive to work in his air-conditioned car, and enter a nineteenth century factory, with its danger and discomforts? Of course in the real world one does find certain incongruities, where, for technical reasons, it is not economically feasible to provide appropriate working conditions. For example, the conditions of a skilled plumber would be considered dirty work by most, yet he is quite well paid.[6] Or, in contrast, consider the lower-class youth riding the subway from his slum to an elegant Fifth Avenue office building, where he serves as office boy. However, where the technology of providing working conditions permits, one generally observes that an effort is made to provide better working conditions for well-paid employees.

A very similar logic applies to household production time. One could ask whether a modern American housewife would be willing to work under nineteenth century conditions in order to enjoy a marginally higher living standard when she was done? The answer is equally obvious. In both cases, it is reasonable to suppose that the transfer of resources from providing additional consumption gains to the improving of working conditions yielded a net overall gain in satisfaction.

A second factor, operative in the past 30 years, is the constancy of working time. If the historic pattern had been followed and work time had been cut as the wage rate rose (e.g., by a law requiring a 35-hour workweek), this would very likely have relieved pressures to improve work-time quality. In a sense, the productivity of improved conditions (here the potential gain in work-place satisfaction to be obtained from better working conditions) would have been reduced somewhat. The unusual constancy of hours in this period probably exacerbated pressures to improve on-the-job perquisites.

A third reason for better working conditions is the reduction in the relative cost of providing them at higher wages. As labor becomes more expensive, employers have an increased incentive to make outlays that improve labor productivity. Hence insofar as cleaner, safer, better-lit, temperature-controlled environments promote more efficient labor utilization, one can expect such improvements to be made as economic development progresses. Moreover, a similar logic is at work in household production: since the modern housewife has a larger throughput of materials per hour, efficiency dictates that she be provided with working conditions that encourage a high level of productivity.

Finally technological changes have also reduced the relative cost of providing better working conditions more directly by changing the nature of work. The old labor-intensive industries and occupations have been drastically reduced in size. The dominant white-collar and service industries now have much less demand for heavy physical exertion or for work under unsafe conditions. Analogous changes in the home have been less dramatic but are also important; we know that housewives now do spend more time in marketing and household accounts, and less time in cleaning and food preparation, which many would regard as an upgrading of activities resulting from technical change.

The Quality of Consumption Time

One result of this pattern of distributing the potential benefits of gains in the market wage—allocating most to increasing the consumption of goods and services, with little increase in the amount of time allocated to their consumption—is of course a sharp increase in the amount of money spent per hour of consumption time. Expenditure and time budget data show this quite clearly, at least when it is possible to obtain consumption time expenditures statistics separately. (Some expenditures, such as those on housing and transportation, cover a mixture of consumption and household production activities.) When examining the largest category of purely consumption activities—recreation and reading—we see an increase in real expenditure per estimated hour spent in leisure activity of 100 percent in the 1900–48 period. Most interestingly, there was an increase of 145 percent in real per capita consumption of reading and recreation from 1948 to 1976, despite the leveling off in hours of market employment in those years.[7] In fact the post-World War II years have actually seen a small increase in the proportion of total consumption allocated to leisure spending.

Oddly enough, when one turns from these broad aggregates to a more detailed breakdown, these trends are somewhat obscured. The majority of recreation time is actually spent in a very cheap activity—watching television. Consumption spending tends to be in spurts: for example, when entertaining, going out on a weekend evening, on a weekend out-of-door excursion, or on a vacation trip lasting a number of days. To a large degree, the spurts in spending seem to correspond to the energy rather than the time available.

The inexpensive activity, television watching, is heavy on weekday evenings, when the worker is fatigued from his job (and his commuting and share of the housework). On the other hand, the expenditure spurts are concentrated on weekends and vacations, when a worker has a full day for consumption (or at least can sleep the next morning to recuperate). But these particularities average out in the larger aggregate: the overall picture is one of increasing expenditure per hour, however unevenly distributed, and hence presumably of increases in the quality of consumption time.

Conclusions

A more sophisticated model which permits a three-way division of time produces a number of interesting results. Two basic conclusions emerge. First, despite rising wages and all the timesavers yielded by improvements in household technology, little if any decline has been observed in household production time in the recent past. Second, this negative picture is relieved by the evidence of improvements in the quality of working and household production time, paralleling the gains in the quality of consumption activities.

Overall, one might then read the evidence as pointing to an effort by Americans in the past 30 or 40 years to use the potential benefits of wage increases to improve the quality of their lives by improving the quality of paid work, household production, and consumption times, rather than to seek amelioration by any substantial reallocation of time in favor of the more pleasant activity, by reducing work, and increasing recreation and other consumption activities.

Notes

1. See Vanek (1973 and 1974); Robinson and Converse; Walker and Woods; Campbell and Converse; Komarovsky, Lunderg, and McInerny; and J.P. Robinson.

2. See Ford.

3. Much of what follows holds equally well if S_H is improved through better education of the working populace or other factors. The analysis is further complicated if S_L, skills of technology in consumption, is also improved. This issue is considered in appendix E. See also Michael.

4. Of course some commuters, in some cities, still travel under these conditions.

5. See also the mathematical treatment in appendix F.

6. Actually, the "equalizing differences" theory of wage determination predicts that relatively poor working conditions will be compensated for by higher wages, at least for workers of similar qualifications and equal access to good jobs.

7. *Survey of Current Business,* July 1977; *Economic Report of the President,* 1978; *Statistical Abstract of the United States, 1977;* and *The National Income and Product Accounts, 1929–74.*

5 Rigid Schedules and the Quality of Time

This model really offers a rather positive view of the effects of recent economic progress on time use: that while free time has not increased substantially, there have been steady improvements in the quality of both leisure and work experience. But many Americans would regard this analysis as a bit Pollyannish. They see themselves as being in a rather unpleasant time bind, and would recognize themselves less as happy busy people, as perhaps implied in I. Sirageldin's image of the *Productive Americans,* than as the subjects of S.B. Linder's *The Harried Leisure Class.*

Effects of the Rising Price of Time on the Quality of Life

This malaise has a variety of sources; many quality of time problems are really indirect effects of the high market value of time—the basic cause of the leveling off in consumption time growth itself. For example, the increasing level of female labor force participation (in large part a result of the higher market price of female labor) leads not only to less free time in general but to a decline in those labor inputs into family life that had previously permitted a pattern of more graceful living. It is often the case that when a wife goes out to work, the family takes full account of the additional income she will earn, but underestimates the cost to the quality of family life of her absence, since this is more subtle, and its effect may be perceived only indirectly over a long period of time.

Another effect of the rising price of time is that the cost of hired labor services increases, also making it more difficult to maintain an elegant or gracious life-style. For example, 60 or 70 years ago, a family which enjoyed the possession of a fine new home outside the city, two recent model automobiles, annual vacations at a summer home, and an occasional European trip would almost inevitably have one, two or more servants in its employ. Today these good things are in the reach of a large proportion of the American population. But rather obviously all these people cannot have a staff of servants. In fact the proportion of paid servants in the population has declined. Hence the expectation that the hard work and sacrifice of many Americans would pay off in a good life has only been partially realized. They can buy goods, but the price of complementary market services—especially those of unskilled or semiskilled labor—has risen at the same rate or faster than the wages of the purchasers. In consequence, Americans are forced to do the scut work of maintaining their extraordinarily high standard of living, removing much of the sweetness from their dolce vita.

This problem also emerges even at a more modest level, when we consider the average home or car owner, who requires home, auto, or appliance repairs. In a world in which there is very imperfect information about repairmen, in which there are high time costs in locating, selecting, and scheduling a visit with a repairman, and in which the cost of the repairman's time is as high as one's own, owners often must manage to make do without repairs, engage in an inefficient do-it-yourself patch-up operation, or replace repairable items with a new purchase.

As another illustration of the impact of a high cost of time, the economist is able to prove that it "pays to be ignorant" about some consumer matters—one's time is too valuable to inform oneself fully about many items we purchase. But this elegant argument does little to relieve the frustration and irritation we all feel when we realize that we have overpaid for inferior merchandise.

These are some of the reasons why the quality of both household production and consumption time may not seem to be ameliorated to the degree predicted in our more abstract analysis. The common element in these examples is that a rising value of time—or more specifically increases in goods consumption without any corresponding increase in time, raising the relative scarcity value of time—has meant that gains in consumption quality are less than was expected.

Rigid Scheduling: A Cause of Time Management Problems

However, the problem of the harried leisure class is not fully explained by a scarcity of time. Poor management of time by society, institutions, and individuals has greatly exacerbated the basic difficulty.

Many social time management problems derive from the question of the scheduling of activities, especially the scheduling of work time. It will be argued here that scheduling practices in the United States are an important factor deteriorating the quality of time. In its broadest interpretation, work scheduling has several dimensions, including the two discussed at some length in chapters 1 through 4—the number of people who work and the average duration of work schedules—but also encompassing the assignment of work among individuals (i.e., the degree to which individuals depart from the standard) and work scheduling in the narrowest sense, the timing or "whenness" of work schedules. Even given the total number of hours worked in society, the degree to which individuals can choose the number, or even the timing, of their hours is a principal determinant of their satisfaction with the quality of their time, and one which will concern us throughout the remainder of this book.

In the United States today, the average employee cannot set his hours of work. One result is that the 40-hour workweek becomes a binding constraint for millions of Americans. Forty hours may be a good average number of hours, in the sense that it is a satisfactory level for the average employee. But employees vary widely in their needs, so that many find the standard workweek either too short or too long. Employees with another source of income (e.g., a pension or the earnings of another family member), with other demands on their time, or simply with an above-average preference for leisure or household production time are likely to find it too long, while those with few time demands on them, but several financial dependents, are more likely to find it too short. Under these circumstances, some individuals will turn to the part-time labor market, absenteeism, or casual labor to shorten their hours, while others seek moonlighting and overtime opportunities. The majority, however, find these alternatives unattractive and must tolerate the 40-hour schedule.[1] (Some of the problems faced by those who have sought alternatives to the standard workweek are discussed in chapters 7 and 8.)

In terms of the model developed in previous chapters, the fixed working hours constraint provides employees with a suboptimal combination of goods and time. For those who prefer a shorter schedule, an additional hour of time off (whether it be applied to household production or consumption time) would be more productive in yielding satisfaction than would be the necessary loss in money income (with its expected negative effect on household production output). For those who find their hours of work to be too short, the reverse argument would hold.

A second basic scheduling problem arises because even those for whom the 40-hour workweek is acceptable typically find that the lack of control of the timing or whenness of their work provides a constraint. To some degree, the quality of household production, leisure or consumption time, and work time are each depreciated by rigid scheduling practices.

The worst examples occur in household production time. Here the most obvious case is provided by the rush-hour commuter congestion caused by many enterprises establishing the same beginning and ending times. The result is a less productive experience. On many city streets, congestion is so bad that an observer of traffic moving at a snail's pace at rush hour would find it difficult to believe that the revolution in commuter technology had had any positive effect on commuter speed. Moreover, for most drivers, commuter congestion (with the resulting traffic jams and stop-and-go movement) markedly reduces the satisfaction they get from this experience. Another area that is adversely affected by work scheduling practices is the utilization of retail trade and professional services. It is true that many retail establishments now remain open on evenings and weekends to accommodate the employed shopper, but some establishments do not. Moreover, the providers of many professional services typically restrict their hours to the normal daytime schedule. Child care is also negatively affected. Those families in which both parents work full-time will have a difficult time in looking after their children in any event, but if their schedules are rigid, their problem is considerably exacerbated. (For example, if the parents have the same 8:30–5:00 schedule, then neither parent can be with their children during most of the latter's waking hours.) Consumption activity is also adversely affected by rigid work scheduling, if indirectly. Crowded highways and beaches on summer weekends (or similarly crowded ski slopes on weekends in the winter) provide obvious examples. Finally the quality of market work activity of some employees also suffers. Some people are natural early or late starters and dislike a schedule designed for the average person. Moreover, some prefer to carry a job through to completion rather than to have to interrupt it at a standard quitting time. More generally, others would simply prefer to start work when they choose and find a rigid schedule confining.

A number of similar disadvantages of rigid scheduling could be cited. Each of these makes a specific, limited contribution to reducing the quality of time. Together the effects of rigid scheduling provide a considerable deterioration in the quality of time.[2]

These phenomena may be interpreted through economic analysis by arguing that the supply of labor to the market is actually greater than would be deduced from the simple statement that the average worker is putting in, say, 40 hours a week. If the worker were to rank possible arrangements of his 112 waking hours a week[3] (perhaps with zero hours of market work at the top, and 112 hours of work at the bottom of the list), an allocation of 40 hours at times chosen by the worker would be well ahead of an allocation of 40 hours chosen at the convenience of the employer. Similarly within a group of workers, an allocation of 40 hours for every worker would presumably be ranked inferior to one which averaged 40 hours per worker, but which permitted those with an above-average need for time off to work fewer hours.

In a sense then rigid schedules mean that workers are supplying more time or at least a distribution of time that imposes more costs upon them than would hours freely chosen by themselves. One of the principal questions that will be asked in the next several chapters is whether we are likely to see a reduction in this dimension of labor supply, that is, a movement toward employee-chosen hours of work, whether or not we move toward a reduction in labor supply in the more conventional way by reducing the number of hours worked by the average person.

Notes

1. Plus compulsory overtime, when this is demanded.
2. These problems are discussed in greater detail in subsequent chapters.
3. Allowing 8 hours a night for sleep.

6 The Determination of Work Schedule Rigidity

It is obvious that a rigid pattern of work scheduling makes the workweek more onerous to the individual than would be one which allowed him greater choice over its timing and duration: rigidity deteriorates the quality of time in household production, recreation, and work. But this observation does not resolve the question of whether rigid schedules are on balance useful or harmful, or the resolution of related questions: if these practices are not absolutely essential on the basis of economic considerations, can a case be made for social intervention, by government regulation, to prevent employers from maintaining rigid schedules given their obviously negative effects on employees? Or if a sufficiently strong case cannot be made for government intervention, can we at least ascertain dynamic forces at work, which afford realistic, if longer-term prospects, for changes that will eventually provide greater scheduling freedom?

Employer Determination of Work Schedules

The determination of the timing and variability of work schedules, like the determination of the average number of hours worked, is generally made by employers (subject to government regulation and, in some cases, union negotiation to improve their profits). In establishing schedules consistent with maximum profits, firms must balance the needs of production, customers, and suppliers against the needs of their employees. And of course their decisions must be exercised in the context of institutional limits imposed by their own bureaucratic, corporate structures.[1]

In considering production needs, employers are faced with two quite different types of situations: those in which it is important to have workers interacting with each other, which require that they work in the same time interval, and those where production needs are best served by nonoverlapping shifts. The need for cooperation in production is found in most job situations; it is perhaps most rigid in blue collar occupations in manufacturing, mining, and railroads but is also found in an attenuated form in the majority of white-collar jobs. It is an inevitable result of the extreme specialization of function which is so necessary to economic productivity.

However, employers are concerned about the productivity of their capital as well as the input of labor, and this often requires that labor be used in shifts so machinery will not be idle. Technical conditions impose further reasons for shift-

work in continuous process industries and in railroads and some other transportation industries. In practice, the two principles are combined in that the
shiftworker is usually as bound to a rigid schedule by the requirements of specialization on his shift as the day worker is by his situation.

Employers argue that production needs are also served by standard shifts in
ways that might more properly be regarded as institutional than as technical.
Under our capitalist system, employers must concern themselves with enforcing
rules against tardiness, and avoiding the invidiuous distinctions that would result
if those workers who were not required to adhere to a standard schedule were
allowed to set their own hours. (If this were permitted, some low-status workers
might have more on-the-job freedom than some medium-status or higher-status
workers.) A standard schedule system is thought to be much easier to administer
under these circumstances. Similarly the employer wishes to avoid the increased
administrative costs which result when employees work differing numbers of
hours. (For example, the question of adjusting fringe benefits to hours worked
not only imposes more paperwork but can create morale problems as well.)[2] In
many lines of industry, especially the large retail trade and service sectors, the
needs of customers play as large or larger role in determining work schedules
than do those of production, in the narrow sense. Insofar as goods are offered or
services provided to firms during business hours, no conflict between the two
types of demands need arise.[3] But when services or goods are offered to nonbusiness consumers, evening and weekend hours are often required in addition to
the regular weekday hours schedules. Finally the needs of employees must be
considered if the employer is to compete for workers and maintain their morale.
For many workers, the standard schedule is quite satisfactory. But for others a
variant is much preferable. This creates incentives for those employers whose
production conditions permit it to introduce nonstandard schedules in the interest of obtaining good labor more cheaply.

It is easy to cite instances of the ways in which individual employers actually
balance these competing needs. We observe numerous compromises among the
production and sales schedule needs of employers, and between the needs of
employers and those of their employees. For example, some retail outlets stay
open in the evening while others close. Hence the employed consumer can usually do most of his shopping after hours, even if he has to travel further to find a
retail outlet, to sacrifice variety, and in many cases to pay a higher price. Similarly many employers will opt for a two-shift operation rather than seeking a
third shift, because of the difficulty of obtaining good quality labor for shiftwork. Sometimes the extent to which employee interests are considered is obscured by a large area of overlap in the concerns of employers and employees.
Thus the choice of a standard workday centered on the noon hour was originally
chosen in the interests of productivity to take maximum advantage of the day-

light hours. But it also serves employees well because of the common aversion to traveling to or from work in darkness.

There are exceptions of course and all interests are not compromised. For example, high-status professionals, such as medical specialists, will only offer their services to employed clients during normal working hours, so that the client must miss work and the productivity of the client's employer must suffer, when the specialist is consulted.

Economic Evaluation of Scheduling Practices

Following this approach, it would be simple to find dozens of examples of the ways in which enterprises weight different interests in coming to a scheduling decision. From this, it might also be possible to forecast the immediate effects on a typical company's profits of new scheduling practices, and even to allocate this profit's effect among impacts on production, sales, and personnel costs. Unfortunately this study of the rationale of individual employers does not suffice for the more difficult task of predicting the long-term, social effects on production and consumption of a nationwide change in scheduling practices.

Again the comparison with the average number of hours case is instructive. If average weekly hours were reduced by, say, one-half day per week, we could make reasonably well-informed guesses about the long-term economic impacts. The results would be similar to (though of course not identical to) a simple multiplication of the effects of reducing the labor supply of one worker by one half day. But by way of contrast, consider the effects of permitting workers to begin work one-half hour earlier each day. If one worker did this, the result would probably be a production loss, but if all workers were given an earlier schedule, they could still cooperate in production and it is possible that no such loss would result.

More generally, scheduling changes in one sector create a series of indirect effects which are difficult to predict. For example, if manufacturing were to adopt a different standard schedule (e.g., a 4-day, 10-hour-day workweek), profound effects would be likely on the work schedules of those employed in the retail trade, recreation, education, and other service industries. These schedule changes would initiate still further changes among those providing services to employees in the service industries. Thus a series of ripple effects would have to be worked out before a new equilibrium was reached. Under these circumstances, it is difficult to predict the long-term impacts of change. One does not know whether current practices are socially optimal and if they are not optimal, how one might approximate optimal arrangements.

This lack of knowledge makes it harder to assess the economic costs of reforms which would give individuals more choice.[4] As a result, it is much more difficult to develop a sound case for or against government intervention to bring about such change. It is true that there are specific situations where a good a priori argument for regulation of schedules exists. For example, the social disadvantages of rush-hour congestion are so obvious that measures to reduce rush-hour traffic by making some modest alterations in work schedules appear justified to most observers, even if we cannot predict all the social and economic consequences. But apart from such arguments relating to the congestion of social overhead capital (see pp. 56–58), the economic analysis of scheduling is generally much too rudimentary for the design of truly optimal regulatory policies.

The Dynamics of Alternative Work Schedules:
Past Developments

However, a more interesting assessment is obtained when one turns from this abstract problem of whether an airtight argument can be made for government intervention to give employees more choice in their schedules to a consideration of the dynamic forces that are in fact working for change. For the long-term trends in the social, economic, and governmental factors influencing work scheduling practices do seem to predict greater employee choice in the years ahead.

If one were to draw a graph with time on the horizontal axis and employee choice of work schedules on the vertical, the result would be a roughly U-shaped pattern. A century or a century and a half ago, schedules were quite destandardized. Most Americans worked on family-run farms or in family-run businesses. In this structure the scheduling of work for market sales, of housework and household manufacture, and of time for leisure or cultural purposes were all done within the family.[5] It was only in the next two or three generations, in the late nineteenth and early twentieth centuries, that most American families lost control of the means of production—the farm or business that had supported them—and went to work for an employer, who set their schedule.

In this same period of rapid industrialization, employers increased the degree of control they could exercise over the movements of their employees. Skilled workers who had practiced their crafts in the same way for many years and who had considerable autonomy on the job often found their job structure reorganized and themselves reduced to the status of semiskilled employees. Resistance to this employer effort was generally without much success. Tighter employer control permitted the introduction of new mass production techniques, which considerably raised productivity and eventually living standards. The new technologies required very close coordination among extremely specialized workers. Under these circumstances, one is not surprised to learn that hours of work came to be extremely standardized.

Nor is it surprising to find that this emphasis on standardization spread from the economically dominant manufacturing sector to office work and other situations where the technological imperatives were not so strong. Here, too, increased specialization of function provided a rationale for more rigid scheduling. However, for the past several decades we have seen the development of trends which have undermined the social rationale for standardization. These trends are likely to have a still greater influence on work scheduling in the years ahead.

Factors Supporting the Development of Alternative Work Schedules

Changes in the Employer Interest

In the first place, the needs of employers have been changing. As a result of ever-higher labor productivity in manufacturing and agriculture, the majority of the labor force is now in the white-collar and service sectors. The trend to white-collar employment offers at least passive support for the development of alternative work schedules by weakening the production efficiency argument for standardization. White-collar work generally is fairly well suited for standardized hours, but very often it is also consistent with a high degree of flexibility. White-collar jobs are usually much less specialized and closely coordinated than those in heavy manufacturing. Hence white-collar work often lends itself to a division of tasks between those an employee has to do in conjunction with others and those he can do by himself. As a result, it may permit the introduction of a limited degree of schedule flexibility. Moreover, studies of alternative work schedules indicate that, for a number of bureaucratic reasons—payroll periods, billing periods, and so forth—there are actually regular fluctuations in much white-collar work which can make nonstandard hours more profitable for the employer.

The most dramatic change in the employer's interest has been the relative growth of those divisions of the retail trade and service industries that directly serve the public. The impact of this shift is increased by two other trends; first, the rise in female labor force participation to the point where a majority of married women now work. Obviously workers in the retail trade and nonbusiness service industries are dealing with people who are not at work. But with a majority of adult women and most adult, prime-aged males now members of the labor force, the purchaser of a good or service is most likely an employee himself. Clearly then the buyers and sellers cannot always work the same hours. Sometimes the buyer makes the adjustment, as when an employee takes a long lunch hour to have an appliance repaired or pick up some forms in a government office (as we saw in chapter 5). But more frequently it is the supplier of the service who must work an alternative schedule to meet the customer's needs. For example, such industries as recreation, retail trade, food preparation, automotive service, and a variety of repair trades must now maintain long schedules.

A second supportive trend is the long-term decline in hours of work. Many years ago, retail trade and service outlets also maintained long schedules, in part because they wished to attract the business of those who worked 10-hour or 12-hour days in manufacturing and other industries. But in that era, stores were staffed by the simple expedient of extending the workdays of retail trade and service employees (since their labor was lighter than factory work, they were expected to endure a longer day). Today that alternative is no longer open to management (in fact hours of work in retail trade are now much shorter than those in manufacturing). Instead, long hours of operation demand the use of either part-timers or shiftworkers, or both (see chapter 7).

Finally another group of employees in the service sector have nonstandard schedules because they are supplying emergency services. As our demands for better health care, better police and fire protection, and other emergency services increase, a larger proportion of the work force finds employment at nonstandard hours. Thus changes in the nature of work have greatly increased the number of job situations in which the employer's objective interests are furthered, or at least are not seriously impaired, by the introduction of alternative work schedules.

A second factor changing employer needs is the development of new personnel management techniques, broadly associated with the dominance of large corporate or government employers. It may seem paradoxical to associate size with a weakening of standardizing forces, since large organizations destroy the informality of the smaller firm (which might have a permissive attitude toward nonstandard hours schedules) and since the large firm also lends itself to greater specialization of function (and hence to more interaction among employees, with consequent constraints on hours schedules). However, an increasing number of corporation and government organizations have come to recognize the deleterious effects on efficiency and morale of offering an impersonal image to the employee, and have developed personnel programs to provide a less alienating experience for the employee. These include both measures to give the worker an opportunity to schedule his own time and the development of complementary programs which mesh well with scheduling reforms, where these seem desirable on other grounds (these innovations are discussed in greater detail in chapter 9).

Moreover, while the large organization does give maximum scope for specialization of function, there are apparently limits to which specialization can be economically carried. In such vast organizations one usually finds a number of people doing the same or similar jobs. Experiments with alternative work schedules also find that this condition, a number of people doing the same job, greatly increases the prospect for success with the new schedules.

Employee Demands

Another set of factors challenging the logic of standard schedules and supporting the spread of alternatives derives from the changing position of American employees—their new needs and their much enhanced ability to secure their goals.

An important source of change lies within the family. In the same period of industrialization in which most adult American males were reduced to employee status, the scheduling of family life was further complicated by the introduction of compulsory primary education. However, in the typical household the mother (and perhaps a grown sister, a grandmother, or a maiden aunt) were available to close gaps in the family schedule. Neither a capitalist employer nor an educational bureaucracy constrained the schedules of the females in the house; they could be counted on to make sure that all family members went off to work well groomed and well fed, to look after the children when they came home after school, and to help the employed adults to enjoy their leisure in the evenings.

All this has changed. Partly as a result of social security and other income maintenance schemes for the aged, older relatives generally do not live with their children or their nephews and nieces. Even more important, more and more wives have been entering the labor force, so that a majority of adult women are now employed.

This has created very intractable scheduling problems in millions of families: witness the demand for day-care facilities and our concern over the so-called latch key child. A potential solution for these scheduling dilemmas is some form of staggered working hours. If the daily work schedule of husband and wife can differ by as much as 3.5 to 4 hours, then even if both parents must commute and work an 8-hour day, it will be possible for one parent to stay at home until their child is ready to go off to his 6 hours of school, and for the other to be at home when the child is through for the day. Flexible work schedules provide one alternative (see the discussion in chapter 9). Permanent part-time work provides another alternative solution in this situation. But a standard workweek offers the worst possible arrangement.

Another trend in the family with consequences for the development of alternative work schedules is the later age at which children enter the full-time labor force, partly as a result of the higher levels of formal education that have now become common. But many of these youths are employed at part-time jobs at schedules that fit in well with their class times. Finally as a result of a declining birthrate and death rate, the proportion of elderly has increased sharply. This group constitutes another important source of employer demand for alternative schedules.

These changes in the needs of employees are complementary with changes in their position. It was argued in chapter 3 that a basic factor affecting working schedules (hours reduction) was secular increases in the demand for labor reflected in ever-higher real hourly earnings (due in turn to long-term processes of capital accumulation and technological advance).

The analysis in chapters 4 and 5 would predict that higher real wages would also be a factor supportive of the development of alternative work schedules. In recent decades, rising real wages have generally brought improvements in the quality of time, though not in its quantity (since hours of work have leveled off). However, it was argued that the rigid scheduling of work and other activities has prevented the quality of time from rising as rapidly as one might have hoped, given the vast increase in consumption spending per hour of free time. This would predict some pressure for change: that is, as increases in goods per unit of time reduced the expected marginal gain in satisfaction from still more goods, while rigid schedules continued to provide a major obstacle to the enjoyment of these goods (or rather of the activities in which the goods are employed), one would expect that employees would now be willing to trade off more goods to obtain a modicum of schedule freedom.

Moreover, if employers at the same time were finding that the relative cost to them of providing alternative work schedules was declining, for the reasons given above, this would provide additional force to the movement to schedule freedom as a result of decisions made by profit-seeking employers. If we accept the expanded definition of labor supply developed in chapter 5, a movement toward schedule flexibility might be considered as a reduction in labor supply, analogous to the reduction in hours of work observed in earlier years as wage rates rose and the relative cost of leisure declined (see chapter 4).

The Interest of Government

Finally the interest of government in working schedules is increasing, in large part because of an increased concern with better utilization of our social overhead capital. The long-term growth in population and in per capita income in this country, with the consequent drain on domestic resources, has, as we all know, generated an acute interest in reducing pressures on the environment and in conserving materials and energy. This new interest in a more intelligent use of our social overhead capital has led planners to focus on the scheduling or timing of activities as one important area in which savings can be made.

The French social thinker and government planner, Jacques de Chalendar, believes social demand for a more rational use of social overhead capital will be the primary factor in generating effective demands for alternative work schedules. In his excellent monograph on alternative schedules, *l'Aménagement du Temps,* de Chalendar begins by asking us to consider which items in our households are provided on an individual basis and which must be used in rotation? A bed is used for 8 hours a day, and so, in all but the most depressed circumstances, each individual will have his own space in bed. But a bathroom is used much less; de Chalendar estimates about one-half hour a day per individual. And so, in most families, individuals will have to share bathrooms. One can go around the house, predicting which items must be shared: on the basis of the time each is used during the day or week, the cost of providing one for each family member, and the difficulty of working out a sharing arrangement.

Then de Chalendar turns his attention to the business enterprise where a similar logic is used in deciding which facilities shall be shared among employees and which facilities—for example, a secretary's typewriter or a machinist's lathe—shall be reserved for the use of one worker.

Finally de Chalendar asks, why don't we use the same hard, dollars-and-cents logic in allocating those facilities which we use socially? His most telling examples are drawn from the journey to work. Whether one is talking about a space in an office elevator at closing time, a lane on a freeway at rush hour, a seat on a bus, or a place on the train, logic would appear to demand a staggering of commuters so as to permit many uses each day of the same facility. Similarly the recreationists offer us many examples of the benefits we could obtain from a more staggered use of leisure time; for example, if summer weekends could be scheduled during the week rather than on Saturdays and Sundays. Then that favored spot on the beach or that popular picnic site could be used much more efficiently.

As individuals live ever further from their jobs and embark upon ever-more ambitious recreation activities, we can expect a continued upward trend in demands that we economize on our social overhead capital. The strength of this reaction will most likely continue to be focused on scheduling issues both by environmentalist concerns about overcrowding of outdoor recreation areas and by an awareness of the extra energy costs imposed by commuter congestion.

The implications for work scheduling of this interest in conserving our social overhead capital are rather obvious. In general, the worst possible work schedule for economizing on social overhead capital is a standard workweek, which forces nearly everyone into standard commuting and leisure-time patterns.

Hence one can expect social pressures for destandardization. Of course the distribution of work schedules which makes the most efficient use of social overhead capital will not be the same as the one which would maximize employee satisfaction. For example, many people prefer to take their vacations at the beach when the weather is warmer, to have a workweek that provides Sunday or

Saturday off (for religious reasons), to center their workday on the daylight hours, and so on, and are willing to tolerate some crowding to obtain these preferred schedules.

Nevertheless, there is sufficient overlapping of interest—given the very negative effects of standardized schedules on the utilization of social overhead capital—to give government an incentive to support employee-chosen alternative work schedules. This government interest is not likely to be an idle one. Relatively little emphasis was put on the role of government as a determinant of the past evolution of working schedules, but this may well change in the future as pressures build for better utilization of social overhead capital. Already the past several years have seen a number of bills in Congress, supportive of alternative work schedules. These have attracted widespread interest and have generated extensive hearings.

This legislative history has also emphasized another factor supportive of change: a number of employee-oriented groups—especially of feminists and the militant aged—are no longer content to rely on employer decisions to create jobs at schedules that a mother or older person would find convenient. Increasingly they are turning to legislative action to force employers to take these initiatives. These groups are now playing a prominent role among those working for favorable legislation.[6] This development has important, if difficult-to-predict, implications for the future of alternative work schedules.

Summary and Conclusions

An analysis of the dynamics of alternative work schedules suggests that a number of factors are working together to generate demands for a departure from standard schedules.

1. Employers have the principal role in determining whether work schedules should be rigid or flexible, since they set these schedules, though employers must also respond to demands from employees and to government pressure.

The employer's own needs are influenced by the industrial and occupational mix, which has been changing in ways favorable to the development of alternative work schedules, reducing the relative cost to employers of providing them. Rising wage costs also provide an inducement to develop personnel technologies, such as alternative work schedules, which might better motivate labor. At the same time, a willingness on the part of the labor force to pay a larger relative price to obtain schedule freedom will provide a further inducement to the cost-conscious employer.

2. Employees are likely to become increasingly willing to pay a higher price for scheduling freedom as a result of their increased affluence; the tighter time constraint under which families must operate as an increased proportion of the adults in the family enters the labor force; and the larger number of students,

older workers, and others who are interested in a limited participation in the work force.

3. Finally governments are also moving to support the development of alternative work schedules (as large employers themselves, and possibly by changing regulations which affect schedules in the private sector). The government interest derives from concerns about the efficient utilization of our social overhead capital and about methods for increasing the labor force contribution of marginal workers. This interest gains strength both from the increased concern with conservation of material resources and from the projected slowdown in labor force growth.

Notes

1. The following analysis relates to problems of variability in the number of hours as well as variation in the timing of work. There are, in addition, specific problems for employers if hours are either very long or very short. These considerations also impact upon the question of extreme variability in hours (e.g., schedules that would allow employees to work 20 or 60 hours a week); but because of the complex questions they raise, those issues are discussed separately in chapter 3 (long hours), chapter 7 (the part-time job market), and chapter 12 (a future reduction in hours), and in appendixes A and B. The rationale for employer scheduling decisions is also developed in more detail in the description of the flexible scheduling systems given in chapters 9 and 10.

2. See the discussion of part-time employment in chapter 7.

3. But here too periodic variations (e.g., certain busy hours of the day, week, month, and year) may create a demand for nonstandard work hours. See chapters 7 and 9.

4. Though an attempt is made, in the second part of the book, to use available research findings in a discussion of the likely effects of some important alternative working schedules on key economic and leisure time variables.

5. Though the need to work in daylight hours did introduce a common sunup-to-sundown schedule in many occupations, before the improvement of artificial lighting.

6. See passim, U.S. House of Representatives, Hearings before the Subcommittee on Manpower and Civil Service (1975), and Hearings before the Subcommittee on Employee Ethics and Utilization (1977); and U.S. Senate, Hearings before the Subcommittee on Employment, Poverty, and Migratory Labor (1976).

Part II
Alternative Work
Schedules and Leisure

We turn now to the second part of our inquiry: a more specific discussion of the realistic prospects for relief from pressures on leisure time through changes in work schedules. The principal innovations considered will be schedules which offer individuals greater choice in the number of their hours of work, in the timing of these hours, or alternatively those which yield a general reduction in hours of paid work.

There will be some change of focus in these chapters. Because we are interested in a realistic forecast of future schedule changes and because, as we saw in chapter 6, the specific needs of employers play a major role in schedule determination, we cannot limit the analysis here to a consideration of the aspiration of employees or even of their market choices. At least as much attention must be given to the demand-side factors that influence employer behavior as to the supply-side factors that shape employee preferences in determining schedules. Similarly where they are most relevant the concerns of trade union organizations, or the government, will also be treated in considerable detail.

7

Conventional Alternative Work Schedules

Introduction

The dominance of the standard work schedule is obvious. Yet a surprisingly large minority works at some other schedule. For the most part, these nonstandard schedules are conventional in that the employer, not the employee, sets working times. As a result, they provide an imperfect system from the point of view of the employee; there are still many round pegs in square holes. While some employers make concessions to employee needs when setting working times and many individuals with special schedule needs will gravitate toward employment offering an appropriate schedule, there is no reason to expect any perfect matching. Employers must weigh other factors along with employee needs in setting schedules and employees must consider a number of variables before changing jobs to obtain a better schedule. However, despite their obvious imperfections, the options these alternatives offer do make it possible for millions of Americans to find schedules that, if not ideal, are at least preferable to the standard workweek.

Conventional alternative work schedules are a difficult "system" to study empirically, inasmuch as the data on them are scattered and incomplete; but it is essential that the available evidence be analyzed in any objective discussion of the prospects for change.

The Extent of Nonstandard Schedules

The principal forms of employer-determined alternative work schedules of interest to us here are voluntary part-time work and, to a lesser extent, shiftwork and compressed workweeks. Of course this is not the full list of what we might in the broadest interpretation regard as alternative work schedules. About 11 percent of those employed are farmers or self-employed businessmen;[1] members of this group set their own hours and typically work irregular schedules (though often with much more weight given to the needs of their businesses than to their own personal convenience). The issue of developing suitable alternative schedules has only been a problem for the other 89 percent, the members of the nonagricultural wage and salary work force, and this group will claim most of our attention here.

Even within this group, a lack of work provides another, if perverse, form of alternative work schedule. About 6 percent of the nonagricultural wage and salary labor force is unemployed. Moreover, among the approximately 17 million workers who are employed less than full-time, 18 percent are classified as involuntarily part-time.

But among employed nonagricultural wage and salary workers, about 14 percent voluntarily work less than 35 hours per week.[2] Another 5 to 6 percent are moonlighters, most of whom are part-timers. (Only 1 out of 20 moonlighters actually works two full-time jobs.)[3] About 12 percent are shiftworkers (shiftworkers are defined here as those who neither begin work within the 6:30 A.M. to 9:30 A.M. interval nor end it during the 2:30 P.M. to 6:30 P.M. period). Finally about 1.7 percent of the work force are on compressed schedules, where these are defined as lasting for at least 35 hours a week, scheduled during four or fewer days.

The inclusion of shiftworkers in this grouping is somewhat questionable, at least if we are interested in attractive alternatives to the standard schedule. The literature on shiftwork indicates that workers are mostly attracted to these schedules by the high wages they offer (or because day work is difficult to obtain). Nevertheless the same literature also indicates that the schedule is an attractive alternative on its own grounds for some employees who dislike day work.

On the other hand, voluntary part-time work presumably does provide a generally attractive alternative work schedule for those who accept it. Those who would prefer full-time work are excluded by the definition of voluntary part-timer. Moreover, as we shall see, part-time workers pay a rather steep economic price to obtain this schedule, affording further evidence of its nonpecuniary attractions to those who seek it at such cost. As a principal alternative to the standard schedule, actively sought by millions of Americans (about one-fifth of the labor force if we include part-time moonlighters),[4] the market for part-time jobs will receive the major share of our attention in this discussion of conventional alternative work schedules.

Part-time Labor Market as a Source of Employment

Part-time employment has been helpful in permitting many individuals to balance the scheduling demands of work against those of family and other private concerns. This has both eased the lot of those employed and enabled more people to enter the labor force. Thus the dramatic increase in the adult female labor force participation rate in the past 20 years has been greatly assisted by the development of the part-time labor job market. In the same period, the proportion of part-timers in the labor force (male and female) rose from 1 in 12 to over

1 in 7. In all, about two-fifths of all the new jobs for women in this period have been part-time.

Part-time jobs are attractive to women for several reasons. Given the existing sexual distribution of labor,[5] the great majority of women have an alternative source of income and so are not completely dependent upon their earnings (in the absence of a working husband, a social security or a welfare check is likely to be available to supplement part-time earnings). Moreover, partly as a result of that same division of labor, women are likely to have extensive nonmarket work responsibilities: housework, child care, and so on. Some of these women could handle a full-time job it it were scheduled at a time which meshed with their own nonmarket work tasks (e.g., if it permitted them to be home in the late afternoon when their children arrived from school).[6] But most jobs are still on a rigid nine-to-five or eight-to-four schedule. The responsibilities of other women are such that 40 hours would be too much, even if they did have full freedom to schedule them.

Of course many women do not work for pay, and many others work full-time. But part-time job opportunities often play a significant role in their lives as well. For many women, part-time employment is important in a transition period between childbearing, when they do not work for pay, and a later period, when the children are grown and full-time work becomes more attractive. In the years in which child rearing, though still time consuming, does allow more time for other activities, part-time work can be used to provide both a source of income and, in some cases, a way of maintaining old job skills.[7]

Part-time work also appeals to many young people who are making the transition from school to work. The post-World War II period saw a vast increase in the number of young part-time workers, as student employment rose from 1 percent or less of the labor force in 1940 to over 6 percent today.[8] This occurred partly as a result of the earlier baby boom, partly as a result of the rising proportion of young people going to college. Demographic changes may reduce the relative size of the college age population, but the proportion of youths staying in school is not expected to decline. In fact given the difficulties many families now incur in paying college costs and the inability of financially hard-pressed colleges to meet these needs through scholarship aid, the future demand for part-time jobs for students could continue to increase, despite the leveling off in numbers of young people. Moreover, other young people, not in school (but not yet fully attached to the labor force), will continue to prefer part-time over full-time work. Hence this role of part-time employment is likely to continue to be important.

Finally part-time work can and sometimes does help ease retirement from the labor force. A less than optimum use of part-timers is now made here. Phased retirement (a gradual reduction in hours and responsibility to coincide with the slow diminution of the worker's physical capacity) has been recommended by many experts in the field of gerontology.[9] In this ideal model, the employer gradually phases out the employee; in practice, employers generally prefer an abrupt retirement for their workers. Hence the older worker must seek part-time employment elsewhere, where he can only utilize a portion of his acquired skills, as a beginner in a new organization. Another limit on part-time work by older workers is imposed by the social security system. Under present OASDHI regulations, if the worker makes more than $4,500, he loses his pension (at the rate of fifty cents for each dollar earned over this limit). Hence both employer practices and the operation of the OASDHI system ensure that much less than optimal use is made of part-time work as a way of providing gradual retirement. Nevertheless the existing opportunities for part-time work are utilized by a large number of older workers.

Moonlighters

Each of these groups—mothers, students, and retired workers—is in a sense marginal to the labor force: they have some alternative source of income and some limit on the number of hours they can work. The labor force participation of these groups is significantly lower than that of the groups from which the average worker is drawn.

Yet the part-time job market also serves another group: those who are so solidly attached to the labor force and so specialized in market employment that they regard the standard workweek as too short, and also work at a second job. This group of part-timers is drawn mainly from the married male labor force, with little representation by women or students.

The data in table 7-1 give the proportion of voluntary part-timers among different demographic groups. Voluntary part-timers are defined here as those who voluntarily work 1 to 34 hours a week (i.e., do not wish full-time employment). Young is defined as less than 25 years of age; prime age as 25 to 49 years; and older as 50 or more. The data in table 7-1 support the hypotheses that the demographic groups expected to desire part-time employment in fact are much more likely to have such jobs.

Employer Demand for Part-time Labor

Employer Resistance to the Use of Part-timers

These opportunities for part-timers depend upon employers finding it profitable to hire them. In fact an increase in the number of those who find part-time work

Table 7-1
Distribution of Demographic Groups over Types of Employment[10],[a]

| | All | Voluntary Part-timer | | | | Full-timer |
| | | Single Job (Part-time Job only Job) | | | Part-time Moonlighter (One Part-time, One Full-time Job) | (Full-time Job Only Job) |
		All	Working Late Afternoons	Free Late Afternoons		
All	100%	12.9%	9.5%	3.5%	3.8%	81.2%
Married men	100	2.4	1.7	0.7	6.2	89.7
Single men	100	25.6	21.2	4.4	2.0	70.4
Females with children under 15	100	29.5	20.2	9.3	0.8	66.9
Other females	100	17.8	12.8	5.0	1.7	78.1
Young males	100	25.9	21.5	4.4	2.9	66.3
Prime-age males	100	1.3	1.0	0.3	6.7	89.9
Older males	100	5.0	3.4	1.7	4.1	89.2
Young females	100	33.0	25.8	7.3	1.7	64.4
Prime-age females	100	18.7	12.1	6.6	1.2	78.6
Older females	100	21.1	14.4	6.7	1.5	76.6

[a]Nonagricultural wage and salary workers.

is occurring in spite of a long-standing preference for full-time over part-time workers for most jobs.

Obviously if employers were paying the same weekly wage to both groups, they would prefer full-time help. But even when they must pay the same hourly wages, they have usually preferred full-timers. This is not to argue that employers will always be willing to pay a higher hourly wage to employees willing to put in longer hours. On the contrary, there is evidence that when hours of work were reduced from high levels after World Wars I and II, production losses were minimal.[11] Workers gained in health and energy from the diminished fatigue and related effects of long hours. Accidents were less likely to occur, quality control of product was improved, and other similar benefits were obtained. But this type of dramatic gain, characteristically observed when hours of work are reduced from a weekly total of 60 or more to 35 or 40 per week, is generally not expected as one goes from 35 or 40 hours to 15 or 20 hours per week. Moreover, there are a number of reasons why unit labor costs will generally increase with very short hours schedules.

Training and Promotion Problems

First, the economics of training and promotion make the part-timer relatively more costly. Many companies and government organizations provide formal training programs for their employees, largely or altogether at the company's expense. In others, formal training is limited, but an employee learns his job through experience, gradually becoming more valuable to the firm. Eventually he will be promoted through the various skill ranks of his job. In some cases, the worker will then move up to a managerial or other higher position in the firm.

Part-timers are generally regarded as unsuitable for beginning jobs in these mobility chains: a basic argument against the use of part-timers here is that the expected total number of hours worked in the firm by a part-timer will be much less than that worked by a full-timer. In the first place, many managers believe that the turnover rate of part-timers exceeds that of full-timers. Others point to contradictory experiences, leading to some question about the relationship between turnover rate and part-time status.[12] But even if turnover rates are assumed to be exactly the same for the two groups, the part-timer will still put in fewer hours with the company by reason of his reduced weekly schedule.

The implications of this difference for the economics of training can be elucidated with a simplified example.[13] Let us make the assumption that it takes an employee 800 working hours to become fully skilled in a particular job. Over this period as a whole, his net value to the company is assumed to be zero: the contribution he does make as he approaches full-skill level is offset by extra costs in the earlier period, such as that of providing instructors, disrupting other workers (who informally help him to continue to improve his job skills after the formal training course), spoiled work, and so on. The hypothetical employee is paid $2.00 an hour during the training period and $3.00 afterward. After his training, he is worth $4.00 an hour to the company, so that the firm then receives a net benefit of $1.00 an hour from the trained employee.

Assume also that the average employee puts in 80 weeks with the company before quitting or otherwise being separated. Under these assumptions, the average full-timer (whom we will assume works 40 hours a week) will finish his training in 20 weeks (800/40 = 20); this will leave him 60 weeks to work as a fully skilled employee. The employer pays $1,600 (800 X $2.00) in training costs, but receives $2,400 (60 X 40 X $1.00) in posttraining benefits for a handsome net surplus of $800 on its $1,600 investment—a 50 percent return.

The case of the part-timer is rather different. Assuming a 20-hour week for the part-timer, he will take 40 weeks to finish his training (800/20 = 40), leaving a 40-week pay out period. The training costs are the same as in the full-time case ($1,600) but the payoff is now only $800 (40 X 20 X $1.00) so the company loses $800 on its $1,600 investment. Of course this example would in practice have to be modified in a number of ways to make it more realistic. (For example, the learning of some tasks benefits more from an intensive 8-hour-a-day exposure than others. And individuals also vary in the extent to which they will profit from a more concentrated work experience.)[14] But the basic logic of the example does help to explain the reluctance of managers to hire part-timers for jobs that require much training (see figure 7-1).

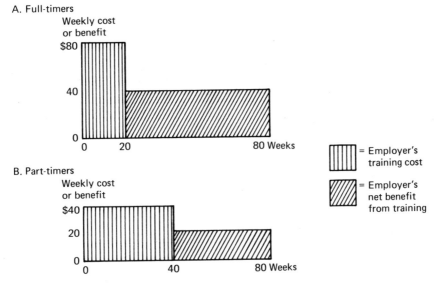

Figure 7-1. Economics of Training Part-time and Full-time Workers[a]

[a]See text for explanation.

Another factor that helps to explain this employer reluctance to train part-timers is the restricted option value of the trained part-timer. Writers in the field of the economics of education and training have in recent years stressed that we should consider as part of the return to training not only the benefit that will be derived if the trainee spends the rest of his life (or at least the rest of the period with the company that trained him) doing just the task for which he is trained but also the gain that will be obtained if the employee is subsequently subjected to still further training for a higher position (or for a horizontal move if demand conditions change).

These additional options are more limited for the part-timer for two reasons; first, because it may be that the economics of training argument detailed above would make further, more complex training uneconomical for the part-timer. Second, because the time restrictions—hours per day and time of day—imposed by the part-timer often sharply limit the number of jobs an individual can fill. For example, a housewife available mornings only may make a perfectly good switchboard operator, but might not be thought of as eligible for a job as, say, assistant office manager.

Supervision, Coordination, and Communications Problems

A second objection to part-time employment relates to supervision, coordination, and communications costs. If a set of full-time jobs is divided into part-time jobs (say, on a two-for-one basis), the size of the direct labor work force may be just doubled, yielding no change in direct labor costs. But indirect costs are likely to be increased. The probable increase in training costs imposed by the use of part-timers has already been discussed. But there are other costs which might also be increased as a result of using more people to do the same work.

There is a fairly extensive literature by economists and especially by organization theorists on the influence of the size of a business or government organization on its efficiency. It is generally agreed that size has both advantages and disadvantages.[15] But most of the advantages of scale that are adduced can be restated as due fundamentally to gains from specialization: as the number of employees is increased, it is argued, they can be trained for ever-more specialized tasks. Similarly in a larger business, specialized departments can be developed and utilized to assist in the management and administration of the enterprise. However, none of these advantages is obtained when the number of workers is increased by replacing full-timers with part-timers. The economics of training argument developed in the preceding section predicts that less, not more, training will be given the part-time work force. And no increase in production or sales is expected which would provide an economic justification for creating a more specialized departmental structure.

But if increasing the number of part-timers does not bring the advantages of

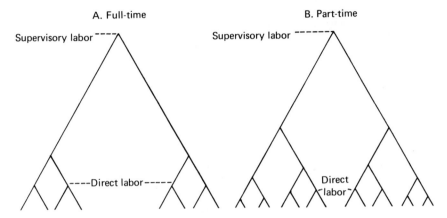

Figure 7-2. Supervisory Costs of Part-time and Full-time Workers[a]

[a]Simplified illustration of organization chart: see text.

size, it does impose the disadvantages of a larger work force, discussed in the size economy literature. More specifically, an increase in the work force will, ceteris paribus, increase supervision, coordination, and communications costs. As the number of employees is increased, either the span of supervisory control is increased, so that each supervisor must oversee more workers, or the number of layers of supervision is increased (as in figure 7-2). Hence one would predict either a reduction in productive efficiency or an increase in administrative costs, depending upon whether managers are utilized more intensively or their ranks are increased.

Coordination and communications costs are also increased. Figure 7-3 presents the classic view of how these could increase as the number in a simple work group is increased. If the initial size of the group is large, the number of links quadruples as the number of employees doubles. For smaller groups, a more rapid rate of increase is predicted. If interactions among combinations of workers—pairs, trios, and so on—as well as among single workers are considered, the increase in the number of possible interactions will, even for a quite small work force, quickly reach astronomical proportions.[16]

In practice, communications and coordination costs need not rise quite so rapidly. In the first place, not all workers have to interact with each other, or with all possible subgroups of workers. In the second place, the flow of work and information is to some extent controllable by management and, at some cost it is true, can be modified by various types of job redesign plans as the size of the organization grows, limiting the rise in communications and coordination costs.[17]

On the other hand, the use of part-timers imposes an especially difficult set

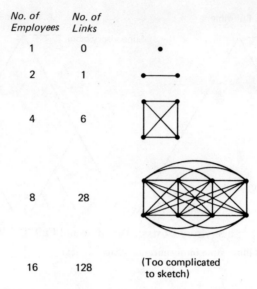

No. of Employees	No. of Links
1	0
2	1
4	6
8	28
16	128

(Too complicated to sketch)

Figure 7-3. Communications Links with Increased Number of Employees

of supervisory, communications, and coordination problems when the part-timers are used sequentially: for example, when two or more shifts of part-timers are employed to maintain a needed service over an 8-hour period or to obtain a more economical use of work places (see the discussion in the next section). Then two or more groups are formed, with no obvious means of communication and coordination. Here it is necessary to improvise—to use a full-time worker, a full-time supervisor, or overlapping shifts—to establish some type of interaction.

Work Place Utilization Problems

Another cost of increasing the number of employees needed for a given work output is that it may require much more capital stock. This is most dramatically true in such industries as manufacturing, mining, and railroads, and in fact is probably the chief reason for the low level of part-time utilization there. However, it can also be important in other situations; for example, clerical work in a high-rent office district.

A typical managerial response to this problem is the use of shiftwork. When full-time labor is used, the addition of an evening or night shift can be employed to double (or triple) the utilization of capital equipment. But in practice, even the manufacturing industries make a limited use of shiftwork: shiftworkers are hard to obtain, require an hourly pay differential, and are very often not as productive as day workers.[18]

The shiftwork principle is sometimes employed in part-time employment as well. For example, one clerk can be employed in the morning and another in the afternoon to maintain utilization of a desk. But the shiftwork principle is no panacea here. In the first place, the supply of morning workers and afternoon workers may not be equal. In the second place, using part-timers in shifts considerably increases communications problems among the work force. Hence in situations where the employer wishes to maintain operation of his facility, full-time help have a competitive advantage over part-timers.[19]

Disadvantages from Part-time Work as a Nonstandard Schedule

These disadvantages are inherent in the small number of hours worked by part-timers. They would hold whether or not the hours of all workers were reduced to the part-time level (see chapter 12 for a fuller discussion of this point). But there are additional disadvantages which result just because part-time work is an alternative or nonstandard schedule. The discussion in chapter 6 emphasized the importance of productive interactions among employees as a factor supporting a standard workweek. In practice, part-timers are generally not used where interactions between full-time and part-time workers are an important consideration, unless management strategies can be devised to reduce its significance; for example, by the employment of consecutive shifts of part-timers.

A second class of difficulties is generated by the institutional problems of employing workers on nonstandard shifts (see the discussion in chapter 6). These considerations are not so rigidly binding as are the more technical constraints, but they do serve as a deterrent to some potential employers of part-time workers. Surveys of employer usage of part-timers both here and in Europe indicate that such institutional problems are often a major reason for underutilizing part-timers. For example, the question of the prorating of fringe benefits for part-timers imposes some administrative costs upon management. Moreover, unless this prorating is done skillfully, the morale of full-time employees sags when part-timers are given what the others regard as excessive privileges. This morale issue is not necessarily resolved by an arithmetically correct division of cash benefits; it can also require some more visible distinction between the two groups of workers. For example, part-timers may be denied access to the company cafeteria or to recreational facilities in order to reassure the full-time workers that they are still held in higher esteem by management.

These administrative and morale problems have been resolved in a variety of ways. But the survey results indicate they are still given a perhaps unduly heavy weight in decision making by some tradition-bound managements, unwilling to make the necessary administrative investment in change.[20]

Factors Supporting Increased Usage

This list of disadvantages helps us to understand the relatively limited use now made of part-timers, but does not explain the rapid growth in the use of part-timers that has taken place.

Better Supply of Part-timers

The most obvious advantage to the employer of hiring part-timers is that there is now available a very substantial supply of potential part-time workers as a result of the changing needs of employees (see chapter 6). This abundant supply has a number of implications for employer decision making. In some job situations, it means that part-timers can literally be paid less per hour for just the same work. In other situations, institutional considerations—union rules, company practices, civil service requirements, considerations of employee morale, and so forth—prevent such wage differentiation, but the abundance of potential part-time labor still makes it more attractive. Even if he cannot vary the money wage, the employer may still be able to obtain better quality labor for the same hourly wage.[21]

Neglect of this very important point has often led to misunderstanding of the operation of the part-time labor market. In the empirical survey method, employers are asked how their experience with part-time and full-time help compares. The employer often cites a number of favorable experiences he has had in using part-time employees which, if not correctly understood, can be mistakenly interpreted as denoting the efficiency of part-time work rather than the ability of the employer to tap a wider pool of labor if he opts for part-time workers. More specifically, the better supply of part-timers permits employers to obtain workers who are mature, experienced, and well educated, or depending on the nature of the employer's need, workers with such specific characteristics as a strong back, nimble fingers, or an attractive appearance.

Moreover, the personal qualities of the part-timer cannot only outweigh the disadvantages of part-time work for the employer, under some circumstances a supposedly negative characteristic can in a sense actually be converted into a positive feature of using part-timers. For example, it was argued that a disadvantage of using part-timers was that it was generally not economical to train them. This was a formally correct argument for the average employee. But as any employer knows, workers vary very widely in the speed with which they learn a new job. If the supply of applicants for part-time jobs consists overwhelmingly of those whom the employer perceives as quick learners, at least in comparison with those whom the employer can hire at the same hourly wage among full-timers, he will have to rethink his opposition to employing part-time workers on these grounds; under some circumstances it will be more economical to train part-timers than full-timers, despite the obvious technical argument. More generally, the formal objections to part-time employment in terms of hiring, screening, training, supervision, and communications costs can all be turned around when the "human factor" argument strongly favors the part-timer.

In practice, this factor gains importance because of widespread differences in the quality of part-time workers and because of the heterogeneity observed among job situations in terms of the relative importance of human and technical factors. Part-timers span the range of educational levels. Their average attainment is quite similar to that of full-timers. Sometimes the formal education of the part-timer provides a skill which enables him to move directly into a high-status job, without any further on-the-job training. (A part-time schoolteacher would provide a good example here.) Other types of schooling, for example, a liberal arts education, may simply make the worker a better learner as well as a generally more productive person after he is broken in on the new job.

Part-timers vary considerably in the amount of job experience which they have acquired. Housewives who are reentering the labor market or older workers who are stepping down from full-time jobs often have substantial amounts of useful job experience. True, they are not likely to find work as part-timers with the same firm that trained them as full-timers; but if they can find work in the same field, that aspect of their training which is of general use in the field, as opposed to that of benefit only to their previous employer, will still have value. (This distinction corresponds to that made between specific and general training by the human capital school of economists.) And even in the unlikely case that the mature part-timer has never worked full-time, he will still have some general job experience, though probably at rather low-level jobs.

Such advantages are of course lacking in the young part-timer, but he may have other specific, attractive characteristics for the employer. The broad back of the young male athlete, the native sales ability of the attractive young coed, or the intelligence and ambition of the straight-A student will recommend them for specific openings in the part-time labor market. The job experience of part-timers with such characteristics will often be quite different from the experience of those with more average qualities. In fact many of the more successful may be able to compete with full-timers for relatively good jobs.

Changing Industry and Occupation Mix

Job situations also vary in the degree to which technical conditions are adverse or favorable to part-timers. In some jobs, technical conditions make the use of part-timers very difficult. In others, part-timers are only at a modest disadvantage so that a relatively better quality (or lower cost) supply of part-timers can easily tip the balance in their favor. In still others, technical conditions actually favor the use of part-time work. A second major reason for the increase in the usage of part-timers has been a change in the distribution of jobs in the economy— away from employments where part-timers are at a disadvantage and toward those in which there is a real need for part-time workers.

Not all of the change in the industrial and occupational structure has had a positive effect on the demand for part-timers. One advantage of part-time work is that in very boring or strenuous work there is some gain in productivity as one goes from 8 to 4 hours a day. But with increasing mechanization and a general upgrading of jobs, the proportion of jobs in this category is declining, reducing the importance of this argument for a shorter workweek. At least a partial off-set, though, is found in the greater emphasis put on the responsibility factor in heavily mechanized or automated factory work. The costs of fatigue-induced error here can be much greater than the costs imposed by fatigue in a simpler industrial environment. Another offset arises from the high job expectations of many workers, especially the young, overeducated employee. Managers report that this group is easily bored, and some do find that a half-day shift will significantly raise productivity.

A second negative factor is the increase in professional and technical occupations, and the continued development of what some labor economists call internal labor markets. Workers in the professional and technical occupations generally require, and obtain, more postschool training than others.[22] Internal labor markets in large corporate or government bureaucracies establish elaborate training and promotion ladders; young workers are introduced at the bottom rung and gradually work their way up. Moreover, the size and complexity of these bureaucracies often create complicated problems of supervision, coordination, and communication, which would tend to reduce the use of part-timers (see pp. 70–72). The analysis of training economics presented above suggests that both of these developments would tend to limit the employment of part-timers.

However, a number of changes in the industry and occupation structure have been more favorable[23] to the employment of part-timers. These changes parallel those cited in chapter 6 as tending to undermine the rationale for the standard workweek. First, there has been a dramatic decline in the proportion of the work force employed in manufacturing, mining, and railroads. Part-time work is generally not economical in blue-collar occupations in these sectors because close interaction among large groups of employees is often needed and work stations here are typically quite expensive; when part-timers are used, they must be employed in consecutive shifts, imposing a number of costs.[24]

Similarly the increase in the employment of clerical workers has provided passive support to the growth of part-time work. Clerical work encompasses a rather heterogeneous group of work situations, but in general the technical objections to part-time work or to other alternative work schedules have much less strength here than in the manufacturing, mining, and railroad sectors, since inter-actions among clerical workers are typically less rigidly determined by technical considerations than is the case in industry and work stations are usually much less expensive to provide for clerical workers. Hence where there is a good supply of applicants which is often the case in traditionally female clerical jobs, employ-ers are frequently quite willing to substitute part-timers for full-timers. A more positive reason is that clerical workers sometimes have functions which are heavily overlapping with those of the service sector. As an example, consider a municipal employee in a local hall of records. He will be designated as a clerical employee, though much of his time may actually be spent in dealing with citi-zens' requests for information, a function ordinarily regarded as part of the ser-vice industry. In such jobs, a strong positive case can be made for employing part-timers (see below).

Perhaps the most important demand-side change favoring part-time employ-ment has been the sharp increase in the service industries, where there is often an actual technical advantage in their use. A basic characteristic of a service demand is that it has a time distribution which is imposed by the customers' needs to be served at a specific time, or at least is a compromise between customers' needs and those of the employer and his staff. In contrast with work that is produced for stock, service demands typically have an erratic pattern over the day or week. Even in a highly cyclical industry, a manufacturer can generally plan to maintain an even pattern of production over a week or month; for example, in very good times he may decide to pay overtime and schedule work at 10 hours a day, 5 days a week, and need to revise his estimate only, say, once a month. But a ser-vice industry will typically not have such uniformity of output. There will be certain busy periods during the day or week. In many such industries, much of the customer demand will be found in the evenings and on weekends, dictating long hours of operation.[25]

There are a limited number of methods for dealing with the problem of pre-dictably irregular service demands: (1) employees can be asked to work overtime on a regular basis to maintain hours of service beyond 40 per week; (2) employ-ees can be kept on duty even during slack periods when they are not needed; (3) employees can be hired for shiftwork (using that term now to denote any non-standard but full-time schedule; e.g., 11 A.M. to 7 P.M.);[26] or (4) part-time workers can be employed.

In practice, all four of these alternatives are used, often in combination. But each has special advantages and disadvantages. The drawbacks of the first two are obvious. Premium pay for fatigued workers raises labor costs, often danger-ously above a competitive level. Similarly while semi-idle employees are quite often an inevitable cost of the slow period in many service or distribution outlets, management must regard this as an unavoidable evil to be kept at a minimum.

The use of full-time shiftworkers sometimes provides an optimal solution,

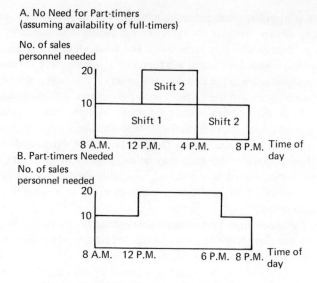

A. No Need for Part-timers
(assuming availability of full-timers)

No. of sales
personnel needed

B. Part-timers Needed
No. of sales
personnel needed

Figure 7-4. Distribution of Service Demands

but this condition requires a special time distribution of orders. For example, if the work flow for the salesmen in a small department follows the pattern in figure 7-4, shiftwork would provide an ideal solution. In this special case, demands would be met perfectly by two shifts of 10 employees each, 8 A.M. to 4 P.M. and 12 P.M. to 8 P.M. But in the absence of such an unusually perfect fit, the result of using the shift option alone is to have idle or semi-idle workers much of the time. In figure 7-4 consider the scheduling problem imposed by only a slight modification: for example, if the peak period extends from 12 P.M. until 6 P.M. Now only the part-time option (or some combination of part-time and full-time workers) would yield a perfect fit. Thus if the peak runs from noon to six, 10 part-timers could be employed from four to six, and full-time shift-workers used to handle the remainder of the business. Or more extensive use of part-timers could be made. This second case is the more common result: full-timers usually cannot fill the schedule need, without some employment of part-timers.

Notes

1. Including unpaid family workers.
2. U.S. Department of Labor, *Employment and Earnings,* January 1978.
3. Brown.

4. Department of Labor, *Employment and Earnings.*

5. See Lloyd, "The Division of Labor between the Sexes: A Review," in Lloyd.

6. This is reported to be one result of the European flexitime schemes. See Allenspach (1975).

7. Part-time work can also serve the female student and older worker.

8. See Owen (1976b).

9. For example, see the discussions in Manney and in Schulz.

10. Data source is matched March–May 1973, U.S. Bureau of Labor Statistics, Current Population Survey tape. Percentages do not add up to 100 since involuntary part-timers (and those few workers who have two full-time jobs) are excluded.

11. See Leveson for a critique of these studies.

12. The empirical measurement problem is complicated here because the quality of the part-time labor force often is different from the quality of the full-time labor force. See pp. 74–75.

13. To simplify the exposition, the argument is made here for the case where the employer pays the cost of training. A similar argument can be made in the case where the employee pays (usually by taking a lower wage while acquiring training than could be obtained by working as an unskilled employee elsewhere). Compare the discussion in Owen (1977c).

14. Very similar results are obtained if it is assumed that there is a constant separation rate q so that t periods after a group of workers of size N is hired, Ne^{-qt} are still employed.

15. See Price, especially the chapters on size, communications, and span of control; Khandwalla, especially pp. 295-97; and Starbuck, "Organizational Growth and Development," and Massie, "Management Theory," both in March.

16. If there are n individuals in a group, the number of possible individual interactions is given by $n(n-1)/2$. The number of interactions among subgroups is $2^n - n - 1$. See Starbuck, p. 497, in March.

17. For example, workers can be organized into groups which keep themselves fully informed, with systematic channels of communications with other groups.

18. See Owen (1976a). In the present economic conditions, depressed product markets and high costs provide additional reasons, in many industries, for staying with a single shift.

19. An intriguing exception is the minishift—a half-time shift of part-timers which comes on the job after the day shift is through, thus providing 12 hours a day of utilization. However, despite the interest in this innovation shown by journalists and advocates of alternative work schedules, it has yet to have important impacts on American work scheduling practices.

20. See Nollen, Eddy, and Martin; and Nollen and Martin (1978b).

21. And hence pay a lower quality-adjusted wage.

22. Only a partial offset would be expected to result from the use of part-time professionals by small businesses, which are unable to afford the services of one or more full-timers.

23. One indirect factor may have been increases in demand in occupations traditionally dominated by females, for example, clerical work, many service industries, and some retailing industries. Then the greater preference for part-time work among females would help to explain its growth. Since more females than males prefer part-time work, an increase in female job opportunities in general would be expected to increase the proportion of part-time employment.

24. See pp. 72–73.

25. In addition, there is considerable unpredictable variation. But this can only be met by defensive management strategies, for example, by overstaffing.

26. Or the 4-day, 10-hour-day workweek. Indeed this is an important use of the compressed workweek.

8 Conventional Alternative Work Schedules: Statistical Analysis

Empirical Analysis of the Part-time Labor Market

The available empirical data offer some support to these hypotheses about how employers use the part-time labor market. The influence of the factors affecting employer demand for part-timers can be seen in the cross-sectional distribution of part-timers among industries and occupations. To study the intersectoral distribution of part-timers, national data on their employment were aggregated by 200 sectors, corresponding to the 20 major industry and 10 major occupation groups of the U.S. census categories.[1]

The analysis in chapter 7 predicts that employer preferences for part-timers would be relatively weak in those sectors in which pay levels are high relative to the education and other background characteristics of the work force. An important reason for relatively high pay in some sectors is the training and promotion opportunities they offer. But survey evidence[2] indicates that employers are most reluctant to extend these opportunities to part-timers; a result predicted by the analysis presented above. A complementary argument supporting the expectation of underrepresentation of part-timers in high-wage jobs is the disadvantage part-timers suffer in large complex organizations. Pay scales are frequently high in such organizations for a variety of reasons. For example, they often develop highly differentiated job structures, which provide training and promotion opportunities. But part-time workers are likely to be barred from these organizations or at least confined to departments or divisions that do not offer opportunities for earning high wages. Apart from the drawbacks of training and promoting part-timers cited above, a complex organizational structure itself provides a disadvantage to the employment of part-timers, because of the costs of supervising and coordinating this type of worker and maintaining communications with and among them. Thus consideration of the organizational problems of supervising and coordinating part-timers and the economic problems of training and promoting them, both tend to support the expectation that part-time workers will be underrepresented in well-paid jobs.

An empirical analysis of the extent to which part-timers are confined to sectors in which labor is poorly paid was carried out by first adjusting the hourly earnings of part-timers and full-timers for background characteristics (sex, race, education, and experience) that would influence their wages, and then aggregating the adjusted wages of each class of worker by sector.[3] The quality-adjusted wage of part-timers was 29 percent below that of full-timers. But this was due in part to part-timers being employed in large numbers where the (adjusted) wage of full-timers was low. When the sectoral averages of adjusted wages of full-time workers were aggregated, using the sectoral levels of part-time employment as weights, the estimated full-time wage level was about 19 percent below the actual full-time level. In other words as much as two-thirds of the gap between the adjusted wages of part-timers and full-timers was associated with the segregation of part-timers into sectors where the wages of full-timers was low.

A second hypothesis is that employers will use part-timers where there is a technical need for them. More specifically, that they will be used where there is an uneven distribution of temporal demands and that they will not be used where the cost of providing work stations is high and where technical interactions among workers are most important. To test this hypothesis, a part-time job need variable was constructed, equal to the proportion of shiftworkers in the sector, except in the mining, manufacturing, and railroad industries.[4] In this data set, the average part-timer is in a sector in which the mean value of the need for part-timer variable is 18.4 percent, almost double the level, 9.6 percent, of that variable in the sector in which the average full-timer is employed. This result supports the hypothesis in the preceding section on the relationship between work flows, the demand for shiftworkers, and the demand for part-timers developed above.

A third hypothesis is that employers do tend to create part-time jobs where the demographic factors are favorable. Table 8–1 offers a test of this hypothesis. The table shows the proportion of part-timers in the sector of the economy in

Table 8–1
Average Proportion of Voluntary Part-time Jobs in Sector by Demographic Composition and Type of Employment[a]

	Voluntary Part-timer	Full-timer
Married males	.247	.110
Single males	.357	.133
Other single females: no children under 15 years	.375	.178
Single females with children under 15 years	.455	.186
Other married females: no children under 15 years	.327	.163
Married females with children under 15 years	.301	.158
Young persons: under 25 years	.380	.146
Prime-age persons: between 25 and 50 years	.295	.125
Older persons: over 50 years	.338	.136

[a]Numbers in body of table are proportion of voluntary part-time employees in the sector where the average member of the specified group is employed.

which the average member of a particular demographic group is employed. For example, in column 2, the average full-time married male has 11 percent part-timers in the sector in which he works, while the single mother, with children under age 15, employed full-time has 19 percent part-timers in her sector. The results in column 2 are thus consistent with this third hypothesis. (In fact it could be argued that this is an exceptionally strict test of the hypothesis since if, when employers replace a full-time job with, say, two part-time jobs, these are given to full-timers with the expected demographic composition—e.g., mothers or students—this would reduce the proportion of full-timers with such demographic characteristics. Hence if employers acted randomly in deciding the proportion of part-time jobs in their sector, one would expect a negative correlation between the proportion of part-time and the demographic characteristics of the full-time labor force.)

A More Sophisticated Statistical Model of the Part-time Labor Market

The cross-tabulation method is a crude way to study the determination of the ratio of part-time to full-time workers in each secor, since some of the independent variables influencing this ratio are correlated with each other. Hence the part-time, full-time ratio was also studied with the help of a more complex method (two-stage least-squares regression) which permits the analysis of the effects of one variable, with the others held constant. This method also affords separate estimates of the effects of changes in the relative price of part-timers on their supply and demand (see appendix G for a further discussion).

Overall, the results obtained from this method showed that there is a flourishing market in part-time labor. The supply of part-time labor to a sector is highly responsive to variations in its price as well as to the demographic composition of the sectoral labor force, for example, the proportion of mothers or of single males. On the demand side, employers were responsive to the relative price of part-timers, the level of wages, and part-timer job need variable. Some of the principal quantitative results are given in table 8-2.[5] (See appendix G for more detail.)

Determination of Wages of Individual Part-timers

But while the market for voluntary part-timers is flourishing in the sense that both buyers and sellers are highly responsive to changes in the relative advantages and disadvantages of using this type of labor, the individual part-timer is still faced with the problem that employers generally prefer full-timers (at least for the better-paid jobs) and will hire part-timers only if they earn less than full-

Table 8–2
**Supply and Demand Analysis of the Utilization
by Sector of Part-time Employees**

Supply Equation

Percentage change in ratio of part-time to full-time employment supplied per
1 percent change in:

Proportion of Mothers with Children under 15 Years of Age	Proportion of Single Males	Ratio of (Quality-adjusted) Wage of Part-timers to that of Full-timers
0.6	1.1	5.5

Demand Equation

Percentage change in ratio of part-time to full-time employment demanded per
1 percent change in:

Sector Wage Level	Part-time Job Need	Ratio of (Quality-adjusted) Wage of Part-timers to that of Full-timers
–3.0	0.4	–4.3

timers or if they are better qualified. Since the qualifications of part-timers are
not, on the average, superior to those of full-timers, the result is that part-timers
are in general less well paid for their work.

Wage Differentials within the Part-time Labor Market

Relatively low wages paid to part-timers do not mean that they are all confined
to an amorphous, unskilled labor market. On the contrary, part-timers vary as
widely in such characteristics as education, sex, age, race, and experience as do
full-timers, and these play as important a role in determining their earnings.

The analysis of employer evaluations of the quality of part-timers presented
in chapter 7 would predict that some part-timers would be preferred. In some
cases, one would predict that the education or prior experience of applicants for
part-time jobs would enable them to begin work at a relatively well-paying job
with just a minimal amount of breaking-in to the ways of a particular employer.
In other job situations, the employer must make a significant investment in the
specific training of a new employee, but if the skills of available part-time job
applicants exceed those of full-time applicants available at a comparable wage
rate, this may outweigh the other disadvantages of training part-timers and lead
to their being hired for relatively good positions.

It is useful here to employ the popular analogy of a labor market as consisting of queues of applicants ranked in terms of their quality, and lists of jobs ranked in terms of their skill level and wages, with the market matching people and jobs with greater or less success. One can then think of part-timers and full-timers as composing two separate but overlapping queues. Within each of the two queues, workers are ranked in terms of their personal characteristics, but between queues, full-timers are generally ranked ahead of part-timers. Part-timers are only able to compete for well-paid jobs with full-timers when they are distinctly better in education, experience, and other personal characteristics that help to predict job performance, especially the costs of training. This model would forecast that part-timers would, on the average, be paid less than full-timers (since the distribution of personal characteristics among part-timers is generally not superior to that among full-timers); but it would also predict significant variation in the earnings of part-timers on the basis of their personal characteristics.

Some Empirical Findings

The empirical data on the wages of part-timers and full-timers support this view. Table 8–3 presents the results of an effort to estimate the effects of characteristics on earnings.[6] The first column gives the percentage gain in hourly earnings obtained (corrected for other characteristics) from an additional four years of school for members of each subgroup. The second column gives the percentage gain in earnings from the first 10 years of experience (again corrected for other characteristics). A statistical technique, multiple regression, was used to deter-

Table 8–3
Earnings Variations among Part-timers[a]

	Percentage Gain in Hourly Earnings from:	
	Additional Four Years of Schooling	*First Ten Years of Experience*
Males		
Voluntary part-timer	33.5	28.2
Full-time worker	28.4	32.8
Females		
Voluntary part-timer	48.2	20.4
Full-time worker	36.0	16.4

[a]Nonagricultural wage and salary workers.

mine these relationships within each of the four subgroups (other variables held constant include race and, for females, number and age of children).

The results obtained in these estimations support the view that part-timers are less well paid than full-timers: even when all these factors are held constant, male part-timers earned 30 percent less than male full-timers and female part-timers received 17 percent less than female full-timers. (The gross or unadjusted differential was 51 percent for males, 28 percent for females.) But they also indicate the extent to which the wages of part-timers vary with their background characteristics. Table 8–3 indicates that the relative gain in earnings from additional education or experience[7] is about the same among part-timers as among full-timers.

Decline in the Return to Schooling

When, in an alternative statistical formulation, the payoff to education was allowed to vary with years of postschool experience, the average gain in hourly earnings resulting from an additional four years of schooling was found to be much greater for young part-timers than for those who had been out of school for a number of years; in the course of the first 20 years after graduation, this education differential was cut by 40 percent among male part-timers and by almost 30 percent among female part-timers.[8] This would be the predicted pattern if employers would accept either superior experience or schooling in applicants for relatively well-paid, part-time jobs, but at the same time generally bar part-timers from the best jobs (i.e., those at the front of the full-timers queue) which often require large amounts of both experience and education. Then as part-timers obtained more job experience, we would observe a decline in the relative gain from additional education.

Special Scheduling Problems

The special problems of mothers of school-age children who require a work shedule which allows them to be home in the late afternoon, when their children return from school, are of particular interest in a study of time pressures and the role of the part-time labor market in dealing with these problems. Hence female part-timers were further divided into two groups, those with schedules that freed them from 2:30 to 5:30 P.M., and the remainder. Separate analyses were then carried out for each subgroup, identical to that used for the combined group of female part-timers, as reported in table 8–3. Results for the two groups were remarkably similar;no significant differences were observed either in the average, adjusted, hourly wage or in the payoffs to education or experience. Thus these data indicate that on the average the female part-timer suffers no additional disadvantage if she requires a schedule that leaves her free in the late afternoon, beyond that imposed by her status as a part-time female worker. A possible explanation is the large number of students who prefer late afternoon work schedules. Table 7-1 indicates that while, as expected, mothers are more likely to work schedules that leave them free in the late afternoon, young male part-timers, many of whom are students, are much more likely to work in this time interval.

Shiftworkers

A similar analysis of the earnings of individual shiftworkers was carried out. There was relatively little difference between the average wages of shiftworkers and nonshiftworkers, whether or not the wage data were standardized for differences in background characteristics. However, there was much less variation among shiftworkers on the basis of experience and education. Among males, the payoffs to experience and education within the shiftworker group were, respectively, only 80 percent and 46 percent of the payoffs within the nonshiftworker group.[9]

Taken together, these results indicate that while a shiftworker with little experience or education earns more than a nonshiftworker of similar qualifications, among those with higher levels of experience and education, nonshiftworkers receive the higher wage. This pattern could be predicted from our a priori knowledge of the market for shiftworkers. Shiftworkers are generally paid more than nonshiftworkers for the same work. This shift differential is paid to compensate for the preference the average worker has for daytime over evening or night work. At the same time, though, the more highly paid managerial and professional employments are usually scheduled during the daylight hours. Hence advancement opportunities for shiftworkers are eventually limited unless they move to daytime work. Thus one would expect that among highly experienced and well-educated employees—where we would find the highest proportion of upper-echelon workers—nonshiftworkers might be observed to have higher average earnings than shiftworkers.

Compressed Workweeks

Compressed workweek schedules, such as the 4-day, 10-hour day or the 3-day, 12-hour-day weeks, fall logically into this category of employer-determined alternative working schedule. However, unlike part-time work and shiftwork, their growth is a quite recent phenomenon. Moreover, they are often installed by employers simply as a means to improve employee morale, not as a way to meet the demands of production or sales.[10]

Four-day workweeks grew rapidly at the beginning of the 1970s, attracting an enormous amount of journalistic interest. However, in the past several years the proportion of workers on these schedules has leveled off at about 1 in 60. Experience has shown that these schedules are a boon to certain types of workers: especially those doing light work and not fatigued by major family responsibilities at home. For this group, the extra leisure opportunities provided by the extra day off each week is more likely to offset the disadvantages of the 10-hour day.[11]

However, the three-day or four-day workweek, without a substantial reduction in weekly hours, definitely appears to be a minority taste among employees. While obviously important to this relatively small group who are on compressed schedules, the new workweeks now appear to be unlikely to develop into a major alternative to standard hours.

Summary and Conclusions

About one-third of the nonfarm wage and salary work force are on conventional alternative work schedules, including moonlighters or other voluntary part-timers, shiftworkers, or those on compressed schedules.

The major category, part-time workers, are employed in a large, flourishing labor market. Part-timers now serve a variety of economic purposes. Yet they are typically regarded as less valuable than full-time employees for a variety of reasons. In consequence, part-timers are generally paid substantially less than full-timers, suffer a higher rate of unemployment, and are usually confined to lower-status jobs. Nevertheless a large and rapidly growing number of Americans are sufficiently discontented with the standard schedule that they are willing to endure the economic and social disadvantages of part-time work.

Notes

1. This chapter presents results from an analysis of a tape of the matched March–May, 1973 Current Population Survey, made available to the author by the U.S. Department of Labor. Sample size was 13,515. See Owen (1977b and 1978) and appendix G for greater detail on the calculations made with these data.

2. See Nollen, Eddy, and Martin.

3. Data for individuals were adjusted for background characteristics by first running multiple regressions similar to those described on pp. 85–87. The

residuals obtained here were then aggregated by sector. See Owen (1977b), p. 84.

4. A shiftworker continues to be defined as a full-timer who neither begins work between 6:30 and 9:30 in the morning nor ends work between 2:30 and 6:30 in the afternoon.

5. The economic and statistical analysis on which this table is based is described in appendix G.

6. In the estimates summarized in table 8–1, the logarithm of hourly earnings of male full-timers was regressed on race, years of schooling, experience, and experience squared. The logarithm of hourly earnings of male part-timers was regressed on these variables and student status. The logarithm of the hourly earnings of female full-timers was regressed on race, years of schooling, experience, experience squared, number of children under 6 years of age, and number of children under 15 years of age. The logarithm of earnings of female part-timers was regressed on these variables and student status. Only voluntary part-timers were included. No wage data were available for moonlighting part-timers.

The race variable was equal to 1 if the individual was white, zero otherwise. (Race was a significant determinant of the earnings of full-timers, but generally not of part-timers.)

The coefficients in table 8–3 were all significantly different from zero at the 1 percent level of confidence. Tests were also carried out of the significance of differences between the coefficients in the part-time and those in the full-time estimations. The constant terms were significantly higher for full-timers. Experience and education coefficients were significantly higher for female part-timers, but such differences were generally not significant between full-timers and part-timers within the male group. See Owen (1978).

7. A possible explanation of this result is offered by a finding from the ongoing research of Ethel Jones: Jones's longitudinal study of mature females indicates that there is a very high degree of movement between full-time and part-time jobs. This would tend to reduce differences in the average level of accumulated experience between those who are currently employed part-time and those who currently work full-time.

8. A much more modest decline was found for full-timers; the decline was two-to-four times as high among part-timers. In still another alternative estimation, the payoff to schooling was allowed to vary with years of schooling. Here no significant diminishing returns, or other variation, were found for the part-time group.

9. The data source is described in note 1.

10. This schedule also meshes well with the needs of some industries, which benefit from a 10-hour-day operation. Automobile repair service is one such case. Here the three days off are likely to be nonconsecutive, so as to permit five-day or six-day operation of the business.

11. See Poor; Wheeler, Gurman, and Tarnowieski; and Maklan.

9

The Economics of Flexible Working Schedules

Development of Flexible Working Schedules

The part-time jobs and other conventional alternative working schedules discussed in the preceding chapters offer a degree of flexibility in hours of work, but usually at a substantial cost to the employee. However, recent experiments indicate that it is possible to open up very considerable flexibility to the individual in the scheduling of his work time, that is, in the timing but not the total number of his hours, without any comparable economic cost. Where this is possible, majority group workers can continue to hold their better-paid, possibly upward mobile jobs, while enjoying a considerable measure of flexibility in their allocation of time.

Types of Flexible Work Schedules

Staggered work hours provide one of the most elementary types of schedule flexibility. In a typical hours staggering scheme, offices in a downtown area will agree to change their closing hours from a common 5:00 P.M. to one ranging from 4:45 P.M. to 5:15 P.M., at five-minute intervals. Corresponding changes are then made in opening hours. In the interests of reducing congestion, hours staggering has been introduced in major firms in a large number of the world's metropolises—New York, London, Paris, Tokyo, Washington—as well as in many medium to large cities.

Hours staggering does not have a negative impact on productive interactions among a firm's employees, since they all work the same new staggered schedule. It can have a small negative effect on interactions among firms; effective communication among firms may be difficult in, say, the first and last half-hour of each working day.

The principal advantage of the system is the social contribution it makes in reducing commuter congestion. However, it often brings some advantages to the individual as well. There are obvious gains in reducing commuting time and allowing the employee to commute under less stressful conditions. In addition, employees are often given some voice in determining the timing of the new schedule (voting as a group), which can bring less obvious benefits. For example, it is quite common for them to opt for a somewhat earlier schedule, allowing more daylight leisure in the late afternoon.

The new flexible-hours scheduling programs, popularly known as flexitime, provide a much greater degree of individual freedom in hours scheduling than do staggered hours. Since rigid scheduling practices now deteriorate the quality of time in household production, leisure, and paid work (see the argument in chapter 5), the introduction of flexitime can provide significant improvements in the quality of each of these activities.

In a typical pure flexitime system, the employer sets a core time during which all employees must be present, for example, from 10 to 12 in the morning and 2 to 4 in the afternoon. He also sets a bandwidth within which all hours must be worked—say, 6:00 A.M. to 6:30 P.M. In addition, certain restraints must be imposed in the interest of the worker's health; for example, he may have to take at least 45 minutes for lunch and limit his hours to 10 on any one day. The worker is still required to put in the same total working time, say, an average of 40 hours a week. In the most limited variant, schedule flexibility is confined to daily starting and ending times, and the worker must continue to put in a total of 8 hours each day. In less limited plans, he may vary his total daily hours. In still more generous plans (more common in Europe than in the United States), he may even carry hours forward from week to week and month to month. (In practice, an upper limit is usually placed on these carryforwards; e.g., in some firms no more than 10 hours per week and 20 hours per month may be accumulated.)

Flexitime is not restricted to this pure type. It is sometimes said to include three types of flexible-hours schedules:

1. The employer offers the employees a more or less wide variety of hours schedules to choose from. Having chosen, the employee is expected to remain on that schedule, at least for a fixed period of time.

2. The employee decides upon a weekly hours schedule for himself. But once chosen, he must stick with it.

3. The employee is free to choose his schedule of hours, without advance notice, from day to day, if he so desires—the pure type usually described in the newspapers.

In practice, this pure type is often modified. In one variant, highly regarded by the advocates of flexitime, central management retains the formal freedom given by the original flexitime plan, but insists that whatever schedule arrangements are chosen and however often these are changed, productivity must not suffer. Here each work group and its supervisors must arrange hours and work flows in such a way that the individual employee is allowed the flexibility which he values most, while still maintaining the productivity of the group.[1]

The Spread of Flexitime

The flexitime system is said to have been first installed in the research and development division of a German aerospace company, the Messerschmidt-Bolkow-

Blohm division outside Munich, in 1967.[2] The access road from the M-B-B establishment to the autobahn had become clogged with traffic. The local management considered an elaborate system of staggering hours schedules, but rejected this as too complicated. Instead, workers were told they could pick their starting and ending times (within broad limits). The system not only resolved the local traffic jam but brought considerable benefit to both management and labor.[3]

The flexitime system has spread rapidly since 1967. At the time this is written, a third or more of the Swiss labor force is said to be on flexitime. In Germany, 5 to 10 percent of the white-collar labor force is reported to have the system. Substantial, if somewhat lower, proportions of the work forces in France, England, and other European countries have flexitime. Though mainly concentrated in white-collar occupations, flexible-hours scheduling has also been extended to some European blue-collar workers in the manufacturing and service industries. In some sections of Switzerland, a majority of the work force (including white-collar and blue-collar employees) are said to have flexitime.[4]

The system is also making progress in Canada, Australia, and Japan. The United States was relatively slow in introducing flexitime, but it has been estimated that several hundred thousand Americans—perhaps as many as 1 million—now have the system.[5]

Installations of flexitime in this country have largely been in white-collar work. A number of large insurance companies each have thousands of employees in the system. Banks and other employers in the financial industry are commonly found in the group. In addition, the white-collar divisions of many manufacturing firms have introduced the system.

The federal government now has several hundred thousand employees on the plan, almost all in the white-collar group. Other large concentrations exist among research and development personnel at several federal establishments. The U.S. Civil Service is now developing plans to increase substantially the number of federal employees on flexitime.

Can Flexitime be Compatible with Productive Efficiency?

Insofar as rigid scheduling practices deteriorate the quality of time in household production, leisure, and paid employment, the introduction of flexible working scheduling practices would be expected to provide welcome advantages to employees. But would it be compatible with productive efficiency? The flexitime system as described in the newspapers would appear to be feasible in only a relatively few sorts of jobs—employees coming and going as they pleased would lead to production anarchy in most cases. However, the journalistic accounts describe only the purest form of flexitime, where the workers have unrestricted freedom to determine their starting and finishing times. But as we have seen, when such formal hours rules are given to each small work group and its supervisor as minimum requirements, central management can, and often does, add the all-important proviso that any departure from the standard hours schedule must be consistent with an efficient, profitable operation. Consequently the real effect of the new rules may be to challenge the group and its supervisor to devise ways in which individuals can choose their own hours without damage to company profits. Central management can and often does assist the work group's effort in many ways, ranging from providing consultant services to radically reorganizing job structures so as to facilitate the introduction of the new system.

The Applicability of the Flexitime System: Under these ground rules, the success of flexitime will depend in each job situation upon the ingenuity of the work group and its supervisor and upon the cooperation and support of central management. However, the degree to which work efficiency is consistent with meeting individual preferences on hours schedule depends on the extent to which job requirements permit hours choice and on the practicality of altering these requirements so as to make hours choice more feasible. There are three principal factors here: (1) the extent to which the employee's or worker's interaction with others in the production and distribution process is necessarily continuous or is intermittent; (2) the number of people in the work organization capable of doing the same job; and (3) the extent to which there are regular, predictable variations in the demand for a worker's services over the day, the week, or a longer period.

1. While almost every member of the labor force must interact with others in the production and distribution process (there are very few true Robinson Crusoes in modern industry) for some workers such interactions are so infrequent that a very considerable degree of choice in hours is possible. The person writing a novel or the mathematician endeavoring to prove a theorem provide obvious examples; less obvious ones are frequently found in more mundane occupations. Each of the 350 clerks in the Social Security Administration offices in Baltimore, the subject of a widely publicized experiment in flexitime, works in isolation from the others: they compare data from written reports with computerized data which they flash on a TV screen.[6] A manufacturer of power lawn mowers has introduced a very generous (and again widely publicized) system of flexitime among a group of workers in the small town of Betzdorf in West Germany. Members of this group each work on a given part, which is shipped in from another region; when the part is finished, it is trucked to another company installation for assembly.[7] In these situations there is no real need for an employee to adhere to a standard schedule. In the more general case, employees are less isolated.

In perhaps the most common job situation, each worker or employee receives an input, performs a task, then passes the result on to the next employee, a customer, or some other person outside the firm. This category includes most production workers in manufacturing (both those in job-shop and those in assembly-line layouts), probably a majority of white-collar workers (who generally process and transmit information), and some service workers (e.g., those carrying out nonemergency repairs). Since few such employees are as isolated as are those in the Betzdorf installation, the "disconnection" of their efforts to provide flexitime will impose a cost. However, this disconnection can be accomplished by increasing the level of in-process inventory between each pair of successive workers in the system who choose a different time schedule. Broadly speaking, the increase in costs will depend on how closely the workers have been interacting and on the space and other costs of holding more in-process inventory. Thus job-shop layouts are generally more suitable to flexitime arrangements than are assembly lines, since operatives in the former situation usually work from an inventory of raw materials and produce an inventory of piece parts, even without flexitime, while assembly-line workers generally interact more closely. However, the Swiss watch industry, which does use an assembly-line type of production layout, has been able to adopt flexitime with profit; industry spokesmen explain that a tray of watches does not take up much space.[8]

The costs of introducing flexitime when employees are in a series producing or distributing a good also depend on whether each employee comes and goes as he pleases or whether choices are constrained somewhat, in the interest of efficiency. Costs will be reduced if workers in adjacent positions agree to moderate the differences in their time schedules or at least inform each other about expected departures from the regular schedules. For example, suppose that by agreement Jones generally gets to work about 30 minutes after Smith but that once a month he is a full 2 hours late. If the day of Jones's 2-hour lateness is a random event due, say, to oversleeping, a 2-hour inventory of his finished parts must always be maintained to avoid an out-of-stock situation. But if Jones can warn of his monthly lateness in advance, the 2-hour inventory will only be accumulated on 1 day in 30, with a half-hour inventory stored on the other days.

In a third and common type of job situation, an employee must constantly supervise a process or provide service on demand. An example of the first case would be a traffic policeman or a control-room operator in an automated factory. A receptionist or a retail clerk provide examples of the service-on-demand job. When each employee is providing a unique service, the flexitime system is hard to introduce. Jobs which require coordination among a work team also provide a difficult case for flexitime, for example, a lighting technician, a sound technician, and other members of a small film crew. However, in this case the group as a whole may choose a nonstandard schedule without damage to efficiency if the members wish to do so.

2. The number of people in a job situation who are doing the same job, or who are capable of filling in for each other if one is absent, generally has an inverse effect on the costs of introducing flexible-hours scheduling. For example, consider a factory in which workers are arranged in series but where there are 50 workers carrying out each operation. In a large apparel factory, 50 women may

be sewing sleeves on coats, while a similar number of women are engaged in the preceding step (basting the sleeves) and in the following step (lining the coat). Then even if the sewers were to come and go according to their whims, much of the random variation within the group would be self-canceling and, unless there were systematic differences between the schedule preferences of the sewers and those of the basters and liners, inventory costs would not be increased by much. Or consider the impact of numbers in the teamwork case, mentioned above. If there are a number of teams, each doing the same operation and each deciding on a mutually agreeable time schedule for the group, it becomes possible for a specialist on one team (say, a late-rising electrician in a team of early birds) to trade teams, and hence schedules, with a similar specialist (an early-rising electrician) in another team.

3. The larger the regular predictable variation in the flow of work demands, the more feasible is the flexitime system; if there is an absolutely even flow of work over the standard workweek, standard hours are probably most efficient; even if there are a number of workers available to do each job, the absence of some will impose a cost. But if work flows are variable over the day, week, or month, the standard workweek is not optimal for the employer, and some alternative is better. For the system to be advantageous to management, though, the flexitime choices of employees will generally have to be decided by compromise with the employer, since there is no guarantee that the unhampered choices of employees would lead to departures from standard hours that, on balance, would yield a net gain to management.

Variability in work demands is most likely to occur when a service is supplied on demand, as in retail trade or the service industry. For flexitime to work well here, however, there must be more than one person available to provide the service. A larger number can be on duty during the busy time of the day or week while still providing a minimal level of service during off-peak periods. In contrast, flexitime would not work at all well in a smaller, owner-operated retail outlet, inasmuch as the owner would probably not be willing to close shop altogether during the hours when business is relatively slow.

Ways of Expanding the Applicability of Flexitime: The compatibility of individual needs and job needs can generally be much improved if management endeavors to restructure jobs and job rules so as to improve the prospects for flexitime. In some instances, much of the initiative for change will come from the small work group and its supervisor; in practice, there are often just too many details about employee preferences and individual job needs—too much information—for central management to acquire, absorb, and translate into optimal scheduling decisions. In fact one could regard the allocation of scheduling responsibility to the work group and the supervisor as central management's important first step toward finding new opportunities for flexible scheduling. However, the greater resources available to central management for initiating change provide a rationale for its active participation in the scheduling process.

Even in the simplest work situation, some management adjustments are needed with flexitime. Sometimes it is only necessary to make few changes in bureaucratic and supervisory procedures. For example, in the case of the social security clerks working in relative isolation, personnel regulations had to be changed to permit flexitime, an orientation program had to be mounted to explain the program to the clerks, and a reorganization of supervisory schedules had to be worked out so that the entire 6:30 A.M. to 6:00 P.M. period was covered.

A more ambitious management goal would be to increase the number of people doing or capable of doing the same job, either by job rotation or job enlargement programs. For example, if a number of machinists are working on a product in a series, each carrying out a specialized operation, a program of job rotation which provides each worker with the skill needed to substitute for an absent member will reduce the costs of flexibility. Actual job enlargement provides a more ambitious solution; each worker could be trained to do, say, five successive operations and consequently could have four potential replacements if he were absent, which would further reduce scheduling costs. This type of reorganization need not be confined to blue-collar workers. One large English insurance company, which introduced flexitime after a considerable investment in preparatory planning, found it profitable under the new system to apply job rotation or enlargement not only to clerks but also to such very specialized and technical occupations as that of insurance underwriter.[9]

Much more complex changes are also possible. Jobs can sometimes be broken down into elements, some of which require continuous interaction with others and some which do not, and the work so assigned as to permit maximum schedule flexibility to the members of a work group. To take a very simple example, if a group of secretaries are first pooled rather than each reporting to a different executive and their work divided into operations which require interaction with others, such as taking dictation and answering the phone, and those which do not require interaction, such as typing, a schedule for the group can be developed which will provide for some people to be always on duty during standard office hours to answer the phone and take dictation while much of the typing can be done outside of standard hours if the group prefers this.

In all these reorganization efforts, neither the small work group and its supervisor nor central management has a monopoly on suggestions for change. Many instances of creative thinking are reported as coming from the bottom as well as from the top of the management hierarchy.

Schedule Bargaining

Some of the most positive gains to the company are secured when the supervisor is given authority to work with his group to determine where there are regular fluctuations in work needs and then to bargain forcefully with his group over deviations from the standard schedule. The standard workweek is now used in many job situations where it does not meet management needs. For example, if there is a weekly cycle of effort, employees on a standard schedule typically will simply work more slowly on some days and push on others or, if necessary, put in some overtime. In many job situations, especially in white-collar work, any suggestion by management that some employees take a "slow" morning or after-noon off and make up the time on the evening of a busy day would be met with indignation and an increase in the company's quit rate. However, flexitime can produce this result if the supervisor handles the situation adroitly. For example, a British insurance company had a weekly billing period so that one day, Wednes-day, was the busiest for its clerical staff. When flexitime was installed, employees who wanted to take some time off on a slow day were often told that they could do so if they consented to make up the time by putting in longer hours on Wed-nesday. As might be expected, the company found that its Wednesday overtime costs were cut under the new arrangement. Of course the use of this strategy re-quires the greatest discretion and flexibility on the part of the supervisor. If such management-oriented deals were all that emerged from the system, it is unlikely flexitime would get much support from the staff, and all empirical studies show that enthusiastic employee support is a prerequisite for the plan's success. How-ever, it is important to realize that flexitime does hold a potential for solving problems like this one which should help to stimulate management's interest in the system.

Empirical Findings from Case Studies

Unfortunately, there is no reliable body of macrostatistical data which can be used to test these arguments on the advantages and disadvantages of flexitime in a concise and reasonably accurate manner.[10] In this respect, we are in a less desirable position than when discussing the economics of the part-time job mar-ket, or when analyzing changes over time in the allocation of time between work and leisure. However, there is a fairly large, and growing, number of case studies on the progress of the new system. These studies have generally supported the positive assessment predicted by theoretical considerations.[11]

Employee Reactions

In general, employees both here and in Europe react favorably to the flexitime system. In a typical survey, a majority of employees regard the system favorably, a minority are more or less indifferent, and only a very few are actively opposed.

Employee use of the system is extremely varied. Some employees stick with the standard schedule, which is their right under the flexitime rules. A large percentage will make some regular adjustment in their schedule, essentially treating it as employee-chosen staggered hours rather than as flexitime, though perhaps making an occasional, irregular departure.

Others make more steady use. In fact in Germany, where the system is well-established and employees can "carryforward" time from week to week, employers sometimes go beyond the formal flexitime system and informally allow workers to have half-day, or even full-day, holidays under the system.

Employee use of this schedule flexibility, as it is described in the various case studies, generally bears out the theoretical expectations. Perhaps the most common use is to improve the quality and productivity of household production time. A very common finding is that flexitime eases the commuting problem of the individual worker. Some workers simply find that without having to worry about meeting a rigid schedule, they no longer rush to work, reducing the probability of an accident and easing anxiety and stress. A few workers report that they now take local streets rather than the expressway for the same reason. Other workers make a more ambitious adjustment, actually changing their starting and quitting times so as to avoid the rush.

Another reported benefit is easier access to retail outlets, service establishments, and government offices, which are open only during standard hours. This is commonly accomplished by taking advantage of the lunch hour flexibility available under the system.

A widely reported and important benefit is the enhanced ability to manage child care and other family activities. Workers report that they have more time for these purposes, though their workweeks are not reduced. This is more commonly reported as a benefit by employed wives. Choice in the scheduling of hours can make an obvious contribution to resolving the time problems of the two-earner family, especially that of providing supervision for school-age children. An example of how this schedule freedom is sometimes utilized to maximize parental supervision may be instructive. Suppose a child's school schedule requires him to be away from home from 8:45 A.M. to 3:00 P.M., 6.25 hours (we will assume that he gets to school by himself and that the school provides his lunch). If each parent has a half-hour commuting trip to work, a 45-minute lunch, and an 8-hour workday, he must be away from home 9.75 hours. To ensure that someone is always there when the child is at home, the parents may, with flexible scheduling, arrange their time so that one parent leaves home at 8:45 A.M. (and so arrives home at 6:30 P.M.) while the other arrives home at 3:00 P.M. (having left at 7:15 A.M.).

Apart from these regular schedule changes, some forms of flexitime permit changes in schedules at the whim of the employee. This permits a working mother or father to take off time to tend to a sick child or to handle some other emergency at home. In practice, these and other family advantages have been appreciated by employees obtaining flexible scheduling. For example, in the social security experiment with flexitime for a group of female employees, about

75 percent reported that their new schedules allowed them more time with their families, even though no reduction in their hours was offered them.

Of course the flexitime system does have its limits in improving the situation of the two-earner family. For example, if the working couple follows the schedule described above, they will be making an extreme sacrifice of spouse interaction time in order to maximize child-care time. The 3.5 hour difference in the starting and finishing times of husbands and wives used in this example would grossly limit the amount of time the parents have to spend with each other. Assuming that the early riser goes to bed 8.5 hours before he must go to work, he would be retiring just 2.25 hours after his spouse, who is on the late schedule, comes home from work. On the other hand, if they had the same work schedules, they would have almost 7 hours together in the evening and would also be able to breakfast together, rather than one parent going off to work while the other slept. Thus the working parent still faces a hard choice, even with flexitime.

Moreover, it is by no means certain that parents under this flexitime system will adjust their schedules so as to meet child-care needs. Other factors may take precedence in the thinking of parents, so that the hypothetical example outlined above will not be fully realized. For example, a large English insurance company found that six months after the introduction of flexitime, the median departure from standard hours was only 20 minutes. Indeed some employees will actually use the freedom they gain from flexitime to link their work schedules more closely with that of their spouses, allowing less time for parental supervision of children than is provided under standard schedules. A German publishing firm introducing the system found a very common use of flexitime was to match the working schedule of spouses more closely in order to be able to use one rather than two cars for commuting.[12]

Education

Flexitime also brings obvious advantages to those trying to combine a job with a program of formal study. Many courses are offered only in the day. Moreover, even when courses are offered in the evening, the school may be at the other end of the metropolitan area from the individual's work place. Or the course may require some preparation time from the student, or at least a psychological breathing space between work and class time. Hence a common usage of flexitime is to leave work early on the day a night student is attending class.

Another advantage arises if the enterprise itself is offering courses, as some European firms do. The enterprise can then lay out a schedule for their instructors throughout the day, counting on the employee's use of flexitime to take advantage of the opportunity. Messerschmidt's research and development facility found that this was a major use of flexitime.

Flexitime also contributes to the quality of recreation and other consumption time in a number of ways. First, workers often opt for earlier hours of work, which enable them to take better advantage of the daylight hours for leisure. Second, many use the system to provide an occasional extended week night celebration: to leave early, go home and dress for an evening out, then come in late the next morning (this is said to be a common use of the system among young European workers). A more ambitious use, popular among both families and single people, is to extend the weekend; for example, to begin the holiday at 3:00 P.M. on Friday afternoon and then return at 10:30 A.M. on Monday morning. This avoids weekend traffic and permits a much more ambitious weekend trip. In some European establishments workers are allowed to cut into their core time, usually by special permission, so that a three-day or four-day weekend is possible, with the employee making up the hours at another time, or he may take a day off during the week.

Flexitime has also produced benefits in the quality of work experience. Workers appreciate the right to come to work when they feel like working, coming in late after the occasional night on the town or coming in late routinely if their biorhythms make this more acceptable.

The right to choose one's schedule appeals to workers in very different stations of life. Flexitime can raise employee morale even in situations that are quite alienating. Where the worker is doing a very routine job in which he has almost no decision-making functions, flexitime does give the worker at least one very important freedom; a study of several hundred federal workers doing this type of work found that after the introduction of flexitime they hated their jobs somewhat less. On the other hand, experience with higher-status workers employed on variable length projects in research and development establishments indicate that these workers value flexitime because it permits them to work on a job until it is completed (taking compensatory time off later) rather than having to work on a routine work schedule, regardless of the needs of the work. More generally, workers report that they simply value the right to vary their beginning and ending times if they so desire, whether or not they decide to use this power, and quite apart from any specific gains that deviations from the standard gives them. The right to vary hours implies employer trust, may confer status, and often raises morale.

In summary, case studies of flexitime show employee benefits in all three types of time: household production, consumption, and paid employment.

Employer Gains

The case studies also show that employers often obtain important benefits from the flexitime system on a number of grounds. The most common benefits derive from the popularity of the system with employees. The resulting increase in employee satisfaction and morale is frequently cited as a source of numerous gains to management, sometimes including both lower quit rates and higher labor productivity. In the longer run, some managements see an additional advantage in their being able to recruit for full-time positions more women and other persons for whom, for whatever reasons, a standard schedule is unworkable.

Moreover, management also derives some more direct benefits. The company no longer has to administer a tardiness control system. In fact the employee must now make up any late time (a not unimportant benefit in times of labor scarcity, when management is reluctant to dismiss workers for tardiness or taking a long lunch hour). Absenteeism rates may be lowered somewhat. The argument is that, since late arrivals are now legitimized, the tardy employee is no longer so strongly tempted to take the day off, feigning illness. The empirical evidence on this is mixed. However, some case studies have found an effect of flexitime on absenteeism.

Further, under the flexitime system employees doing interesting or creative work are sometimes reported to stay at work late, if need be, to finish a project (taking time off later during a slack period), even without any pressure from management. Workers at less interesting tasks are psychologically more ready to begin work when they arrive at a time of their own choosing than when they are forced to adhere to a standard work schedule. More generally, a better tailoring of work times to work performance is frequently obtained under the new system. When given the choice, many employees will come to work at a time when they are psychologically ready to work and will stay until they have finished a task. For example, there is no longer a "let's sit down and discuss the morning traffic jam coffee break" when the workers arrive. As each worker arrives, the others are at work, providing him little incentive to delay his own start-up. Otto Bassler, Personnel Director of the Messerschmidt-Bolkow-Blohm Company, has said that this better matching of work time and work performance was the major gain to his company from the flexitime system.[13] One indirect effect of this better allocation of work time can be a reduction in overtime payments. Where management has made a creative effort to exploit further the advantage of flexitime, additional gains are obtained as predicted (see pp. 97-98).

The attention given to work-flow variations under flexitime can also produce some unexpected benefits for management. Whether or not a company has the flexitime system, production must be maintained when workers are absent due to sickness, vacation leave, enrollment in a company training program, or some other cause. The development of management strategies to deal with employment absence under flexitime—for example, job enlargement, accompanied by extra training for the worker—can produce the unexpected benefit of reducing the economic cost of full-day absences.

In summary, a closer examination of the effects of the flexitime system shows that it need not lead to production anarchy, and indeed can lead to improvements in efficiency. It would seem that in many cases flexitime has "squared the circle" by meeting the needs of both employers and employees.

Employer Problems with Flexitime

This optimistic description of the employer's interest in flexitime should not obscure the fact that it has not always been successful from the point of view of the employer; in fact the system has on occasion proven to be disastrous and quickly withdrawn.[14] Often the cause of failure has been due to some error in the process of installing flexitime.

1. A failure to use some time-recording device: Under a rigid scheduling system an honor system for tardiness will often suffice for white-collar employees. But this honor system may in fact rely on the circumstance that, with a common starting time, the tardy worker is conspicuous. Under flexitime, workers arrive continuously and tardiness is not so obvious, so that a time-recording device may be necessary.

2. Errors in dealing with first-line supervisors: The provision of supervision is made more difficult by the institution of a 10-hour or 12-hour day bandwidth. The system may fail if it opts for either of two obvious methods of dealing with this problem, leaving the supervisor on his old 8-hour schedule and so providing no supervision in the early and late hours or insisting that the supervisor work the entire 10-hour or 12-hour bandwidth, thus providing him with every incentive to sabotage the new system to demonstrate its impracticality. A more helpful solution is to provide overlapping shifts of supervisors. This may require some retraining of supervisors so that they can work with a group normally under another supervisor's direction (e.g., so that in the early morning hours an early supervisor can work with the employees usually reporting to a late supervisor).

3. Employees have to be prepared for the new system: Flexitime is a complicated system which affects many job practices. Employees have to be oriented to the new ground rules and given advice as to how to obtain the most schedule flexibility, subject to management's productivity constraint. Failure to do so can produce negative results and possibly a premature withdrawal of the system.

Notes

1. See Elbing and Gordon for a discussion of the positive uses of small work-group autonomy under a flexitime system.

2. See Baum and Young.

3. Interview with O. Bassler, Personnel Director of Messerschmidt-Bolkow-Blohm.

4. See Elbing, Gadon, and Gordon. See the discussion by CATRAL (Comité pour l'étude et l'aménagement des temps de travail et des temps de loisirs dans la région parisienne) in *L'horaire libre en 1974* for additional estimates.

5. On the basis of her survey, Martin estimated that in 1975 as many as 1 million American employees already had some form of flexible-hours schedules.

6. U.S. Civil Service Commission presents information from interviews with representatives of the U.S. Civil Service Commission who are monitoring the experiment.

7. Site visit at WOLF-Geräte GmbH, Betzdorf/Sieg. Interviews with management and works council representatives. See also "Betriebsvereinbarung zwischen der Geschäftsleitung und dem Betriebsrat der Firma WOLF-Geräte GmbH, Betzdorf/Sieg" ("Shop Agreement between the Management and the Shop Committee of the Firm WOLF-Geräte GmbH, Betzdorf/Sieg").

8. At the Omega watch factory in Switzerland, inventories permit a margin of 3 to 8 hours between employees. See the statement by the Federation of Swiss Employers Association, "L'horaire variable en Suisse," in *L'horaire libre en 1974*.

9. The company first reorganized all work units into sections of at least 12 people, then had workers within each section learn the jobs of some or all of the others in the group, and then gave the section chief autonomy in allocating work assignments and work-time schedules with the group. (Interviews with D. Jubb, General Manager, London and Manchester Insurance Company; and Maurice Reynolds, National Secretary, Insurance Section, Association of Scientific, Technical and Managerial Staffs, representing the London and Manchester employees.)

10. For a discussion of American experience, see First National Bank of Boston; U.S. Social Security Administration; Golembiewski, Hilles, and Kagno; Holley, Armenakis, and Feild; Evans (1975); Martin; Schein, Maurer, and Novak; Nollen and Martin (1978*a*); and Cohen and Gadon. For a survey of European experience, see Racke; Wade; Baum and Young; Bolton; Elbing and Gordon; Allenspach (1975); and Evans (1973). See Plowman for a useful survey of Australian experience.

11. There is a probable positive bias in these studies in that unsuccessful flexitime experiments are often canceled before they can be studied by an outside researcher.

12. This was an extreme case, however, because of the special commuting situation provided by the firm's location (in a large industrial park) and because of the small minority of mothers among the women employed.

13. Interview with author.

14. See Legge.

10 The Long-term Prospects for Flexible Working Schedules

Trade Unions and Flexitime

Despite the net advantages of flexitime to employers and employees, only a small minority of Americans now enjoy the system. One reason for the relatively slow growth of flexitime in this country lies in the role played by legal and other institutional factors in determining the speed with which the new system can be introduced. The institutional framework is unfavorable to the spread of flexitime in the United States in two senses: there is a set of rules that is unfavorable, and behind these rules there are organized interests which resist change.

The principal legal obstacles are the Walsh-Healy and Public Contract Acts and the Fair Labor Standards Act, which together require time-and-a-half overtime premiums to be paid after 40 hours a week in most nonagricultural wage and salary employment, and that time and a half be paid after 8 hours a day in government employment and in departments of private companies that do at least $10,000 annually in federal government contracts.

Additional restraints are imposed in the union sector, which represents almost a quarter of the nonagricultural work force. Unions typically impose stricter overtime penalties than the law prescribes: time and a half after 8 hours, even when no government contract work is done, double time on Sundays, and so on. They frequently specify shift differentials and narrowly determine the range of each worker's job.

The legal and union overtime rules were originally imposed primarily to reduce the length of working hours. They also serve other useful purposes: to discourage employers from compelling workers to adhere to an irregular schedule of hours, to limit employer-imposed shiftwork, and to protect the employment of each category of worker by preventing others from doing his job. However, these rules now stand in the way of more employee choice over hours; they prevent the employee from working a nonstandard schedule of his own choice.

These institutional "rules of the game" are more unfavorable to the spread of flexitime here than they were in a number of major European countries. But this inheritance is only a very partial explanation of the difficulty. Such legal and union rules could readily be changed to accommodate the new hours system. They have not, largely because of strong opposition by trade unionists and their supporters. Despite the popularity of the system with employees, some spokesmen for organized labor have offered serious resistance, while the attitudes of others range from skepticism to mild hostility. Only a few labor spokesmen have praised the idea, and very few indeed have actually urged its adoption; the initiative for introducing flexible scheduling has come almost entirely from employers.

Perhaps most important, segments of organized labor have led the opposition to changing the legal rules which would permit the extension of flexible scheduling systems already in operation. As a striking example, during recent hearings on a bill to permit widespread experimentation with flexible-hours systems for federal employees, the principal opposing witness at the hearings was the president of the American Federation of Government Employees, the largest union representing federal employees.[1]

In general, labor opposition has been much stronger in the United States, as in Europe, in locals and in national unions which have had no experience with the new system and simply regard it with distrust as a new management ploy than in those who have more concrete knowledge of flexitime; in other words union opposition is in some cases a function of ignorance or of ideological prejudice.[2] Nevertheless there are some significant industrial relations problems related to flexitime that must be solved to make the new system acceptable to organized labor. Some believe that union opposition is so rigid that it will successfully block the spread of flexitime by lobbying for restrictive legislation to prevent its spread to nonunion workers as well as by rejecting it for union members. Because of the potential strength of this opposition, we will now digress to discuss at length some of the labor relations issues raised by the new flexitime system. Those readers who are willing to assume that these issues will somehow be resolved may skip ahead to the next section (p. 111).

Union Organization Issues

Union attitudes are conditioned by the treatment of the union organization in the flexitime scheme as well as by the bread-and-butter issues raised for the membership by flexible hours. Negative reactions by some unions in this country may be ascribed, in part, to the fact that such schemes have typically been sponsored by employers. In any event, there is strong evidence from European experience that a negative union response to flexible-hours schedules will more easily develop if the employer introduces the system without involving the union organization in its design and implementation.[3] Close labor-management cooperation cannot only help to head off a union suspicion that flexitime is a purely management-oriented policy, but also assure prompt resolution of specific problems of the union organization under the new system. For example, if a union local customarily holds meetings at lunchtime or just after work, the introduction of flexible schedules could have a bad effect on attendance. A labor-management compromise, often adopted in Europe, is to revert to a common luncheon or quitting time on the days when union meetings are planned.[4] In addition, labor representatives can also bring to light and help to resolve amicably specific problems of hours, earnings, and work intensity that affect the economic interests of members and that might otherwise lead to conflict.

Membership Issues

Labor union spokesmen have argued that under some circumstances flexitime will increase the amount of time given by the employee for the same weekly wage, reduce the employee's monthly earnings while increasing the intensity of his work, and encourage longer hours of work. They have also claimed that flexitime increases management profits without raising wage rates, though the increase derives from a more effective and often a more intensive use of labor.

Each of these points requires serious consideration. An obvious corollary of the claim that management gains from reductions in tardiness or part-day absences (because workers are now more likely to make up lost time) is that more labor will actually be supplied for the same wages.[5] Where the lost time is the result of oversleeping, taking time out for a haircut or hairset, or some other frivolous cause, most employees will agree that management is within its rights to expect makeup time, but they will not extend this principle to other occasions, such as a visit to a doctor. Moreover, some labor spokesmen have argued that when increased employee time is put in under a flexitime system, even where it results from makeups for frivolous latenesses, the earnings of the workers should increase or there should be some other form of compensatory reward.

Overtime Effects

The claim that overtime payments are reduced under flexitime leads to another corollary, that employees' gross earnings will be reduced.[6] Moreover, if management can obtain the same amount of work from employees while reducing overtime, there has usually been an increase in the intensity of work as well. A reduction in overtime is more likely to occur when the worker's choice is subject to management-imposed limits over and above those embodied in the formal flexitime agreements. As we have seen, employees may spontaneously decide to stay late to finish a job, voluntarily offset these hours by taking time off in a slack period on another day, and so reduce overtime costs (at least if overtime premiums are calculated on the basis of weekly or monthly rather than daily hours). Or they may simply work more effectively while on the job (presumably because they are at work at a time when they are psychologically prepared rather than at times determined by a time clock) and hence need less overtime to complete their task.

There is much greater scope for reducing overtime under a flexitime system when the worker's hours choices are further limited by management. The gains to management here are likely to be greatest where the demand for employee services varies over the week or month. A very crude method which management can use to ensure that the distribution of hours inputs under a flexitime system will match company requirements, thus reducing overtime payments, is for the employer to tell the employee the schedule he should "volunteer" to work, threatening him with sanctions, either directly or by implication, if he should "choose" otherwise. It is difficult to find examples of such gross violations of both the spirit and the letter of the flexitime agreement in the various experiments with flexible-hours scheduling, and under collective bargaining agreements grievance procedures are available to eliminate such coercion. Nevertheless well-informed European trade unionists and government officials have expressed fears that such practices will become common, especially in small-size or medium-size businesses in the trade and service sectors if flexitime becomes widely accepted there.[7]

It is easier to find examples of a more subtle form of management pressure which, without violating the flexitime agreement, does induce workers to change the distribution of their working hours so as to minimize overtime payments. Thus consider a hypothetical example in which under a flexitime system insurance company clerks are often denied permission to take time off on other days of the week unless they agree to work late on the one busy night of the week, with the result that overtime is sharply curtailed or eliminated. In a sense, this is an entirely legitimate management policy. Each worker retained the option of working the standard schedule but voluntarily chose an alternative. However, the net result of the flexitime system could be that all workers have been made worse off. If they make $5.00 hourly, then:

A. If in the original situation hours of work were 44 per week (the standard workweek plus four hours of overtime), weekly pay was $230 (if overtime is compensated at time and a half).

The employees worked Wednesday nights but had a relatively easy time Mondays and Fridays.

But with flexitime the employer in effect has offered the worker a choice between:

B. Forty hours of work per week, at a weekly pay of $200, with employees working Wednesday nights, and taking either Monday morning or Friday afternoon off. Because overmanning is eliminated on those days, the worker must exert himself more on the Mondays or Fridays he does work.

C. Forty hours of work per week, at a weekly pay of $200, with a standard

8:00-to-4:30, five-day workweek. Because overmanning is eliminated, the worker must exert himself more on Monday and Friday.

Under flexitime, alternative A is no longer available to the worker. The employer can now meet his Wednesday night needs without offering overtime.

Some workers may well rank the three alternatives: $A > B > C$. These workers could be worse off under the flexitime system, since their most preferred option is no longer available.[8] In work situations where the average employee has become dependent on overtime earnings to maintain his living standard,[9] those made worse off by the system could constitute a majority of the work force.

Some unionists also fear that flexitime could lead to longer working hours. This objection has particular force in the United States, where it is feared that the flexitime system would undermine legal limitations on working times. The Fair Labor Standards Act requirement of overtime premiums after 40 hours a week and the Walsh-Healy and Public Contract Acts requirements (for those employed in government or in companies working on government contracts) of overtime payments after 8 hours a day, now cover millions of employees; they are especially important for those workers whose schedules are not already regulated by a union contract. But the advocates of flexitime argue that workers should be allowed to carry hours forward from day to day, or even from week to week, to gain the full benefits of the system. (If this is not done, flexible scheduling would necessarily be confined to variations in daily starting and quitting times or, at most, in weekly hours.) To facilitate these carryforwards, American labor laws could be modified to continue to require the payment of overtime premiums only in those situations in which extra work time in a day or week was ordered by management; when an employee chose a long workday or week to have compensatory time off at another date, no overtime premium would be required by law. But this revision of the federal statutes would clearly make it more difficult to enforce the hours laws. Moreover, union spokesmen have argued that the introduction of a flexitime system can make enforcement more difficult, even if the law is not revised to permit carryforwards of time from one day to the next. Under the flexitime system, normal business hours are extended, and each employee has a different starting and stopping time, complicating the job of the government inspector.[10]

Because of the various problems flexitime raises in the enforcement of hours legislation, some union opponents actually regard the spread of the system as a step backward in the historic struggle for a shorter workday and workweek.

Another possible source of controversy between labor and management is over the distribution of benefits. Even if makeup time, overtime loss, and similar problems are resolved in a satisfactory manner (at least in the sense that most of the workers feel that any losses here are well worth the gains that result from being able to set their working hours to some extent), unionists question the rationale for permitting management to retain all residual benefits from the introduction of the system. In their view, insofar as higher productivity results from a more intensive use of labor, at least a portion of the resulting gain should be distributed to labor in the form of higher earnings.[11]

Resolution of Hours, Earnings, and Work Intensity
Problems under Flexible Scheduling

Experience with the flexitime system under union conditions presents examples of the successful resolution of all these problems either through collective bargaining or preventive management action designed to head off a potential union objection. European experience shows that the makeup time issue can be settled, in part, by breaking down incidents of lost time into those from justifiable and those from unjustifiable causes; the overtime problem can be alleviated if management avoids pursuing an aggressive policy of overtime reduction in situations where there is a tradition of large overtime payments, leading workers to regard them as a permanent perquisite. These and similar problems are further alleviated as productivity gains, including those resulting from makeup time or a reduction in overtime payments, are divided between higher hourly wages and higher profits so that workers actually obtain a financial benefit as well as greater freedom in rearranging their schedules.[12]

On the other hand, the nonunion or weakly organized sectors present a different problem. There the most pressing concern must be for those groups which are economically weak but which now enjoy legal protection from competitive market pressures on their wages and hours. There is no doubt that the extensive development of flexitime systems could make enforcement of the wage and hours provision of the FLSA and Walsh-Healy and Public Contract Acts more difficult, especially if the laws are amended to permit voluntary carryforwards of work time. If the use of flexible scheduling continues to spread, one can predict that the wage and hours division of the U.S. Department of Labor will have to allocate more resources to the effective enforcement of hours and overtime payment regulations. In Europe, a special commission of the French government to study the management of work and leisure time, CATRAL, examined this issue and proposed that a random sampling procedure be used by French labor inspectors to deal with the problem. In this way, CATRAL believes, sufficient resources can be expended in intensive investigations at the selected sites to assure that the rights of the employees are being fully protected under flexible-hours systems. It is hoped that the threat of inspection will act as a sufficient deterrent to all employers so that the expense of a full census of employers need not be incurred.[13]

But while there is an obvious need to assure that bogus flexitime schemes are not used to victimize workers, there does not appear to be a very strong case for going further and arguing that the interests of organized labor demand that legislation be used to restrict or eliminate genuine flexitime schemes. The experience with flexitime in this country to date[14] suggests that the effects of flexitime on employees tends, on balance, to be positive or neutral; that is, that drawbacks such as the need to make up time missed or a possible loss in overtime income are offset or more than offset for most workers by the positive advantages of the system. This is not an accidental result. If an employer is to obtain a profit advantage from a genuine flexitime system, he will, in most circumstances, have to obtain an improvement in employee morale, with its related personnel benefits. Otherwise it simply is not worthwhile to introduce this rather complicated new system with its unpredictable effects on productive efficiency. A further constraint on the employer is provided by the need for a high degree of employee cooperation to make a genuine system of flexitime work. Otherwise there are just too many ways in which an unpopular flexitime system can be sabotaged, ranging from a simple refusal to choose schedules which conform to job needs (in the more sophisticated variants where management has delegated autonomy to the small work group) to actual, physical interference with the individual time-recording devices. Hence it has not been in management's interests to endeavor to take such advantage of this system's full potential for reducing overtime income and increasing work effort that the employees become disenchanted with flexible scheduling as a result.

Prospects for Change

If union resistance to the flexitime system is relaxed and legal and institutional barriers are lowered, the prospects for its expansion would of course be considerably improved. But fairly good opportunities for the eventual spread of flexitime exist even within the present institutional restraints. A great deal of flexibility can be provided within the bounds of FLSA, Walsh-Healy, and other hours laws, either in the nonunion sector or where unions are not hostile to the plan. Certainly daily freedom to fix hours—that is, the freedom to fix hours within the constraint of an 8-hour day, simply varying daily starting and finishing times—could be easily arranged under current rules. (In fact the AFL-CIO has given its qualified support to this version of flexitime.) Moreover, the FLSA itself permits day-to-day variations in hours, without payment of overtime, as long as the 40-hour weekly limit is not exceeded. Tens of millions of workers are covered only by FLSA, since they are neither working on government contracts nor are represented by a trade union. This still allows considerable room for experimentation with the day-to-day version of flexitime.

One might conjecture that if the new system can prove itself to labor within these confines, bringing obvious gains to employees and not damaging the interests of union organizations where they permit its introduction, union attitudes would very likely relax and eventually become less antipathetic to new rules that would permit much more flexibility in individual hours in a much wider variety of job situations.

Some further grounds for optimism here is to be found in the long-term factors listed in chapter 6 as tending to support the development of alternative working schedules. The development of a postindustrial service economy, with an ever smaller proportion of the work force in heavy industry; the increasingly diversified demographic composition of the work force, with even greater employment of females, youths, and semiretired individuals; increasing materials, energy, and environmental problems, with a concomitant concern for more efficient use of social overhead capital; and increasing bargaining power of labor along with more sophisticated approaches by management in utilizing group psychology to motivate labor are all likely to continue to gain strength and to generate pressures for individual scheduling of hours. Favorable developments, in the institutional framework as well as in more basic long-term trends, could lead to a large proportion, perhaps even a majority of the work force, having the flexitime system.

Variations in the Number of Hours Worked

The same constellation of underlying factors would also be likely to increase the degree of choice over the number of hours worked. Moreover, the spread of flexitime may itself be a factor encouraging this development. On the supply side, one would expect that, for example, as employees become accustomed to taking a couple of afternoons off a week, some of them are going to prefer not to make up the time and to be willing to suffer an income loss for the privilege.

On the demand side, the spread of flexitime might also reduce management objections to part-time employees. In many flexitime plans employees learn to confine most of their interactions with each other to the core period. Hence if a part-time worker is employed during just the core period, he will have much the same opportunities to interact with others as do the full-timers.

Similarly when the introduction of flexitime compels management to investigate the regular flows of variations in the demand for labor in the enterprise, it often finds that there are more regular "peaks and valleys" than it had thought. This experience in tailoring work time and work flows can generate a demand for part-timers during peak periods.[15]

Hence it is at least possible that the more modest step of introducing flexibility in the timing of hours would in some enterprises gradually lead to the introduction of scheduling practices that actually gave individuals some control over the number of their hours of work.

Other Strategies for Introducing Schedule Flexibility

Flexitime is not the only new strategy for providing individual choice over schedules. The pure form of flexitime, in which each individual chooses his starting and quitting time without regard for the needs of the enterprise, is quite inappropriate in many job situations. As we have seen, this difficulty can sometimes be resolved by deputizing schedule decisions to the small work group, with the instruction that the efficiency of the department must not be impaired. But this is not the only solution; rather than deputizing decisions to the small work group, the relevant information—the schedule preferences of employees and the productivity needs of the enterprise—can be fed into a computer and a set of optimal schedules determined. An important advantage of this alternative is that it need not be confined to a small work group. For example, it might be used in a factory layout, with two or three shifts of workers, where schedules for a very large work group must be determined simultaneously. The disadvantage of this method is that it will of course be impractical to feed all the relevant information about individual preferences and company needs into the computer, so that a less refined result will necessarily be obtained.

Nevertheless the computerized system could be helpful in many situations in which the introduction of ordinary flexitime would be impractical because of the size of the relevant work group. For example, one might think that individual scheduling would be impossible in a continuous process industry, operating on three daily shifts. But workers could vary their hours, only averaging 8 per day and 40 per week, over a very long period of time, perhaps once a year. At the beginning of each year, workers would enter their preferences on the computer and an optimizing result obtained (with ties broken by seniority). Insofar as possible, each worker would be given his ideal schedule. Presumably, devoted skiers would have light schedules in the winter, while scuba divers would have vacations and long weekends in the summer.[16] In this way, a considerable degree of schedule flexibility could be offered even in a heavy manufacturing industry, where it might otherwise appear to be impractical.

Notes

1. Webber, on proposed federal legislation to authorize employees and agencies of the government to experiment with flexible and compressed work schedules as alternatives to present work schedules.

2. See Baum and Young for a review of English and German experience.

See also the union position papers in *L'horaire variable ou libre* and *L'horaire libre en 1974*.

3. See the position paper by the Confédération Général du Travail in *L'horaire libre en 1974*, and Webber.

4. See discussions in *L'horaire libre en 1974*. See also Bernard and Ghanadian.

5. See Bernard and Ghanadian.

6. See the discussion of the overtime problem in Bernard and Ghanadian; *L'horaire libre en 1974*; and Webber.

7. *L'horaire libre en 1974*, p. 26.

8. This is based in part on a real example in which many of the objective conditions were as described in the text. However, in practice management recognized the possibility that a sharp reduction in overtime would alienate the staff and so did not take full advantage of the opportunity to cut overtime costs.

9. See Bernard and Ghanadian for a discussion of this problem among low-paid British workers.

10. See the position paper by the Confédération Général du Travail in *L'horaire libre en 1974*.

11. See the discussion in Racke.

12. Of course the replacement of standard hours schedules by the new flexitime system will require an additional union effort to negotiate the continued protection of employee rights under the new system. Where union resources are already strained, this additional cost may itself constitute a reason for union resistance to a proposed change in schedule provisions.

13. See *L'horaire libre en 1974*, pp. 18-19.

14. See the discussion in chapter 9.

15. If the work is especially fatiguing, a shorter day may increase hourly productivity. This may become apparent under flexitime, when a company can compare workers' outputs on days on which they work only the core time with days on which they work the standard 8 hours. This knowledge could also stimulate the employment of part-timers.

16. I owe this example to Richard Dudek, professor of Industrial Engineering at Texas Tech University.

11

Long-term Social Effects of Flexible Working Schedules

Any forecast of increased schedule flexibility, even as a long-run possibility, must be highly speculative. Nevertheless it is useful to consider the probable effects on time usage and related issues (especially the likely long-term effects on leisure time and on the management of household production time) if this forecase were realized.

This discussion must start with the available evidence: the individual firm studies of the effects of flexitime. But we must also go beyond this evidence and ask two key questions. Would the effects on individuals observed in these relatively few studies of enterprises continue to be seen if the system were applied to the labor force as a whole or to a substantial portion of it? Since most of these before-and-after studies cover only a short period of time, can we assume that the observed effects will persist in the long run?

The individual studies indicate that on-the-job productivity could often be maintained or improved, while employees would obtain better opportunities to deal with their time management problems, both reducing the amount of necessary household production time and improving the quality of paid work, household production, and consumption time. In general, there is little reason to believe that these advantages would be lost as one extended the system to a larger proportion of the work force.[1]

Flexitime and Social Gains from Reducing Commuter Congestion

Rush-hour traffic control does constitute one area[2] where the effects on the community of widespread adoption of flexitime would not be of the same magnitude as those on the individual who now obtains more freedom to arrange his schedule. Congestion control provides a classic case of a spillover effect, where the individual is not properly rewarded by the market for his positive action, in this case, commuting outside the rush hour. (The commuter who changes his schedule reduces both his own travel time and congestion among the remaining rush-hour travelers, but is only rewarded for the first of these contributions.) Hence individual and social gains will not be the same.

Diminishing Returns to Flexitime?

On the other hand, there is some reason to believe that the gain to the individual from commuting outside the rush hour is reduced as a larger portion of the work force gets flexitime. If, say, a third or a half of a community is on the system, one might expect to see some leveling out of traffic flows, with less concentration at the peak time and more utilization of facilities in the adjacent hours. Hence as still more workers get the right to vary their hours, their incentive to commute outside the peak time is somewhat less. If other considerations lead at least some of them to prefer a standard starting and finishing time, somewhat fewer of this group may opt for a variant schedule.

Community Studies

However, the importance of this last point should not be exaggerated. When one turns from theoretical considerations to an examination of actual outcomes, a positive assessment emerges. While it is true that there are only a few cases of metropolitan areas where a large proportion of the work force has flexitime, the experience in these communities indicates that substantial community savings are obtained despite the problem of diminishing returns. Gordon and Elbing studied one city, Winterthur in Switzerland, in which a majority of the work force is on the system. They report that "from 1970 to 1973, the amount of traffic using the buses in this city increased, but the number of buses necessary was reduced by 10 percent since the peak operating periods were significantly reduced."[3] More generally, traffic congestion was eased, and the individual commuter ride made more pleasant and efficient.

A similarly favorable conclusion has been reached in more recent studies of several Canadian cities where a large proportion of the work force is on flexitime.[4] Such studies show how flexitime not only improves the commuting situation of those on the system but also that of their fellow commuters, who now have fewer competitors for transportation facilities at the rush-hour peak, as well as assisting the municipalities which must provide these facilities.

How Some Urban Planners See the Role of Flexitime

The basic positive spillover argument—that the social gains of the reduction in commuting time exceed the individual benefits—has been perceived by some policymakers as a reason for government to take the initiative in speeding the introduction of flexitime. Indeed some planners have argued that flexitime, despite its shortcomings, is the best available work scheduling scheme for dealing with the social problem of traffic congestion.

At first, this preference for flexitime over staggered hours appears to be counterintuitive. It would seem that staggered hours could in principle be set so as to minimize the commuter congestion problem; and since this is the basic, or even sole, purpose of hours staggering, it would appear that hours would in fact be set so as to maximize commuter benefits. In contrast, flexitime allows the worker a choice. While he wishes to reduce his commuting time, he is also trying to maximize on a number of other variables (see the discussion in chapter 9). Moreover, he would not be expected to consider the effects of his contribution to commuting congestion on the travel times of others. Hence one would expect a suboptimal solution of the commuting problem, and certainly one that did not maximize commuter benefits.

However, flexitime has important practical advantages. European planners offer the following reasons for preferring flexitime over staggered hours as a method of easing rush-hour congestion:[5]

First, while staggered hours might work best if all the workers in the downtown section left from the same building and took homeward routes that fanned out in a pattern like spokes from the hub of a wheel, in the real world commuting patterns are much more complicated than that, partly because the downtown area itself is spread out—in some cities over a number of square miles. As a result, many commuters must spend some time, often a quarter of an hour or more, in crossing the downtown area on their way home. For the employee in the southwest corner of a large downtown area who lives in a northeast suburb, the departure time which will minimize his rush-hour problem is different from that which would be suitable for a coworker who not only works in the southwest corner of the downtown business area but also lives in a southwest suburb; this second employee does not have to cross the downtown area at rush hour, but can immediately enter a suburban expressway. Staggered-hours systems are limited in their capacity to deal with this type of situation because each employee in a business establishment is assigned the same starting and quitting time, regardless of his individual commuting problem; under flexitime the individual can adjust his hours so as to minimize his rush-hour delay.

Second, employers are generally reluctant to accept staggered-hours schedules which would put their starting or ending times completely outside the main rush-hour period (e.g., outside 8:00 to 9:00 A.M., the morning rush hour). A compulsory starting time of 7:00 or 7:30 A.M. would alienate the office staff and would also require unusual opening and closing hours, which might reduce the level of service a government agency can perform or lose some business for a private firm. However, under flexitime a certain proportion of the employees in each enterprise will choose such nonrush-hour starting times and so will help to reduce commuter congestion.

A third advantage of the flexitime system in dealing with commuter problems arises when there are certain routes that are relatively lightly traveled, say, an express bus to a particular suburb. Then there may only be enough business on that route for one or two trips during each rush-hour period. When hours are staggered, many employees will necessarily find that their work times no longer fit well with the bus schedule. In contrast, flexitime permits workers to pick their arrival and departure times to coincide with those of an express service.

Of course this does not mean that the flexitime system—or any other work scheduling scheme—by itself provides an optimal strategy for reducing commuter congestion. For example, flexitime might produce much better results if it were combined with strong cash incentives for using routes outside peak times (various toll systems have been suggested to achieve this end). Nevertheless even without this feature, it may yield better results than are obtained by hours staggering.

In summary, the principal case in which the social effects of flexitime differ sharply from the individual is congestion. Here the social gains exceed the individual benefits, though both the social and the individual gain from additional workers having flexitime is reduced as more workers are on the system.

Long-term Effects on Leisure Time

However, a less positive answer must be given to the second question: whether the short-term or medium-term effects of flexible working schedules can be extrapolated to the long run, that is, after sufficient time has elapsed for people to change jobs or residences, purchase new durable goods, and make other permanent changes in their life-styles. It is true that long-run adjustments would permit even better use of time. For example, schools could eventually adjust their scheduling practices, allowing children more freedom in their starting and quitting times so as to mesh better with parents' schedules or to serve other goals. It can be argued that a 12-month school year, team teaching, teaching machines, and modular instruction would further this goal. The technology needed for these innovations is there; under the right impetus it could readily be adopted. It is probably not too farfetched to speculate that a broad movement toward flexible-hours scheduling in the labor market would prove the needed stimulus to the adoption of complementary technologies in education, which would provide more individual student flexibility in school scheduling. Other examples of this type could also be cited, in which long-term adjustments would provide a technical basis for further gains in leisure from flexible-hours scheduling.

But it is not at all likely that such technological potential for "saving time" would be realized, in the sense that individuals would in the end have significantly more free, or consumption, time. It is more likely that much or all of the gain from flexitime would go to the development of a more ambitious life-style than that it would lead to any substantial saving in household production time or a resulting net increase in leisure.

The principal reason for this pessimistic prediction is provided by our earlier experiences with devices developed to assist the time management of the employee or householder. True, these devices—the timesavers discussed in chapter 4—were mechanical in nature, automobiles, vacuum cleaners, and the like, and flexible hours is a social technology, but the analysis of their effects is rather similar. In both cases, a substantial improvement is obtained in the productivity of household production time, which permit the same product to be obtained with less time. For example, both the automobile and flexitime will generally increase commuter speed, enabling the same distance to be traveled in less time. But the automobile (like earlier timesavers in commuter technology) also enabled individuals to adopt a more ambitious life-style by gradually adjusting their jobs and residences to take advantage of the new commuting possibilities. The long-term result was a remarkable increase in commuter distance, with an indeterminate effect on commuting time.

A similar argument can be made about other timesaving improvements of flexitime. For example, there is little reason to believe that access to retail outlets at times when there is less time needed to wait in line or at hours of the day when more outlets are open, reducing the necessary driving time, will actually lead to any reduction in shopping time. It is likely to lead to more bargain hunting, with an indeterminate effect on shopping time. (After all, shopping time appears to have increased, not decreased, in the past several decades, despite the development of a variety of devices to save time in shopping.)[6]

The theoretical model developed in chapter 4 can also be used to discuss this long-term impact of flexitime at a higher level of abstraction. It was argued there that a technical improvement in household production time would reduce the time required per unit of household production output, thus saving some time. But insofar as household production time could be substituted for goods in producing household production output and insofar as this output could in turn be substituted for time spent in consumption activities, more rather than less household production time might be required, and less rather than more leisure or consumption time would be enjoyed (see chapter 4 and appendix E). Applying this result to the commuting example, insofar as increased commuter time and distance would enable the worker to live in a better residential environment and insofar as he would be willing to spend time commuting to upgrade the quality of his residential environment rather than increasing the time available for enjoying this environment, no increase in leisure time need result.

The second reason for some skepticism about the long-term effects of flexible-hours schedules on leisure gains is that it would very likely increase female labor force participation. The flexitime system makes the employment of women more feasible, partly because it enables the working mother to provide better care for her children by permitting husband and wife to work out regular schedules that will permit one of them to arrive home early enough to fill part or all of the gap between the school and workday schedule. This effect appears to be better appreciated in Europe, where there has been more experience with the system.

Mlle. Lecoultre of the Social and Manpower Directorate of the Organization for Economic Co-operation and Development, points out that, under some variants of this flexitime system, "working parents can take time off [as needed, making up the time at a later date] to take care of sick parents or children or to fulfill other . . . obligations."[7] Heinz Allenspach, Director of the Central Union of Swiss Employers Associations, argues that it would be "difficult or impossible for married women . . . to accept [full-time] work if they were not allowed a certain individual flexibility in their hours of arrival and departure."[8]

In a number of interviews, managers in European institutions on the flexitime system remarked that many women who had thought that they could handle only part-time jobs found that they could accept full-time employment if they could choose their hours of work. Increased female labor force participation has been a principal cause of the time bind described in part I. Continued increases in market work time by women would presumably lead to additional problems in the allocation of leisure and household production time in the future.

A third reason for skepticism about flexible-hours scheduling as a solution to the time pressures is that it is likely to yield more ambitious, goods-intensive consumption experiences, with a resulting increase in the type of stresses and strains described in Linder's *The Harried Leisure Class*. A not uncommon use of flexitime in Europe, where the system is broad enough to permit it, is to take longer leisure-time modules: an extended weeknight (leaving early on a weekday and arriving late the next day); a full weekday off; or a three-day or four-day weekend. This pattern would very likely be repeated in the United States, where the trend in the past half-century has been to take leisure in larger modules (so that we have had the 5-day workweek, the 3-day holiday weekend, and nearly universal vacations, but no reduction in the basic 8-hour day). In chapter 4 we saw that there is a very marked tendency for complicated and expensive recreation experiences to be concentrated in these expanded leisure-time modules, in contrast to the passive, inexpensive pursuits followed on a normal weekday evening. It is likely that a proliferation of four, three (or even two and one-half) day weekends would give a boost to a more ambitious leisure life-style: more second homes, campers, boats, and so on. These possessions do bring consumption benefits to their owners, but they also mean large installment loans to be repaid and the myriad of repair and maintenance tasks described by Linder and other social critics.

A final reservation has been put forward by leftist critics in Europe. They see government, and corporate capitalism in general, as only very imperfectly responsive to the needs of working people. They point out that some of the factors mentioned in this book—especially the dominance of the two-earner family and the suburbanization of the working class—have put pressure upon the ruling classes to provide more and better commuter facilities, shopping facilities, housing, day-care centers, and the like. In this context, they regard flexitime as a very inexpensive palliative: a way to avoid expensive and politically difficult transformations of the social overhead capital.

One does not have to accept Marxian class analysis to agree that a possible effect of flexitime in this country would be fewer resources allocated to new expressways, day-care centers, and the like. This would also tend to limit the long-run potential effect of the new system on leisure time.[9]

It is difficult to assess the relative importance of each of these four arguments. But taking them together, it is apparent that flexible scheduling may very well not lead to an increase in leisure time. However, this should not obscure the principal expected benefit of flexible-hours scheduling. It was argued in chapter 5 that rigid scheduling practices were deteriorating the quality of time, partly offsetting the gains in quality attributable to massive increases in goods consumption. By widening the area of individual choice, flexible scheduling would be predicted to improve the quality of paid working time, household production time, and consumption time, though its effect on the allocation among these three types of time is indeterminate.

Notes

1. Unless marketplace productivity were deliberately sacrificed to expedite the spread of the system.

2. A similar analysis could be made of several other relevant congestion problems (e.g., golf courses or municipal beaches).

3. See Elbing and Gordon.

4. See Bonsall.

5. See Owen (1975).

6. See chapter 4.

7. Conference of experts in Venice, Italy, on "What Americans Can Learn from European Experience with Alternative Work Schedules."

8. On the effects on female labor force participation, see Allenspach (1972).

9. However, if flexitime provided a sufficient acceleration to the movement to two-earner families and to increased commuter distance, the net result might actually be a net increase in the demand for social overhead capital.

12 The Future of Hours Reducation

A sharp reduction in hours of work, say, from 40 to 30 per week, would be a much more reliable way to increase leisure time. The analysis of historical reductions in the workweek in chapter 3 and of the part-time labor market in chapters 7 and 8 make it clear that further hours reduction would be quite expensive. In fact one could argue that, to a first approximation the cost in national output would be proportionate to the reduction in hours, that is, a 25 percent decline in output and hence in per capita income. Examining the question in detail requires that we look at a number of factors, some of which would decrease and others raise that estimate; but it is not clear that the net effect of all these complexities is to reduce this 25 percent figure.[1]

It is true that some offset might be found in reduced fatigue. But with weekly hours at their present moderate levels, a further reduction would probably not bring very much relief; certainly not a gain in hourly productivity that would be analogous to the improvement that occurred as hours were reduced from their very high levels of the nineteenth century. Of course individuals could compensate for a reduction in hours by working harder. It is rather obvious that a large proportion of the labor force does not work anything near 100 percent efficiency. However, holding back work effort is a behavioral problem, not one of bodily strength. The reasons for this behavior involve a complex of economic, social, and psychological factors, generally discussed as part of the "decline of the American work ethic." There is little if any reason to believe that a reduction in hours would somehow yield a change in these behavioral relationships that would put an end to soldiering on the job.

Similarly while a second offset to hours reduction might be found in an increase in the number of people participating in the labor force, this effect would probably not be all that large. There already is a well-developed part-time labor market for those who wish to work less than the standard schedule. It is not unlikely that this market will be expanded and improved, partly because of flexible scheduling innovations discussed in the preceding chapters. Certainly a reduction to a 30-hour workweek would open up opportunities to still more marginal workers. However, it is unlikely that this gain would provide much offset to the earnings loss of the more productive prime earners whose hours were cut from 40 to 30.

These potential positive offsets must be weighed against a number of negative factors that would tend to exacerbate the effects of hours reduction. The first derives from the analysis of education and hours of work offered in chapter

3; this analysis emphasized the lifetime distribution of work and leisure. In this context, the individual's time in school from age 6 to 18 (or 24) can be thought of as a type of work activity—a way of improving productivity in later years. The value of time of teachers (and of those who build and maintain educational structures, and so on) can be regarded as additional costs of the same activity. The economic return to the worker, and to society, from this investment is obtained in the increase in his earnings, or more precisely in the increase in his hourly productivity times the number of hours that he works. Hence a 25 percent reduction in hours would, other things being equal, reduce the financial return to education by 25 percent. Insofar as individuals are responsive to economic incentives (or since subsidy policies are important in determining the level of educational investment, insofar as taxpayers are responsive to the economic payoff of education), one would expect a lower payoff to result in reduced investment in education. Further, if the earnings of parents were cut by 25 percent by a reduction in hours, their ability and willingness to pay for schooling could also be reduced, reinforcing this effect (see appendix C for a further discussion of this point).

In addition, one could predict some changes in the schooling process itself. As work comes to take up a smaller portion of an individual's time as an adult and as leisure continues to increase, one can expect a continued trend toward "education for life" type courses at the expense of vocationally oriented studies. At the same time, it is also plausible to predict that the leisure orientation made possible by a 30-hour workweek for adults would eventually affect the intensity of student effort and the hours of teachers and students. Taken together, these predicted effects would all operate, with varying degrees of importance, to reduce the amount and effectiveness of schooling as a preparation of market employment and hence tend to lower the productivity of the work force.

Other factors would also contribute to a decline in hourly productivity if workweeks were reduced. It was argued in chapter 7 that most of the economic disadvantages suffered by part-timers was due to the effects of their short schedule on their productivity rather than to the circumstance that their hours were simply different than the standard. Similarly difficult problems could be expected if the hours of all workers were reduced to what is now a part-time level. Thus with a reduced workweek, there would be less incentive to train workers: the payoff would be decreased since (as in the case of formal education) the financial return here is determined by the product of the gain in hourly productivity resulting from training and the number of hours worked. At the same time, complex job structures would become less economic because of the supervisory, coordination, and communications problems imposed by short schedule workers, discussed in chapter 7.

However, the effects of a general hours reduction would differ from those of part-time work in one very important respect. At the present time, part-timers are generally relegated to jobs that require little training and in which there are few complex interactions. But if the hours of all were reduced, it is extremely unlikely that industry could respond by a sufficiently massive redesign of jobs (by a reduction in their complexity, to cut training costs, and by a reduction in the complexity of interaction) to fully offset the effects of lower hours. There might well be some large-scale redesign of jobs, but physical and organizational technology would necessarily limit its extent. In our advanced economy, 30-hour-a-week employees would still have to fill jobs requiring much training and in complex settings, with predictably negative effects on efficiency.

A third problem relates to capacity utilization. We saw that part-timers are at a severe disadvantage where capacity utilization is an important issue, for example, in the mining, manufacturing, and railroad industries. But with a 30-hour workweek for all, these industries like all others will have to suffer a reduction in capacity utilization by one-fourth unless they are able to make much more extensive use of shiftworkers. Lower capacity utilization could seriously increase the economic cost of hours reduction.

Considering the combined effects of these several arguments, it would appear that we are in a position in which a 25 percent reduction in labor input, through hours reduction, could actually yield a 25 percent or larger reduction in output.[2] A variant of this argument was cited in chapter 3 as a major cause of the leveling off in hours over the past 40 years: that is, it was argued that because of the high elasticity of income with respect to effort under modern conditions more leisure appeared to be too expensive to workers and their union representatives. Turning the argument around, we now say that if hours are in fact reduced significantly, a number of factors would combine to make this a most expensive decision.

However, this does not imply that the cost of this choice is so high that it must be ruled out as impractical. In fact if hours reduction took place gradually over a long period of time, very little economic deprivation need result. Unless there is a sharp departure from the historic trend of economic growth in the United States, it would be possible by the year 2000 to have a 25 percent reduction in working times, without any reduction in real weekly wages. This would require an annual productivity gain of only 1.3 percent, but in the past, the long-term rate of gain in output per manhour has ranged from 2 to 3 percent per annum as a result of technological advance and the accumulation of capital. Moreover, it can be argued that there is so much uncertainty about the future rate of productivity growth, the birthrate, and labor force participation rates that, with an acceptable range of high and low forecasts of such variables, we could have a higher living standard with hours reduction (if accompanied by high forecasts of other variables determining living standards) than without hours reduction (if accompanied by low forecasts of the other variables).

In other words there is little question that the nation could afford a reduction in hours: the real question is whether we will be willing to pay the rather steep price. There are at least two plausible paths that might actually lead us to hours reduction in the years ahead: a shorter workweek could result from a constellation of objective long-term factors favorable to gradual reduction, probably yielding a slow decline in hours, or it could occur as a result of an economic crisis, perhaps rather abruptly.

A number of long-term factors could help to generate the first scenario, a gradual reduction in working times:

1. A rapid growth in real hourly earnings: Rising real hourly wages have in fact been supportive of hours reduction in the past and have been the traditional explanation by economists of hours reduction. Certainly if a rapid rate of gain in labor productivity is obtained, hours reduction will have less painful consequences. If an annual rate of 3.2 percent is obtained (the rate of gain in productivity in the 1948-69 period), a 25 percent reduction in hours by the year 2000 would be consistent with a 50 percent increase in weekly or annual incomes.[3] Conversely if material and energy problems, or other difficulties, continue to restrict productivity gains, hours reduction could well mean a decline in incomes. Any rate of gain less than 1.3 percent (comparable to rates which obtained in the mid-1970s) would yield this result.[4]

2. Low birthrates, a leveling off in the increase in number of years spent in school, a reversal of the trend toward early retirement, and continued increases in the labor force participation of women, all would help to raise the ratio of the working to the nonworking population, and hence make it easier to reduce hours without reducing living standards.

Statistical evidence introduced in chapter 3 argued that the war and postwar baby boom, along with the increase in the average school-leaving ages, raised child-rearing costs and so was a principal factor in explaining the leveling off in hours of work since World War II. By the same reasoning, the present low rate of births and leveling off in the proportion going to college might be taken as predicting future hours reductions. However, some feel that the so-called graying of America (the increasing proportion of the population over 65 years of age) together with the trend toward early retirement will impose sharply increased pension payment costs on the working population, unless the retirement age is increased. Steady increases in pension costs could be a deterrent to hours reduction (this point is considered in appendix D). A reversal of the trend toward early retirement—regarded as essential by some analysts of pension costs—would facilitate hours reductions.

Finally increases in female labor force participation may become a factor in hours reduction for three reasons: women traditionally have sought to work a shorter workweek than men, presumably because they are assigned more non-market work chores under the existing sexual division of labor. The family's income need is reduced by the wife's employment and earnings. And the husband's leisure time is reduced as he comes to take over some of his wife's chores. The great increases in female labor force participation observed over the past

several decades have been associated with a vast increase in part-time employment rather than with a reduction in the standard workweek. However, militant
feminists are becoming increasingly interested in general hours reduction as a
method of equalizing the work responsibilities of men and women, and may
increase their efforts to reduce hours in the years ahead if the trend toward increased participation of women continues.

   3. A continued trend toward a welfare state: Hours reduction would impose
severe economic costs upon society, but the extent to which these costs are felt
as such by individuals increasingly depends upon government policy. Through
the welfare system, the government now provides a floor for those who choose
not to work at a fairly generous level by historical standards. In addition, there
is a trend toward providing many consumer goods and services free of charge or
at highly subsidized prices: education, medical care, and outdoor recreation are
three examples. At the same time, progressive income taxes may also diminish
incentives to work. This welfare state trend could eventually produce a paradoxical condition in which perceptions of the sharp social costs of a reduction
in work effort are blurred by government policies which penalize the relatively
industrious; individual workers, or even industrywide unions, might then opt for
shorter hours, realizing that much of the social cost would actually be displaced
to other workers, whose tax rates would be increased as receipts from the taxes
of short schedule workers dropped.

   4. Future changes in the nature of work could help either to encourage or
discourage hours reduction. An increased demand for poorly educated workers
and for those with little on-the-job training, and an increase in simple, easy-to-
supervise jobs might encourage hours reduction. Short-hours schedules impose
fewer diseconomies in this type of work and hence are relatively less costly to
employers. Moreover, the job satisfaction literature would predict that an increasingly high education level of the work force, could lead to hours reduction
in some cases. On the other hand, continued increases in job complexity would
make work-time reduction more costly while improvements in the working environment, including further gains in physical working conditions as well as inno-
vative management changes (e.g., more use of autonomous small work groups
or matrix management) might make hours reduction relatively less important.
The question of the influence of the nature of work on hours of work has
received very little attention from economists, though some observers predict
that this will become an important issue in the years ahead.

   5. Finally changes in individual tastes may promote a reduction in hours.
The catchall term "tastes" (used by economists to describe all factors which
are not susceptible to economic analysis) is most useful, given our inability to
predict many social phenomena with purely economic variables. For example, a
future change in the emphasis that Americans put on the quantity of leisure or
consumption time relative to the quantity of goods and services used in con-

sumption could easily produce a downward trend in hours of work. This movement could also be supported by possible future gains in recreation technology.[5]

In an alternative scenario, an economic catastrophe, analogous to the Great Depression of the 1930s, could lead to drastic hours reduction as a share-the-work remedy. An example of such drastic revision would be a change in the Fair Labor Standards Act so that time-and-a-half overtime premiums would be imposed after 30 rather than 40 hours a week. If the experience of the 1930s and 1940s is a guide to the future, the lower level of hours could then become accepted as a new standard to be defended fiercely by trade union lobbyists even after the reestablishment of full employment conditions.

In practice, this method of achieving workweek reduction would yield less actual reduction in work time than would a gradual market solution resulting from the interaction of long-term factors. In the latter case, employees would by hypothesis be generally interested in reducing their own work time at the expense of market income. But if worksharing is imposed by law then, when full employment is again achieved, workers will presumably endeavor as individuals to extend their hours through overtime and moonlighting, as was indeed the case in World War II and the postwar period. At the same time millions of other workers, the self-employed and those management, professional, and other employees whose hours are not effectively controlled by statute, would continue to work long hours. Nevertheless a significant reduction in labor input could be obtained by changing the hours laws, yielding both substantial reductions in output and potentially important increases in leisure time.

Effects of Workweek Reduction on Free Time

It is not intuitively obvious that a reduction in working hours must yield an increase in consumption of leisure time; it could simply lead to a gain in household production time. It is very likely, however, that a gradual reduction in hours, reflecting increased demand for time off as hourly wages rose (the first scenario), would lead to an increase in leisure. Some calculations (discussed in appendix E) suggest that on the basis of past experience, the most plausible result would be that the increase in time off would be divided in roughly the same proportions as the present leisure—household production mix (so that if 60 percent is now devoted to household production time, a 10-hour reduction in market employment time would yield a gain of 6 hours in household production time and 4 hours in consumption time). There is no guarantee that the future will repeat the past, especially since we are forecasting increases in both time and goods to unprecedented levels of general affluence; one should certainly not rely on any definite forecast of the expected division between leisure and other time. But it does seem rather implausible that no increase in leisure time would result from a decline in working hours, which was a product of an increased preference for time off.

A rather different analysis is called for if hours are reduced by law, with no accompanying change in the preferences of workers for material living standards over increased leisure. Living standards could be at least partly protected by substituting household production time for market production. Since do-it-yourself is a notoriously inefficient substitute for market services, more rather than less total work time would be required if living standards were to be fully maintained. In this scenario, workers might seek to do most home repair and improvement themselves, maintain their own clothes, and even grow a portion of their own food. In the long run they would be expected to gravitate to less expensive residential areas or suburbs, where land was cheaper (thus obtaining a further incentive to grow food). The substitution of household production time for market work time would also be fostered by the use of slower, cheaper transportation modes, for example, by taking buses rather than a private car.

Of course it is not obvious that workers will indeed sacrifice leisure to improve their material living standards under these circumstances. In fact the analysis in Linder's *The Harried Leisure Class* would suggest an opposite conclusion: that a reduction in workweeks, or rather the consequently lower level of income and hence material living standard, would mean that individuals would have to spend less time in maintaining and repairing their consumer goods simply because they had fewer of them. In this analysis, workers would have a twofold increase in their leisure since they would work fewer hours for pay and would need to spend fewer hours in household production.

These two opposed views of the effects of a reduction in market work time can also be analyzed in terms of the more general model developed in chapter 4. The net effect on leisure or consumption time of an enforced reduction in hours would depend upon the relative possibilities of substituting goods for time in household production and consumption. If it is relatively easy to substitute time for goods in household production (i.e., if people are reasonably successful at do-it-yourself activities) and relatively difficult to substitute time for goods in consumption (the case if individuals are unwilling to accept a change in their life-styles which would involve spending more time at less expensive recreational pursuits), more of the potential gain in time would go to household production and less to leisure time.

Some calculations of substitution possiblities (based upon past experience) are presented in appendix E. These suggest that here too these substitution effects may be roughly offsetting, so that the distribution of additional time between leisure and household production time might not be very different from the present distribution.

In summary, past experience indicates that hours reduction, unlike flexitime and similar work schedule changes, would be a plausible way of providing substantial, permanent increases in leisure time. This would be a higher probability forecast if hours were reduced gradually through the market, but would still be likely if hours were reduced abruptly by government invervention.

A Note on the Future of Commercial Timesavers

Leisure time can also be increased without reducing the workweek, by reducing household production time. The most likely method is through gains in household production technology, which would offer potential savings in household time. Some futuristic innovations that could conceivably be developed in the very long run include:

1. The development of driverless transportation (a computerized highway system which could be programmed to guide a vehicle from origin to destination) that would reduce the need for shopping trips and make chauffering of children unnecessary.

2. Computerized ordering of foodstuffs and other necessaries, using telecommunications to link home and store in combination with driverless transportation to convey the goods, could eliminate altogether the need for most day-to-day shopping trips.

3. The development of self-cleaning materials and appliances.

4. Looking to the more distant future, automation may eliminate much housework. Robots are already being used for certain dangerous, unpleasant tasks in industry, and will almost certainly be used much more extensively for this purpose in the near future. They are still very expensive and usually designed to perform just a few simple tasks. Suitable robotlike devices for households are still far from realization.

However, even such futuristic innovations could either yield a gain in leisure time or simply a general improvement in material living standards. As we saw in the analysis of past advances in household technology, the historic record is one of using potential timesavers largely, or even altogether, to increase material living standards. Hence when evaluating the future effects of timesavers, a note of caution or even skepticism must be introduced in predicting the leisure-time gains from even the more "far out" scientific developments that might be forecast.

Effects of Hours Reduction on Other
Alternative Working Schedules

General hours reduction might reduce the demand for part-time jobs or for flexi-time by providing a more easily handled standard schedule. But the importance of this point should not be overestimated. The average part-timer now works only 18 hours per week, far less than the 30 or 32 hours usually suggested for a new standard. And most of the rationale for flexitime remains, even in the context of a four-day workweek. (For example, rush-hour commuting congestion would presumably still remain a problem.)

Moreover, hours reduction would itself make a positive contribution to the development of alternative work schedules. In the first place, a 30-hour workweek would almost certainly increase the proportion of the population which moonlighted; not everyone wants a reduction in income, and those who do want a second job would find it easier to work after 30 instead of 40 hours or primary employment.

But the principal pressures for developing additional alternative work schedules are apt to come from employers. If a 30-hour or 32-hour workweek became the norm, employers would be faced with very serious scheduling problems, providing them with extra incentives to employ shiftworkers and part-timers. This scheduling problem is most acute where capital per man is high (as in mining, manufacturing, and railroads) and capital utilization an overriding concern, but is also important in the service industries. With increased time off, one might find a still further shift in demand toward recreation and other services used in nonworking hours. Owners of service facilities will be hard put to meet such demands with a staff on a 30-hour schedule and so will seek to recruit shiftworkers and part-timers.

However, a final caveat is in order: it is not clear that these employer-demanded alternative work schedules would actually be introduced, if hours were reduced. Chapter 5 introduced an expanded definition of labor supply, in which workers had preferences for the scheduling as well as the number of hours of work. If hours reduction occurs as a part of a reduction in labor supply per worker in this broad sense (due in turn to a desire to improve the quantity and quality of household production and consumption time, even at the expense of market income), it is quite possible that employers will have a very difficult time in finding enough shiftworkers to utilize their plants and to provide services to the public. In that event, only if a proposed alternative shift happened to meet the schedule needs of some group in the work force (e.g., students, moonlighters, housewives, or retirees), could the employers' goals be met.[6]

Notes

1. A distinction has to be made between the short-run and long-run effects of hours reduction. In the short run it would be theoretically possible to concentrate labor in the most modern, efficient facilities through extensive use of shiftwork. This would permit a higher capital/labor ratio, and hence would cushion

the effects of hours reduction. However, it is not obvious that such an advantageous increase in shiftwork would occur (see pp. 130–131).

In the long run new, more capital-intensive machinery could be introduced. (This argument is usually given considerable emphasis by trade union advocates of workweek reduction.) However, while this would be an expected result if just one sector of the economy obtained a shorter workweek, it is not so likely if hours are generally reduced. In the first case, a larger share of new capital might be shifted toward the sector in which hours were reduced. But in the second case, a decline in profits would reduce the aggregate supply of capital, curtailing prospects for mechanization (since investment income is a principal source for new investment funds).

2. That is, in which the elasticity of income with respect to hours worked is greater than unity.

3. Average annual rate of increase in output per unit of labor in the U.S. private/domestic economy; see Kendrick (1977), p. 31.

4. Kendrick (1977), p. 32.

5. Though it may be unlikely that the recreation industry would be revolutionized by a drastic improvement of the type that occurred in the first decades of this century and helped to reduce hours in the 1900–29 period. See Owen (1970).

For other discussions of possible future gains in leisure see, for example, Best, Bosserman, and Stern; Best and Wright; Owen (1976c); and Teriet.

6. Though shiftwork appears to have increased in recent decades despite increased interest in employee-centered schedules, demonstrating the continued power of financial incentives. See C.M.G.F. Robinson.

13 A Concluding Note

Several conclusions emerge from this discussion of the time-pressured American:

1. Prime-aged Americans have less leisure than many believe. Moreover, contrary to a popular impression, there has been relatively little net growth in this leisure in the post-World War II period. Hours of work have leveled off for males, while the labor force particpation of females has steadily increased.

2. The basic explanation of this result is that increasing affluence has taken the form of a higher price of time, in the market and in utilizing market goods in household production. An important secondary factor is the high fixed cost of educating and training the modern employee; this produces a type of economy of scale in lifetime work hours since these fixed costs can be spread over a wider base of work time if hours are longer.

3. The quality of consumption, household production, and work time have apparently increased, primarily as a result of higher-wage rates and consequent increases in spendable income. However, the quality gain has been limited by the inability of the individual worker to determine the number and timing of his hours of work. Rigid work schedules, combined with higher labor force participation rates of women and the inflexible schedules of schools and other institutions, yield a difficult situation for families which must allocate limited resources of time and money to pursue a variety of consumption goals.

4. A number of factors point to some future amelioration of this situation. Hours schedules are set by employers, who balance their production and sales needs against the needs of their employees. But a consideration of recent developments, and of likely future changes, in the needs of both employers and employees indicates that the prospects for improvement are good. The changing industrial and occupational mix, rising real hourly wage rates, higher female labor force participation, and the leveling off of the standard workweek are all supportive factors here.

5. Already about one in three employees is a voluntary part-timer or is on some other variant schedule (part-time, moonlighting, shiftwork, or compressed workweek). Part-timers serve a variety of useful purposes in the service, clerical, and other sectors. However, they are generally barred from the better-paid jobs, largely because of economies of scale for the employer in scheduling employee hours of work. These result from high fixed training costs to the employer as well as from the extra costs of supervising, coordinating, and communicating with short schedule workers.

6. A relatively small but growing number of Americans have the right to

choose the timing, though not the number, of their hours of work through the system of flexitime. Unlike part-timers, workers on flexitime retain the same wages, status, and other benefits which they had when on a standard schedule. This flexitime system—in one or another of its several variants—appears to be applicable to a wide variety of job situations. If union opposition and other institutional obstacles are overcome, tens of millions of Americans—perhaps even a majority of the work force—may eventually get the system. This would very likely improve the quality of time by giving individuals more choice in planning their work, household production, and leisure schedules.

7. The most obvious way of reducing time pressures is to cut hours of work, since this would very likely increase leisure time. Hours reduction would be very expensive; yet Americans may eventually be willing to pay this price if labor productivity continues to increase in the years ahead. Or we may move more precipitately because of a belief (however ill-founded in fact) that job opportunities are limited, and that it is necessary to share the work by hours reduction. In the case of an abrupt reduction in hours, the quality of consumption time would be increased at the expense of a reduction in its quality as spendable income declined.

Technical Appendixes

Appendix A
A New Interpretation
of the Historical
Backward-bending Supply
Curve of Labor

The Determination of Working Hours in Industry
under Semisubsistence Conditions

Introduction

The conventional backward-bending supply curve of labor theory no longer provides a good basis for predicting changes over time in hours of work; while working hours dropped rather rapidly as hourly wages increased in the nineteenth and early twentiety centuries, the subsequent movement in hours has been very much more modest despite continued large gains in real hourly earnings. Moreover, there is no longer the clear-cut negative relationship between hours of work and hourly earnings that was found in cross-sectional data in the nineteenth century. Some writers go so far as to argue that the backward-bending supply curve of labor—as measured by the relationship between hourly wages and hours worked per worker—has now ceased to be operative, though others interpret the data as implying that there is still a modestly negative effect of wage rates on hours.[1]

The present paper offers an indirect explanation of these phenomena, inasmuch as it argues that the large decline in hours of work of industrial workers in the nineteenth and early twentieth centuries can actually be understood as due to a reduction in the relative economic return to long hours of work as the long-term upward trend in efficiency wages finally raised workers well above the subsistence level. (No attempt is made here to analyze fluctuations in hours under the more affluent conditions of the past several decades.)[2] The second section of the paper shows how a tendency for the elasticity of income with respect to effort to be reduced by increases in hourly wages could produce a backward-bending supply curve of labor, with or without the complementary support of the usual explanation of a dominance of the income over the conventional substitution effect of higher-wage rates. The third section examines the income-leisure opportunity locus of the subsistence worker, developing the argument that the declining importance of productive-consumption effects, as wages rose from the subsistence level, did tend to reduce the elasticity of income with respect to effort in the nineteenth and early twentieth centuries.

The fourth section discusses the implications for labor supply of lagged productive-consumption effects, and considers other realistic modifications that must be introduced into an abstract model of the labor-leisure choice under subsistence conditions. Some implications of this analysis for the social regulation of the hours of subsistence workers are set forth at the end of appendix A.

A Relevant Model for the Demand for Leisure under Semisubsistence Conditions

Changes over time in hours of work have been explained largely in terms of the income and substitution effects of an increase in the real hourly wage. The worker is assumed to maximize a utility function which has leisure and income as arguments,

$$U = U(L, Y) \tag{A.1}$$

subject to goods and time budget constraints.

The goods constraint is usually given as

$$Y = wHK + N$$
$$Y = wHK \tag{A.2}$$

where K = hours available for work or leisure (a constant), L = proportion of time spent at leisure (leisure hours $\div K$), H = proportion of time spent at work (work hours $\div K$), w = real average hourly earnings, N = real nonlabor income (assumed equal to zero for the average subsistence worker), and Y = real money income assumed equal to consumption for the average subsistence worker). Since property income is usually neglected in the discussion of historical changes in the labor supply of ordinary workers, variant ($Y = wHK$) is typically employed.

This conventional approach treats the average hourly wage as a parameter. However, since this paper will consider subsistence situations in which it will be argued that the average hourly wage is iteself a function of hours worked, a more general goods budget constraint will be employed, in which income is simply assumed to be determined by the efficiency wage W (the price paid per unit of effective labor input I) and the number of hours worked, without equating the efficiency wage W with average hourly earnings w or otherwise specifying the form of the function.

$$Y = Y(W, H) \tag{A.3}$$

The worker is also subject to a time constraint

$$H + L = 1 \tag{A.4}$$

The first-order and second-order conditions for maximizing utility (see equation A.1) subject to the constraints in equations A.3 and A.4 are, respectively

$$U_L = U_Y Y_H \tag{A.5}$$

$$(Y_H)^2 U_{YY} - 2Y_H U_{LY} + U_{LL} + Y_{HH} U_Y < 0 \tag{A.6}$$

where the subscript denotes partial differentiation.

Taking the total differential of equation A.5 and dividing by dW yields

$$dH/dW = \frac{Y_W(U_{YY}Y_H - U_{LY}) + U_Y Y_{Hw}}{-[(Y_H)^2 U_{YY} - 2U_{LY}Y_H + U_{LL} + U_Y Y_{HH}]} \tag{A.7}$$

where Y_H, Y_W, Y_{HH}, and Y_{HW} are obtained by differentiating equation A.3. Defining $E_{Y,H} = Y_H\left(\dfrac{H}{Y}\right)$ (i.e., the elasticity of Y wrt H) and $E_{(U_H/U_Y),Y}$

$= \left(\dfrac{Y_H U_{YY} - U_{LY}}{U_Y}\right)\left(\dfrac{H}{E_{Y,H}}\right)$, where $U_H = -U_L$, we obtain

$$dH/dW = \frac{\dfrac{U_Y Y_W E_{Y,H}}{H}(-E_{(U_H/U_Y),Y} + 1) + \dfrac{U_Y Y}{H}\dfrac{\partial E_{Y,H}}{\partial W}}{-[(dY/dH)^2 U_{YY} - 2U_{LY}(dY/dH) + U_{LL} + U_Y(d^2 Y/dH^2)]} \tag{A.8}$$

where $dY/dH = Y_H + Y_W\, dw/dH = Y_H$, since W is assumed to be given parametrically to the worker.

In the conventional analysis, in which $(Y = wHK)$ is employed as the goods budget constraint and average hourly earnings w are equated with the efficiency wage W, equation A.8 can be rewritten as

$$dH/dw = \frac{U_Y\left(-E_{(U_H/U_Y),Y} + 1\right)}{-(w^2 U_{YY} - 2w U_{LY} + U_{LL})} \tag{A.9}$$

since now $E_{Y,H} = 1$ and $Y_H = w$. The right side of equation A.9 is often written as $[H(wU_{YY} - U_{LY}) + U_Y]/-(w^2 U_{YY} - 2w U_{LY} + U_{LL})$, that is, as the sum of the conventional income and substitution effects of an increase in the wage rate. In this conventional model a backward-bending, vertical, or forward-sloping supply curve of labor is obtained, depending upon whether the numerator of the right side of equation A.9 is less than, equal to, or greater than zero.

However, the more general expression in equation A.8 yields a less simple result. Here even if $-E_{(U_H/U_Y)} + 1 = 0$ (i.e., even if the conventional income and substitution effects are offsetting), a backward-bending supply curve of labor will be generated in that range of values of W for which $\partial E_{Y,H}/\partial W < 0$. In other words under these conditions hours of work will decrease with increases in the wage rate if the average return to effort rises more rapidly than does the marginal return.

The Income-leisure Choice under Subsistence and Semisubsistence Conditions

The Basic Argument

It will be argued here that under subsistence or semisubsistence conditions, $\partial E_{Y,H}/\partial W < 0$, tending to generate a backward-bending supply curve of labor. The determination of $E_{Y,H}$ under these conditions is not a simple matter. Even if one makes the conventional simplifying assumptions (abstracting from a variety of institutional limits of choice of hours of work, considering only industrial workers selling their labor under competitive conditions in periods of full employment, and hypothesizing that the worker is paid in proportion to his effective labor input) so that the worker is regarded as able to sell his labor at a constant price of efficiency wage,[3] the income of the subsistence worker will not rise in proportion with his hours of work. Thus if the worker's budget constraint is rewritten as

$$Y = WI \qquad\qquad (A.10)$$

where W is the efficiency wage and I is effective labor input, income will increase proportionately with hours only if I and HK have a proportionate relationship. But under subsistence conditions, effect labor input per hours worked (I/HK) will instead vary with the number of hours worked, because of both the direct effect of fatigue and indirect effects upon nutrition, and hence on productivity, which result from variations in labor income.

Moreover, the relationship between income and hours will change as the efficiency wage rises; the basic argument here is that higher efficiency wages will free the industrial workers from the necessity of working long hours to earn a subsistence income. In other words as the worker rises above subsistence, he receives less of a marginal gain in health, and productivity, from the increment in his earnings made possible by long hours of work. This will tend to reduce the elasticity of income with respect to effort in the range of efficiency wages just above subsistence (so that $\partial E_{Y,H}/\partial W < 0$). This tendency for the average return to effort to rise more rapidly than the marginal would, by the analysis of the preceding section, be apt to generate a backward-bending supply curve of hours.

Leisure-income Opportunities under Subsistence Conditions

Under conditions of subsistence or semisubsistence two principal factors will operate to diminish the worker's hourly productivity: fatigue, caused by long hours of work; and the bad health effects of poor food, housing, and clothing, associated with a low consumption level. There is an abundance of data that support the importance of these limits to the productivity of the subsistence worker. Admittedly the quality of these data does not permit us to make parametric estimates of the functional relationships between adequate food and rest, and labor productivity. Nevertheless enough is known about the nature of these relationships, and the type of income-leisure opportunity locus that they would be likely to generate, to understand both how they would act to extend the hours of subsistence workers and how an increase in wages from subsistence levels would encourage a reduction in hours of work.

Subsistence in Time

It has long been recognized that fatigue produces diminishing returns to extended hours of work.[4] There appears to be a certain number of hours the worker's effective input increases only at a diminishing rate. As hours increase further, effective labor input reaches a maximum, then declines. (If hours are sufficiently extended, the worker collapses.)

Figure A-1 offers a schematic representation of the consensus view of the effect of fatigue. The diagram is consistent with the hypothetical data given in Table A-1. Column 1 gives hypothetical values of H, and column 2, the effective input g, corresponding to that level of hours of work.

In figure A-1 the worker's input rises in proportion to his hours worked H up to M. (According to the hypothetical data in table A-1, M corresponds to a workweek equal to one-fourth of the worker's time or about 40 hours per week.) Beyond that point, the worker experiences diminishing returns to his efforts; his effective input is at a maximum at point N. Thus between M and N, the elasticity of labor input with respect to hours of work $E_{g,H}$ declines from unity to zero. (Further increases in hours are uneconomic and will eventually lead to the collapse of the worker at $H = P$.)

Most observers would agree that average working times in England, Western Europe, and the United States have been at or near the point where increases in hours produce proportionate increases in effective labor input, that is, near point M in figure A-1. In the United States the introduction of the 40-hour workweek as the standard in the 1930s probably means that hours have been at this point for at least four decades.

Most would also agree that working hours for unskilled workers in the early

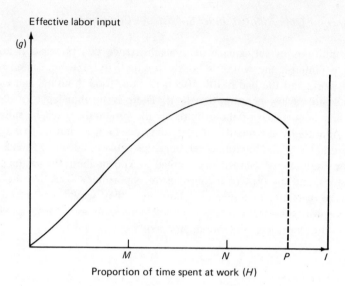

Figure A-1. Illustrative Fatigue Function

Table A-1
Fatigue, Productive Consumption, and Labor Supply

Fatigue Effects			Productive-Consumption Effects				Demand for Leisure Function[a]		
(1)	(2)	(3)	(4)	(5)	(6)	(7)	(8)	(9)	(10)
H	g	$E_{g,H}$	Y	f	$E_{f,Y}$	$\dfrac{Y}{f}$	W	$E_{Y,H}$	w
.25	.250	1	11.00	1.90	0	5.79	23.16	1.00	44.00
.30	.295	.814	3.42	1.59	.37	2.16	7.31	1.29	11.41
.35	.330	.636	2.79	1.44	.61	1.93	5.86	1.62	7.96
.40	.355	.451	2.56	1.36	.77	1.88	5.31	2.00	6.39
.45	.370	.243	2.44	1.31	.90	1.87	5.05	2.45	5.44
.50	.375	0	2.37	1.27	1.00	1.86	4.98	3.00	4.73
(.65	0	-)	(2.20	1.17	1.31	1.88)	–	–	–
			(2.00	1.00	2.00	2.00)	–	–	–

Note that the fatigue effects section of the table (columns 1–3) and the productive-consumption effects section (columns 4–7) are independently determined in this hypothetical example. They are linked here (in the first six rows) by this leisure-demand function and by $E_{Y,H} = \dfrac{E_{g,H}}{1 - E_{f,Y}}$ (derived from the budget constraint $Y = Wfg$. See the discussion in the text). The uneconomic long hours and low consumption levels in the seventh and eighth rows would not be chosen, except under the special circumstances described in note 8.

[a]$H = \dfrac{1}{1 + \dfrac{3}{E_{Y,H}}}$ (derived from $U = L^{3/4}Y^{1/4}$, $H = 1 - L$. See text).

nineteenth century (especially those in the new industries or in the service sector) were often at or near the point (N) at which further increases in hours would make little or no positive contribution to effective labor input. Thus the changes in hours in the period in which the major movement along the backward-bending supply curve of labor was observed, roughly from the second quarter of the nineteenth to the middle of the twentieth century, can be approximated in our diagram as a movement from N to M.

Subsistence in Goods

It is also well recognized that at low-wage levels a worker's productivity is adversely affected by insufficient consumption of food and inadequate levels of shelter, clothing, and other necessaries.

While a certain very low level of subsistence is required for life, at this absolute minimum the worker is so weakened by malnourishment and its related diseases that a more than proportationate increase in his effective labor input is obtained by increasing his consumption level. However, as consumption increases, diminishing returns reduce the marginal gain in effective labor input, until an increase in consumption yields a just proportionate increase in productivity. At still higher levels of consumption, the relative gain in productivity is further reduced, until finally at a sufficiently affluent level no further gain is obtained.[5] Figure A-2 provides a schematic representation of this consensus view.[6] The curve relating a worker's productivity f to his consumption Y is consistent with the hypothetical numbers in columns 3 and 4 in table A-1. The minimum level of subsistence in Figure A-1 is Y_0, yielding a labor input of f_0 (in the numerical illustration, $Y_0 = 2.0$ and $f_0 = 1.0$). In this example, if the worker's income is raised by 10 percent to 2.20, his productivity is increased by 17 percent; further gains in productivity are increasingly more modest, finally reaching a maximum at R.

At point E in figure A-2, increases in consumption yield a just proportionate increase in productivity, so that the elasticity of production with respect to consumption $E_{f,Y}$ is equal to unity. (At the point, the ratio of input to consumption, $\theta = f/Y$, is maximized.) But between E and R, the value of $E_{f,Y}$ is gradually reduced from unity to zero.

At the present time, most workers in the industrialized nations are of course well above point R; further gains in their consumption of food and other necessaries would have only marginal effects on their production. However, as recently as 1915, surveys of the living conditions, health, and productivity of American workers concluded that an increment in the living standard of the average American worker would yield a substantial gain in his productivity. At that time, the real wage of the typical British and European worker was significantly below the American level. In subsequent years the proportion of the work force at such low wages was reduced to a minority—an ever smaller minority in the post-World War II period.

But in the nineteenth century the condition of semisubsistence (as we might characterize those in the range of consumption between E and R in figure A-2) was the lot of the majority of workers. In fact it was often argued by contemporary observers that the poorer workers, especially unskilled workers in the service sector and in the new industries in the early nineteenth century, were actually near point E, that is, were so poor that an increase in their consumption could yield a gain in production almost equal to its cost of wages.

Thus a comparison of discussions of fatigue and productive consumption effects indicates that at very low efficiency wages workers tended to be near subsistence levels in both goods and time. As wages rose, the consumption of leisure increased, yielding the well-known backward-bending supply curve of labor and finally leaving the worker at a point where fatigue no longer imposed a serious limit on his productivity. In the same period, consumption of goods rose to the point where underfeeding no longer curtailed labor productivity.

To a first approximation then, one can summarize the development in this period as (1) a reduction in hours from N to M (in figure A-1), producing an increase in the elasticity of input with respect to hours $E_{g,H}$ from near zero to unity; and (2) an increase in consumption from E to R (in figure A-2), yielding a decline in the elasticity of labor input with respect to consumption $E_{f,Y}$, from near unity to zero.

Joint Effects of Subsistence in Time and Goods on the Income-Leisure Opportunity Locus

A consideration of the impact of the fatigue and productive consumption relations on the opportunity locus, and hence the likely effect on the labor-leisure choice, indicates that such parallel movements in the consumption of time and goods are not coincidental. Under the subsistence or semisubsistence conditions associated with low-wage levels, both the fatigue and productive consumption relationships act to influence the parameters of the income-leisure opportunity locus. Rather obviously fatigue effects will make very long hours uneconomic (i.e., those to the right of N in figure A-1), and act as a discouragement to work within the whole range of hours in which fatigue limits productivity (from M to N).

The role of productive consumption here is less obvious, but may be at least as important. When efficiency wages are very low, one can begin with the common sense observation that the worker is simply compelled by the productive consumption effect to put in quite long hours; he must earn enough to purchase sufficient food to maintain the strength needed to survive. Moreover, at somewhat higher earnings levels, while the worker will have some choice over his

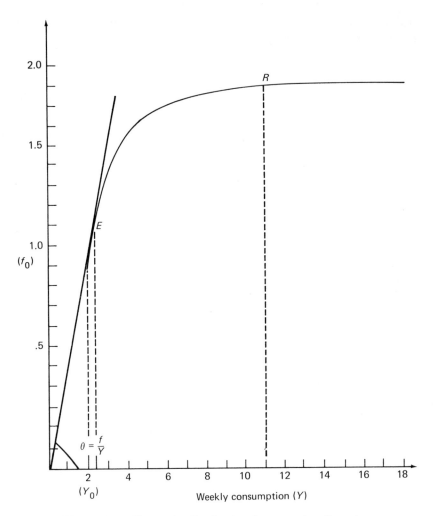

Figure A-2. Illustrative Productive Consumption Function

hours, it is obvious that the productive consumption effect will tend to produce increasing returns to work: there will be a positive feedback relationship to effort, inasmuch as longer hours yield more food for the worker and so an increase in his hourly productivity. There is then both a direct and an indirect positive effect of hours on consumption: more hours of work at a given hourly wage, and an increase in the hourly earnings level. Hence at a low efficiency wage, the productive consumption effect would be expected to generate increasing returns to hours of work, at least partially offsetting the fatigue effect.

The offsetting effects of these functions on the labor-leisure opportunity locus can be analyzed more explicitly. Assume for expositional simplicity that the worker's effective labor input

$$I = I[f(Y), g(H)]$$ (A.11)

can be approximated as

$$I = f(Y)g(H)$$ (A.12)

Then substituting the expression for I in equation A.10 into equation A.12, we derive

$$Y = Wfg$$ (A.13)

Differentiating Y with respect to H, using equations A.11 and A.12 yields

$$dY/dH = W(gf'dY/dH + g'f) = \frac{fWg'}{1 - Wgf'}$$ (A.14)

or in elasticity form

$$E_{Y,H} = \frac{E_{g,H}}{1 - E_{f,Y}}$$ (A.15)

These formulations permit us to analyze changes in a worker's opportunities as increases in his efficiency wage raise him from subsistence to more affluent conditions.

The minimum efficiency wage consistent with survival in this model is found by first rewriting equation A.12 as $W = (Y/f)/g$; W will be minimized where g is maximized and Y/f is minimized. If the fatigue and productive-consumption functions have the general forms shown in figures A-1 and A-2, these conditions will be met where $E_{g,H} = 0$ and $E_{f,Y} = 1$; that is, at N in figure A-1 and E in figure A-2.[7]

In the hypothetical numerical example in table A-1, the minimum value of W is 4.98. At that wage if the worker puts in the input-maximizing number of hours $H = .5$, yielding $g = .375$, $Wg = (4.98)(.375) = 1.866$; but the budget constraint in equation A.13 requires that Wg equal Y/f, and the minimum possible value of Y/f is 1.866 (where $E_{f,Y} = 1$). At this efficiency wage the input-maximizing work schedule is just consistent with survival; no other level of hours will permit survival. Note also that at any lower level of W, there is no hours schedule that will enable the worker to survive.

While the worker's choice is constrained to a point at the minimum efficiency wage, he is given a range of choices as the wage increases. In the case illustrated here, when the efficiency wage rises to 5.31, the worker's choices extend from $H = .39$ to $H = .5$; at one end of the range he has the minimum level of goods, at the other, the minimum level of time. Within this area of semisubsistence, the income-leisure trade-offs open to the worker are still determined by fatigue and productive consumption in accordance with equation A.15. For example, if he opts for $H = .4$, fatigue imposes diminishing returns to effort: in the illustration used here, $E_{g,H} = .45$. However, at $W = 5.31$, consumption is sufficiently low[8] for productive-consumption effects to offset these fatigue effects; in fact in this illustration, $E_{f,Y} = .77$. Hence by equation A.15, $E_{Y,H} = 2.0$, actually indicating net increasing returns to work.

Backward-bending Labor Supply Curve Effect

The interactions among the fatigue and productive-consumption functions in equation A.15 help us to see how a backward-bending supply curve of labor can be generated, even in the case where the demand for leisure is influenced (negatively) by the relation of the marginal to the average return to effort $E_{Y,H}$, but not by the average return to effort w itself (i.e., in the case where $E_{(U_H/U_Y),Y} = 1$, so that the conventional income and substitutional effects of a wage increase are fully offsetting). The argument is that the productive consumption effect $E_{f,Y}$ is reduced as the efficiency wage W increases from low levels; this will tend to reduce the elasticity of income with respect to effort (so that $\partial E_{Y,H}/\partial W < 0$). By assumption, this will yield a decline in hours worked. Declines in hours worked will continue until the wage rate has reached the point where $E_{f,Y} = 0$. Further increases in W, providing for still more affluent living standards will yield no additional gains in labor productivity, so that hours of work may then be invariant to further gains in wages. Hence this factor will generate a backward-bending supply curve of labor within the range of semisubsistence, but not above that range.[9]

This point can be made somewhat less informally by writing

$$\frac{\partial E_{Y,H}}{\partial W} = \frac{Y}{W} \frac{E_{g,H}}{(1 - E_{f,Y})^3} \frac{\partial E_{f,Y}}{\partial Y} \qquad (A.16)$$

Note that $\partial E_{Y,H}/\partial W < 0$ if and only if $\partial E_{f,Y}/\partial Y < 0$. Substituting the right side of this equation in the labor supply relationship in equation A.8, it follows that in the case where $E_{(U_H/U_Y),Y} = 1$, a backward-bending supply curve of labor is obtained as long as $\partial E_{f,Y}/\partial Y < 0$. At higher levels of income, where $\partial E_{f,Y}/\partial Y = 0$, labor supply, in this model, becomes invariant to changes in the wage rate.[10]

This type of labor supply behavior can be illustrated with explicit utility functions. The condition $E_{(U_H/U_Y),Y} = 1$ implies that $(U_H)n(H) = YU_Y$, which would be consistent with utility functions of the form $U = Y^a m(H)$ (or some monotonic transformation of this relationship). Equations A.17 provide three examples of this type of utility function.

$$U = Y^{1/4} (1 - H)^{3/4}$$

$$U = Y/H \tag{A.17}$$

$$U = Y^{1/2} e^{-2H}$$

Equations A.18 describe the demand for leisure relations which result from these three utility functions.

$$H = \cfrac{1}{1 + \cfrac{3}{E_{Y,H}}}$$

$$1 = E_{Y,H} \tag{A.18}$$

$$H = \frac{E_{Y,H}}{4}$$

These demand functions are then used in conjunction with the hypothetical fatigue and productive consumption functions in table A-1 to generate schedules relating hours of work and average hourly earnings, the usual labor supply function. (Some observations in this schedule for function a are given in column 10 of table A-1.) The results are graphed in figure A-3. In each case, hours of work decline as wages increase over the range of semisubsistence in which $E_{f,Y} > 0$; but are not reduced further as wages increase in the range of affluence in which $E_{f,Y} = 0$.

This analysis can also be applied to the case where the income effect of a wage increase is not fully offset by the substitution effect (i.e., where $E_{(U_H/U_Y),Y} > 1$). Here the decline in the productive consumption effect as the efficiency wage rises will tend to accelerate the rate of decline in working time in the range of quasi-subsistence (where $\partial E_{f,Y}/\partial Y < 0$); above that level of income any additional decline in hours of work would be due to the excess of the income over the substitution effects of higher wages.

Some More Realistic Considerations

The model presented in the previous section abstracts from a number of factors that influence the labor-leisure choice. Yet the interpretation of the backward-

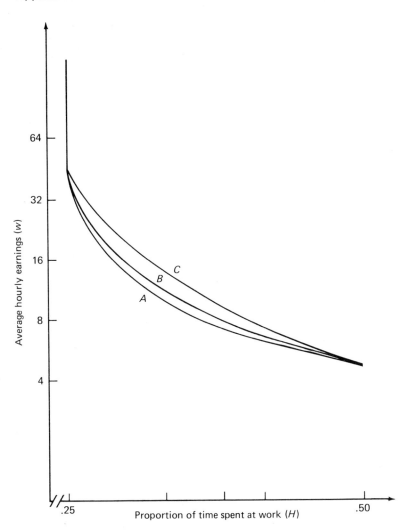

Figure A-3. Illustrative Labor Supply Functions

bending supply curve of labor offered here is essentially unchanged when a number of such restrictive assumptions are dropped.

In the real world, overworking and underfeeding (or living in squalid conditions) have long-term as well as immediate effects on health and productivity. To take these effects into account, one can modify the formulation in equation A.11 by rewriting the fatigue and productive consumption relations as functions of hours of work, and of food and all other consumption in all previous periods as well as the present: $g_t = g_t(H_1, H_2, \ldots, H_t)$ and $f_t = f_t(Y_1, Y_2, \ldots, Y_t)$. In practice, the effects of this modification can be summarized in a simple two-period model: $g_1 = g_1(H_1); f_1 = f_1(Y_1); g_2 = g_2(H_1, H_2);$ and $f_2 = f_2(Y_1, Y_2)$. Then the new budget constraint becomes

$$Y_1 = W_1 f_1 g_1$$

$$Y_2 = W_2 f_2 g_2$$

(A.19)

and the objective trade-offs of consumption and work time for the worker become[11]

$$E_{Y_1,H_1} = \frac{E_{g_1,H_1}}{1 - E_{f_1,Y_1}}$$

$$E_{Y_2,H_1} = \frac{E_{g_2,H_1} + E_{f_2,Y_1} E_{Y_1,H_1}}{1 - E_{f_2,Y_2}} = \frac{E_{g_2,H_1} + \dfrac{E_{f_2,Y_1} E_{g_1,H_1}}{1 - E_{f_1,Y_1}}}{1 - E_{f_2,Y_2}}$$

(A.20)

$$E_{Y_2,H_2} = \frac{E_{g_2,H_2}}{1 - E_{f_2,Y_2}}$$

where E continues to denote an elasticity.

In all three relationships (A.20) productive-consumption effects act to increase the marginal relative to the average consumption gain from an extra hour of work. The first and third relationships are quite similar to those derived in the model presented in equation A.15, inasmuch as they also describe single-period effects. In the second relationship, three separate productive-consumption effects—E_{f_2,Y_1}, E_{f_1,Y_1}, and E_{f_2,Y_2}—tend to generate increasing returns to work. Hence insofar as the worker considers interperiod effects (i.e., does not discount the future altogether), these productive-consumption factors would encourage him to work longer hours.

As the efficiency wage is increased, all these productive-consumption effects will lose strength and finally vanish. Then equations A–20 can be written more simply as

$$E_{Y_1,H_1} = E_{g_1,H_1}$$

$$E_{Y_2,H_1} = E_{g_2,H_1}$$

(A.21)

$$E_{Y_2,H_2} = E_{g_2,H_2}$$

The gradual reduction in these productive-consumption effects as wages rose from subsistence to affluent conditions would tend to reduce the elasticity of income with respect to hours of work and so (if the demand for leisure is a negative function of this elasticity) would tend to generate a backward-bending supply curve of labor. Here too at wage levels above the point where productive-consumption effects are reduced to zero, further increases in leisure would occur only insofar as the algebraic sum of the conventional income and substitution effects of additional wage increases are positive.

This model of subsistence in time and goods can be made still more realistic. For example, in the real world subsistence workers differed in health, partly as a result of their original constitutions and partly as a result of the circumstances of their childhoods and early working lives. They also differed in the number of dependents with whom they had to share their earnings. Hence even among unskilled laborers earning a very low efficiency wage, one would expect to find some (by virtue of superior health or because they have no dependents) to be above true subsistence, while others, less fortunate, would be on the margin of subsistence. An additional complication is introduced because technical or bureaucratic considerations often led employers to impose standard hours for groups of workers who differed among themselves in health and family responsibilities, necessarily imposing suboptimal choices on many individuals.

For these and similar reasons, it would not be realistic to expect to find low-wage workers all at some ideal combination of income and leisure which enabled them to live on a minimized efficiency wage. However, insofar as employers used the average preferences of their work force as a guide in setting hours, one would still expect this average to be at a high level under subsistence conditions. True, even among a group of subsistence workers some individuals, for example, young, relatively healthy, unmarried workers, would be somewhat above true subsistence levels and into the range of semisubsistence; but we have seen that the income-leisure choice of the semisubsistence worker was also biased toward long hours, even if not to the same extreme extent as was the choice of the worker on the margin of survival. Hence the average choice of a group composed of workers at subsistence, and those just above it, would certainly be biased in favor of extended hours of work.

Moreover, here too one would expect that a secular upward trend in efficiency wages would enable a larger proportion of workers to move ever further above the subsistence level, and so, by gradually reducing the relative economic gain from long hours for the average worker, would tend to generate a backward-bending supply curve of labor.[12]

Summary and Conclusions

The major movement in hours of work—the decline in working times from the first half of the nineteenth century to the middle of the twentieth century—

occurred as workers experienced a rise in their living standards from subsistence or near-subsistence levels to a level at which the basic physical needs of the worker could be met by a more moderate workweek. At subsistence or semi-subsistence levels the worker finds that his hourly productivity is enhanced by the improved supply of food and other necessaries which he can obtain by working longer hours. If he is sufficiently poor, this may constitute a powerful offset to the effect of fatigue, which would in itself tend to impose diminishing returns to long hours, and so may provide a rationale for an extended workweek. In fact at very low efficiency wages, the worker has little choice but to work long hours: to survive, he has to earn enough to buy a sufficient quantity of food and other necessaries to maintain his strength, and so be able to compete at a low piece rate.

But as the efficiency wage rises and with it the worker's consumption level, he finds that this pressure to work long hours is diminished, since additional consumption has a relatively smaller positive effect on his productivity. Insofar as the worker is responsive to changes in the elasticity of his income with respect to his effort, the reduction in the payoff of long hours, as the wage rate increases, will generate a backward-bending supply curve of hours of work.

However, once affluent conditions are attained and labor productivity has become more or less invariant to changes in consumption, this factor no longer tends to reduce the elasticity of income with respect to hours of work or to stimulate additional hours decline.

A Note to Appendix A

Overworking, Underfeeding, and the
Social Regulation of Hours

A standard argument for state regulation of hours,[13] put forward in England, the United States, and other industrializing countries in the nineteenth and early twentieth centuries,[14] was that workers who are living in poverty will discount the future at a high rate and so be tempted to "sell their health for wages" to obtain more consumer goods.

However, a consideration of the productive-consumption effects presented in the text of this paper undermines this argument or at least complicates it considerably. The additional consumer goods which a subsistence worker can purchase with an increment in his earnings will make a positive contribution to the health of the worker and his family. Indeed it is quite possible that this positive contribution to health will be more important than will be the additional health cost of more hours of work.

Even in the extreme case where the worker is observed putting in the number of hours that maximize present input (i.e., where $E_{g_1,H_1} = 0$), it is not obvious that an hours reduction would make a net contribution to health: we would have to know just how sensitive is the health of the worker and his family to marginal changes in the consumption of necessaries.

Similarly in the case in which the worker is putting in somewhat fewer hours (so that $E_{g_1, H_1} > 0$), but is still ignoring completely the future effects of his decision, we cannot determine on a priori grounds whether he will tend to overwork or underwork by underfeeding himself and his family: this will depend on the effect on present utility of underfeeding and overworking, relative to the long-term health damage caused by a lack of enough goods or time. The net result would be expected to vary with the individual case; for example, since dependents share food but not long hours or work, one might expect, certeris paribus, the more altruistic worker to tend to err on the side of over-working, and the more selfish individual to tend to underwork and underfeed. Obviously quite detailed information would be needed for a useful policy of social regulation.

However, this analysis would still be consistent with arguments for the regulation of hours of subsistence workers under special conditions:

1. The restrictions of hours of children may lead to a subsidy of children by adults, at least to the extent that the food allowance of the child laborer is not reduced by his parents to the degree that the child's own earnings are curtailed. Under some circumstances this expected induced transfer of resources of children might be regarded as having socially desirable effects. For example, the earnings of the parents may be above the subsistence level, even if the child, considered as an individual consumption-production unit, is at or below that level. In that situation, hours reduction for child labor need not lead to starvation because the parents are able to provide for the child's sustenance. (A similar argument might be made for women workers or other special groups.)

2. More generally, the either-or nature of the leisure-goods choice of subsistence workers may be circumvented if the state (or a private moneylender or some other third party) will lend (or give) a worker sufficient resources to enable him to work fewer hours without reducing his income. Under some circumstances the worker will even be able to repay a subsistence loan, with a reasonable rate of interest: this would be most likely to occur in the semisubsistence labor market, in which the efficiency wage permits the average worker to live somewhat above true subsistence. Then some of those who are temporarily in a below-average position, say, an orphan or an adult worker recovering from sickness, might be good investment candidates for medium-term subsistence loans, even on very narrow economic criteria.

3. The analysis presented here assumes the efficiency wage to be a parameter, as it is to the individual. But the wage itself may be influenced by a social policy of hours reduction. A full analysis of this relationship requires a study of complex macroeconomic and social phenomena, as can be illustrated by considering two extreme cases. Some nineteenth century neoclassical economists believed that a reduction in the supply of labor induced by a cut in hours would, in the short run, increase efficiency wages but, they argued, the long-run

effect would be a compensating reduction in the supply of capital, which would lower the efficiency wage to its former level.[15] In contrast, a Malthusian-type model in which population pressures are expected to limit per capita consumption of goods and services to a subsistence minimum leads to a very different long-run conclusion. Here the eventual consequences of hours reduction would presumably be a smaller population, with more leisure per capita and, by assumption, no change in per capita income. (The efficiency wage would have been increased by the permanent reduction in labor supply.) Clearly one's social assessment of, for example, the medieval practice of observing a large number of annual holidays or the Indian tradition of time-consuming wedding and funeral ceremonies could be highly sensitive to whether one employed this Malthusian-type model, or a modern neoclassical growth model in which the mobilization of human labor in a process of capital accumulation and economic development can permit secular increases in per capita income.[16]

Finally it is important to emphasize that the critique of the social regulation of hours offered here applies only to less-than-affluent conditions. Once wage rates have risen to the point where, say, a 40-hour or 48-hour workweek provides sufficient income to maintain health, there is no longer a health argument to be made for permitting very long hours of work.[17]

Notes

1. See the discussion of this theory in Marshall, Knight, Pigou, Robbins, Gilbert and Pfouts, Lewis (1957), Becker, Owen (1969, 1971), and Barzel and McDonald. Attempts to obtain empirical estimates of the long-run supply response of hours of work to changes in the hourly wage rate include Douglas, Jones (1959), Owen (1969, 1971, 1976b), Barzel and McDonald, Kniesner, and Burkhauser and Turner; see also the discussion of recent work in Lewis (1975). See the discussion of English data in Bienefeld. There is also a growing literature on the cross-sectional distribution of hours of work. See DaVanzo, DeTray, and Greenberg and the references cited therein; see also the recent findings in Borjas. A study of changes over time in the cross-sectional distribution of hours of work found a downward trend in the dispersion of weekly hours in the first half of this century in the United States; see Owen (1959) and the further discussion of these results in Leveson.

2. See Owen (1970 and 1976b) for a discussion of this period.

3. See Owen (1970) for a discussion of the rationale for assuming a direct relationship between hourly productivity and average hourly earnings in analyzing long-term movements in average hours of work. At the individual level, wages would probably vary most closely with effective labor input where piece-rate systems were in force. However, they would also vary with labor input where jobs were graded by the degree of strength and endurance required, and the time

rate set accordingly. This was of course a very common practice in hiring unskilled labor in the nineteenth century.

4. See Barzel, Denison, Florence, Leveson, Northrup, Owen (1969), Reder,
U.S. Bureau of Labor Statistics, and Vernon for representative analyses of the
empirical relationship between hours of work and effective labor input. Some of
these authors make the point that if hours were reduced to very short schedules,
setup costs of different types would impose diseconomies. However, that range
of very short schedules is not relevant for the discussion here.

5. See Leibenstein, Mazumdar, Moes and Bottomley, Rodgers, Stiglitz,
Wellisz, and Wonnacott for modern discussions of this question. See Lauck and
Sydenstricker for a summary and an analysis of empirical studies of American
living conditions that argues that as late as 1915 a majority of industrial workers
were still at a sufficiently low level of consumption of food, clothing, shelter,
and other necessaries that an icnrease in their wage rate would yield substantial
gains in their productivity.

6. The hypothetical function employed was: $f = 0$ if $Y < 2; f = 2 - \dfrac{1}{Y-1}$,
if $2 \leqq Y \leqq 11; f = 1.9$, if $Y > 11$.

7. From $Y = Y(f)$, the conditions for minimizing Y/f are: $(1/f)(1 - E_{f,Y})$
$= 0$, and $(1/f)[(1 - E_{f,Y})f'/f - dE_{f,Y}/dY] > 0$. In the function described here,
minimization takes place at $E_{f,Y} = 1$, since $f > 0$ here and since $dE_{f,Y}/dY < 0$
throughout the range of feasible Ys (a condition imposed in the text).

8. At $W = 5.31, H = .4$, two algebraic solutions are obtained, at $Y = 2.20$
and a $Y = 2.56$. One solution is above, the other below E. (Each is on a ray from
the origin in figure 4-1, $\theta = Y/f = wg = (5.31)(.355) = 1.88$.) As long as the
worker prefers more to less consumption, the higher equilibrium will be preferred. The text discussion proceeds on the assumption that this preference is
exercised. However, if someone other than the worker makes the income-leisure
choice and if the worker's utility enters the decision-maker's welfare function
negatively, the lower equilibrium may be selected. For example, in a penal
colony the administration might deliberately underfeed inmates as a punish-
ment, despite the effects of labor costs. (Similarly they might overwork inmates,
requiring hours beyond the level that would maximize effective labor input.)

9. Labor supply per worker can alternatively be defined as effective labor
input per worker, $I = fg$. As wages increase and hours decrease, the reduction in
effective labor input is mitigated by increases in input per hour as a result of the
reduction of both overworking and underfeeding. In the example, illustrated
in table A-1, effective labor input remains virtually unchanged at about .48, as
H declines from .5 to .25. More generally, $E_{I,W} = E_{Y,H}\left(E_{H,W} + \dfrac{E_{f,Y}}{E_{g,H}}\right)$.

Thus the decline in I depends upon the strength of the fatigue and
production-consumption effects on the one hand, and the demand function on

the other. Under some circumstances an actual increase in I might be observed with increases in W, despite declines in H.

10. Note that if the interaction of fatigue and productive consumption is not constrained to a multiplicative form, so that equation A.11 rather than A.12 is used as the budget constraint, one still obtains $Y = Y(W, H)$, and the text result that a backward bending supply curve of labor will be obtained in the case where $E_{(U_H/U_Y),Y} = 1$, so long as $\dfrac{\partial E_{Y,H}}{\partial W} < 0$.

11. In the t period case—where $g_t = g_t (H_1, H_2, \ldots, H_t)$, $f_t = f_t (Y_1, Y_2, \ldots, Y_t)$, and $Y_t = W_t f_t g_t$—we derive

$$E_{Y_t,H_i} \, (i \leqq t) = E_{I_t,H_i} = E_{g_t,H_i} + \sum_{\tau=i}^{t} E_{f_t,Y_\tau} E_{Y_\tau,H_i}$$

The two-period case in equations A.20 is a special case of these equations.

12. The model can also be amended to take personal uncertainties into account (e.g., by introducing random error terms into the f and g functions and interpreting the results in equations A.20 as conditional expectations). The use of income and leisure time by subsistence workers in ways that do not improve their prospects for survival can also be considered. (Examples here would include the purchase of fish and chips and other expensive cooked foods, and the use of leisure time for drinking alcoholic beverages.) However, none of these modifications significantly affects the conclusions discussed in the text.

13. For example, see Pigou, pp. 468 ff.

14. This analysis has only limited applicability to contemporary third-world conditions for a number of reasons. Hours regulation is often said to be effective only in the advanced sector of the less-developed nation, where wages are well above the subsistence level. Moreover, since employment in this sector is often rationed, hours reduction may actually increase the number of jobs here, possibly reducing employment of surplus labor and expanding the pool of trained manpower. Kabaj uses a similar argument to justify shiftwork in the less-developed countries.

15. Compare the discussion in Marshall, pp. 689–702.

16. See also the interesting discussion in Sen.

17. Moreover, the productivity gains will be much less. For this reason, the results of studies of fatigue effects among U.S. defense industry workers in World War II (when workers were well above subsistence) cannot be applied directly to nineteenth century conditions.

Appendix B
The Supply of Hours of
Work per Worker in an
Affluent Capitalist Society

The recent leveling off in hours of work is also influenced by the productive consumption effects of investing in people. Obviously the levels of nutrition and other consumption, and time for rest and recuperation of the average American worker have long since reached the point where further gains are not expected to yield appreciable productivity improvements (to a first approximation, $E_{f,Y} = 0$ and $E_{g,H} = 1$).

But productive consumption of another sort has become important: investment in education and training. This differs from the earlier productive consumption in that it occurs almost entirely at the beginning of the worker's career. It is also different in that the time and money allocated to education is less obviously a source of direct consumption utility than was the earlier investment in rest and recreation time or in food, housing, and other consumption necessities. (In fact many young people would prefer market employment over studying and remain in school only for the career advantages which they expect an advanced degree will provide.)

It can be argued that rising educational levels have played a major role in retarding the growth of leisure time. Investment in education imposes costs upon the individual family as well as conferring benefits: labor force participation among the young is reduced, lowering their earnings, while direct costs are paid in the form of higher property, sales, and other taxes as well as tuition fees. These costs may be met by debt financing, liquidating assets, or current consumption sacrifices of the family, with each generation assuming the responsibility of making an investment in the next sufficient to maintain the family's relative economic status.

At the same time, investment in education raises the market price of the graduate's time so that an economic return is obtained which is proportionate to the graduate's work effort. The net effect is that income available for consumption now rises more than proportionately to hours of effort ($E_{Y,H} > 1$).

To see this, consider either of two simple models of the leisure-consumption choice of the worker. First, ignoring the time-discounting problem and treating education costs simply as an annual expense C against earnings wH, so that

$$Y = wH - C \qquad (B.1)$$

Then writing $C' = \dfrac{C}{wH}$, it follows that

$$E_{Y,H} = 1/1 - C' \qquad\qquad (B.2)$$

which is greater than unity for those investing in education.

Alternatively one can introduce time preference and consider the direct and indirect costs of education separately. Letting Y^* = the present value of the worker's future net income (earnings, net of direct costs of education) at the beginning of schooling; B = the present value of the direct costs of education (net of student part-time earnings); H = the number of hours of work or study each year (assumed to be the same, for simplicity); s = the total hours of schooling; w = the hourly wage rate after schooling is completed; r = the rate of discounting future benefits; and p = the number of years available for work or study.

To simplify the discussion, differences between the utility of work and study time are ignored and leisure time is defined as the total time available to the worker, net of time spent either studying or working. Assuming that the individual first studies, then works, it follows that

$$Y^* = wH \int_{s/H}^{p} e^{-rt} dt - B \qquad\qquad (B.3)$$

Since e^{-rp} will be close to zero, Y^* can be approximated by

$$Y^* \cong \frac{wHe^{-rs/H}}{r} - B \qquad\qquad (B.4)$$

Similarly it can be shown that the present value of effort can be written approximately as

$$H^* \cong H/r \qquad\qquad (B.5)$$

It then follows that

$$E_{Y^*,H^*} \cong E_{Y^*,H} \cong \frac{1 + rs/H}{1 - B'} \qquad\qquad (B.6)$$

where B' is the ratio of B to the present value of lifetime earnings.

This model of the worker's leisure-consumption opportunities thus implies an elasticity of income available for consumption with respect to hours of work in excess of unity; in fact fairly steeply increasing returns to effort are indicated for workers who make a substantial investment in education. For example, if a worker has 12 or 13 years of school (s/H) and uses a rate of discount (r) in the 8-12 percent range, his effort elasticity of earnings could well equal or exceed two. (This holds even if, as some investigators believe, B' is near zero.)

Both of these models imply that rising educational levels would tend to increase the elasticity of consumption with respect to effort (see equations B.1 and B.4), increasing the financial incentive to work. Hence insofar as rising wages spur increased investment in education or are at least statistically correlated with such increases, these models would predict that the traditional decline in hours in response to increases in the observed hourly wage rate would be reduced or even eliminated.

Appendix C
The Effect of Hours
Reduction on the Return
to Schooling

If we first assume that hours in school (and the intensity of schooling time) are unaffected by the reduction in working hours of adults so that hours in school equal H_0, the approximate expression for the present value of postschooling earnings becomes[1]

$$Y' = \frac{wHe^{-rs/H_0}}{r} \tag{C.1}$$

If the cost of schooling (direct and indirect) is written as simply proportionate to hours of schooling ms, equating costs and returns we obtain

$$ms = \frac{wHe^{-rs/H_0}}{r} \tag{C.2}$$

Taking the total differential of C.1 *wrt r* and H and solving for dr/dH yields

$$dr/dH = \frac{r/H}{1 + rs/H} \tag{C.3}$$

Or in elasticity form

$$E_{r,H} = \frac{1}{1 + rs/H} \tag{C.4}$$

If rs/H is near unity, this implies an elasticity of the rate of return to schooling *wrt* hours of work of about one-half.

Alternatively if the level of work intensity in school is proportionate to that in market employments, so that we can simply write

$$ms = \frac{wHe^{-rs/H}}{r} \tag{C.5}$$

Then again taking the total differential *wrt H* and *r,* dividing by *dH,* and re-arranging terms, we obtain

$$dr/dH = \frac{1/H + rs/H^2}{1/r + s/H} = r/H \qquad (C.6)$$

In elasticity form this yields[2]

$$\eta_{r,H} = 1 \qquad (C.7)$$

As an example, if the rate of return to education is initially 8 percent and hours are reduced by 25 percent, the new equilibrium return is 6 percent if hours of schooling decline in the same proportion. If hours of schooling do not vary, an intermediate result, between 6 and 8 percent, is obtained. (Inserting plausible parameters, e.g., 12 years of school, a reduction in *r* to about 7 percent is predicted.)

Notes

1. See appendix B for notation.
2. This result is also obtained if we write the cost of schooling as $C = aw_0 H \int_0^{s/H} e^{(\pi H - r)t} dt$ rather than simply as *ms.* In this formulation, the cost of schooling rises in proportion to the opportunity cost, or wage of labor, $w_t = w_0 e^{\pi H t}$, where π measures the payoff to schooling (assumed to be constant). Here $C = \dfrac{W_0 e^Z}{\dfrac{\pi}{r/H} - 1} - 1$, where $Z = s(\pi - r/H)$. Y' can be rewritten as $\dfrac{w_0 e^Z}{r/H}$. It can be shown that the constraint $dC/dr = dY'/dr$ implies that $(1-E_{H,r}) \dfrac{\partial C}{\partial(r/H)} = (1-E_{H,r}) \dfrac{\partial Y'}{\partial(r/H)}$. Since $\dfrac{\partial C}{\partial(r/H)} = \dfrac{\partial Y'}{\partial(r/H)}$, this equality will hold only if $1 - E_{H,r} = 0$. Since $H \neq 0$, $E_{H,r} = \dfrac{d(r/H)}{dr} H = 0$ implies that $\dfrac{d(r/H)}{dr} = 0$.

Appendix D
The Graying of America
and Hours of Work

A number of formal models will yield the intuitively appealing result that if the proportion of life span spent working is reduced, the number of hours worked per year when in the labor force will, ceteris paribus, increase. This can hold whether the proportion of time working is decreased as a result of increased longevity or earlier retirement. Moreover, it can be obtained whether the gap between retirement and death results from a failure of medicine to reduce morbidity among the elderly as rapidly as it reduces mortality, or more generally from the phenomenon of physical depreciation of the human agent, obsolescence of education and training, social security or other rules that restrict or tax heavily earnings during the later years, or even from pension plans which reduce income during the early years and increase it later in life, with or without an earnings restriction.

These various developments have one or more of the following characteristics in common: a reduction in the net market price of time sold in later years, an increase in unearned income in later years, and a reduction in income in the earlier years. If the individual is freely allocating time between work and leisure in both earlier and later years, if he is endeavoring to maximize his lifetime utility as a function of consumption and leisure in each year of his life, if consumption and leisure afford diminishing returns each year, and if leisure is a normal good, one would expect that either a reduction in the net market price of time in the early years relative to the later years or (given capital market imperfections) an exogenously determined change in the pattern of unearned income or taxes which reduces income in the early years and increases it in the later years would, ceteris paribus, lead to a longer workweek earlier in life and partial or complete retirement later on.

If the individual completely discounts the future, his present behavior might not be affected by an expected future of low earnings as such. However, he could still be influenced to work longer hours in the early years (if leisure is a superior good) if his current income is reduced as a result of social adaptation to the aging problem; for example, if he is required to give a stipend to his own aged relatives or if a compulsory pension scheme reduces his current take-home pay. The latter circumstance would be more likely to reduce work effort, one would predict, if it did not reduce the marginal price of time. For example, those whose earnings are over the social security maximum or whose overtime and moonlighting earnings are exempt from the private pension plan which covers their first 40 hours of work might work longer hours if their pension deductions were increased.

A potentially important exception to this line of argument must be admitted when the age at retirement is reduced as a result of the same factors which operate to reduce weekly hours, that is, those which wo ild act to reduce labor supply generally. Examples of such factors might inclu. a rapid growth in real hourly earnings or the development of the welfare state (compare the discussion in chapter 12).

Appendix E
Some Thoughts on the
Future of Leisure Time

There has been considerable concern on the part of policymakers over the effects of recent and prospective changes in work scheduling on the long-term demand for leisure. This concern derives not simply from an interest in the free time of individuals but also from the importance of a potential growth in leisure time for planning in such fields as recreation, the spatial location of people and jobs both within and between metropolitan areas, transportation, and energy.[1]

There has been little apparent change in the leisure time of the average employed adult over the past 40 years. However, many feel that we will observe important changes in leisure time in the years ahead. At the present time efforts are being made here in the United States and especially in a number of European countries to improve the efficiency of time use by the introduction of flexitime and similar flexible-hours scheduling systems, which permit employees to choose the timing of their hours of work.[2] It is hoped that this innovation will allow the more efficient use of commuting and house and child-care time, and other types of unpaid work time, and so free more time for leisure.[3] Others believe that a substantial reduction in paid work times is likely. In this view, work time will either be reduced more or less gradually through competitive market and collective bargaining processes, or more rapidly through legislation to share the work in the face of expected substantial unemployment levels. On the other hand, still others believe that we are most likely to see a continuation of the post-World War II experience, in which hours of work are not reduced, despite secular increases in real hourly earnings and hence in weekly income.

It is of interest to consider the likely effects on the demand for leisure of each of these possible scenarios: a continuation of post-World War II experience; the development of flexible-hours schedules; and a reduction in hours through either a resumption of the historical trend to reduce hours or worksharing legislation.

A Simple Model of Leisure-time Demand

In this effort, the conventional economic model, in which all time that is not paid is treated as leisure, is obviously not very helpful. The now-classic Becker model analyzes time allocation in terms of activities which are distinguished by the extent to which they produce money income or alternatively utilize it. The Becker model can be modified, following Mincer, Gronau, and others,[4] and all time divided into three major categories: paid work time; household production time (consisting of unpaid activities, such as commuting, houeshold maintenance, and shopping, which are carried out for an extrinsic purpose); and leisure time.

The considerations raised by these writers suggest a formal model (see equations E.1–E.4.) in which the worker sells M hours of the total time at his disposal (K) in the market at a wage rate w, receiving an income of $X = wM$, which he spends on consumer goods at a unit price, purchasing an amount X. He uses H of the remaining hours $(T = K - M)$ in an intermediate stage, household production, where H and X are combined to produce household production output P. This output is then combined with leisure time, $L = T - H$, to produce consumption activity A. As a typical example, a worker will use part of his income to buy an automobile and gasoline; he will then combine these goods with his own commuting time to produce a household production output "suburban residence," which in turn permits various consumption activities, not practical in a downtown location.

$$K = L + H + M \tag{E.1}$$

$$X = wM \tag{E.2}$$

$$P = P(X,H) \tag{E.3}$$

$$A = A(P,L) \tag{E.4}$$

Utility is assumed to be a monotonically increasing function of A so that the worker will be expected to endeavor to maximize A. Hours of paid work and hence T and consumption X will be assumed to be given exogenously in this paper (to focus on the distribution of time between H and L). Thus the worker will maximize A, subject to equations E.3 and E.4, $T = L + H$, and a given level of X.

If equations E.3 and E.4 are continuous, twice differentiable functions, the first-order and second-order conditions for maximizing A are, respectively

$$-A_P P_H + A_L = 0 \tag{E.5}$$

$$-2A_{PL} P_H + A_{PP} P_H^2 + A_P P_{HH} < 0 \tag{E.6}$$

using subscripts to denote partial differentiation.

These equilibrium conditions can be used to help develop tentative answers to the questions posed above on the likely effects of leisure time of different future scenarios for paid work time.

Affluence and the Demand for Leisure

A continuation of the postwar experience in which hours of paid work showed little change, while consumption rose to new levels of affluence as the real hourly wage rate increased, would have mixed effects on leisure time. While very little has been written by economists on the effects of affluence on the allocation of time between leisure and household production,[5] there has been a long-standing interest in the subject by policymakers and popular writers. Staffen Linder, in *The Harried Leisure Class,* argues that affluence, unaccompanied by hours reduction, will yield a shift from leisure to household production. According to Linder, increases in the level of consumption goods purchased require more time to process them through household production.[6] One can restate his point more positively and consider a number of ways in which higher income can be combined with an increase in household production time to produce a higher material living standard; for example, the shift from downtown apartment living to suburban home ownership made by many families in the affluent 1950s and 1960s. This transition not only required time for commuting but also for servicing and repair of the home, household appliances, and automobiles.

On the other hand, many writers have stressed complementarities between leisure time and consumption goods: from the trade union advocates of work-week reduction in the 1970s and 1980s to the writings of Henry Ford arguing for a five-day workweek in the 1920s to the work of many social thinkers and business journalists today runs a leitmotiv of concern—that American working-men need additional leisure to utilize the higher level of consumption made possible by long-term gains in on-the-job productivity.

The net effect of the offsetting influences of affluence on the allocation of time will depend upon the substitution possibilities in producing P and A. If equations E.3 and E.4 are linear, homogeneous functions, then if X is increased, with no change in T, we obtain (by taking the total differential of equation E.5 wrt $X, H,$ and $L,$ using $dH = -dL$ and dividing by dX)

$$\frac{dL}{dX} = \frac{(\sigma_1 - \sigma_2)}{D} \frac{H}{X} (1-\alpha) \qquad (E.7)$$

where σ_1 is the elasticity of substitution between H and X in producing P, σ_2 is the elasticity of substitution between L and P in producing A, $\alpha = HP_H/P = 1 - XP_X/P$; and $D = (\alpha + H/L)\sigma_1 + (1 - \alpha)\sigma_2$.

Since the denominator D[7] and $(H/X)(1-\alpha)$ are nonnegative, the sign of dL/dX depends on that of $\sigma_1 - \sigma_2$; that is, on the possibilities of substituting goods for time in household production (say, by adopting a more expensive but faster mode of commuting) relative to the possibilities for substituting household production output for time in consumption (e.g., by enjoying a large, well-kept house more than watching television). Only if the first type of substitution is greater than the second will leisure time be increased.

In fact the past 40 years have seen a very large increase in consumption with little observed change in the ratio of leisure to household production time.[8] This experience would tend to contradict either the Linder or Ford hypotheses that $\sigma_1 - \sigma_2$ is, respectively, much greater or less than zero. While the data are certainly not sufficiently extensive or reliable to demonstrate positively that

$\sigma_1 - \sigma_2$ is just equal to zero, it would, on the other hand, be very difficult to reject the null hypothesis that the two elasticities are roughly offsetting.

Flexible Hours Scheduling and the Demand for Leisure Time

Some argue that even if there is not a significant change in the number of hours worked for pay, forthcoming innovations in hours scheduling could and very likely would make the scheduling of household production activity so much more efficient that the same effective amount of household production activity could be produced with much less household production time. The principal innovation in scheduling considered has been the flexitime arrangement, or some variant of that system, that affords workers some choice in determining the scheduling of their hours of work. A number of empirical studies have found that household production time is more efficient after the introduction of flexitime: many workers can commute more rapidly by traveling outside the peak rush hour; working parents can often better balance home and job responsibilities by having one adult home in the late afternoon, after school; and shoppers can make more advantageous arrangements if they are not confined to evening and weekend hours.[9]

However, it is not obvious that increasing the efficiency of household production time will increase leisure time. The efficiency of household production time can be introduced into the model on p. 166 by letting $H^* = s_H H$ in equation E.3, where H^* is the effective level of input of household production time and s_H is an index of the effectiveness of one hour of this time. This yields the first-order condition for maximizing A

$$A_L - s_H P_{H^*} = 0 \qquad (E.8)$$

The ability to choose one's working schedule also improves the productivity of leisure time for many. For example, a day off during the week in summertime may enable the worker and his family to drive on a lightly traveled freeway to an uncrowded beach. Such gains are usually regarded as significant, though probably much less important than gains in the efficiency of household production time.[10] Hence it would be reasonable to conclude that the effect of a reform in scheduling practices would be intermediate between that obtained from a simple increase in s_H (i.e., where s_L, the gain in leisure-time efficiency, is assumed to be equal to zero) and that derived from across-the-board gains in efficiency of both leisure and household production (so that $ds_H = ds_L = ds$). The effects of an across-the-board gain in the leisure and household production time can be seen by writing $L^* = sL$ and $H^* = sH$ in equations E.3 and E.4, and treating P and A as functions of H^* and L^*. The first-order condition for maximizing A is then

$$s(-A_P P_{H^*} + A_{L^*}) = 0 \qquad (E.9)$$

Taking the total differential of equation E.8 with respect to L, H, and s_H, using $dL = -dH$, dividing by ds_H and again making use of the linear homogeneity assumption, yields equations E.10 and E.11.

$$\frac{dL}{ds_H} = \frac{-dH}{ds_H} = \frac{H\,\sigma_1\,\sigma_2}{D}\left[-1 + \frac{1-\alpha}{\sigma_1} + \frac{\alpha}{\sigma_2}\right] \tag{E.10}$$

$$\frac{dH^*}{ds_H} = \frac{H\sigma_1\,\sigma_2}{D}\left[1 + \frac{1}{\sigma_2}\frac{H}{L}\right] \tag{E.11}$$

Taking the total derivation of equation E.9 with respect to H, L, and s, using $dH = -dL$, and dividing by ds yields the results in equations E.12-E.14.

$$\frac{dL}{ds} = \frac{-dH}{ds} = \frac{H}{sD}(1-\alpha)\,(\sigma_2-\sigma_1) \tag{E.12}$$

$$\frac{dL^*}{ds} = \frac{-T}{D}\,[\alpha\sigma_1 + (1-\alpha)\sigma_2] \tag{E.13}$$

$$\frac{dH^*}{ds} = \frac{TH\,\sigma_1}{LD} \tag{E.14}$$

The various results in equations E.10 through E.14 do not suggest that flexitime will in the long run yield any substantial increase in leisure time. In the case where $ds_H = ds_L = ds$, a significant gain in leisure will occur only if $\sigma_2 - \sigma_1$ is substantially greater than zero (see equation E.12). But it was argued above that there are not sufficient grounds for rejecting the hypotheses that $\sigma_2 - \sigma_1 = 0$.

In the case where technical gain is concentrated in the household production sector, leisure time will be increased only if there is relatively little substitution possible between household production time and consumer goods, and between household production output and leisure time (see equations E.10 and E.11).[11] This is perhaps a good short-run assumption, which may account for the fact that some who are surveyed after the introduction of flexitime report that they spend somewhat less time in various household production activities.

But long-run substitution possibilities are certainly large as individuals have an opportunity to change their residence, buy durable appliances, and in other ways permanently adjust their life-styles. We have had considerable experience with a wide variety of technical innovations specifically designed to save time in household production, for example, widespread ownership of internal combustion engines to reduce commuting time, and the use of small electric motors in a number of appliances as well as the availability of prepared foods, easily cleaned clothing, and more efficient cleaning agents, all to save time in housework.

But very little if any reduction in household production time has resulted in recent decades. For example, studies of the distribution of residences and jobs in metropolitan areas indicate that the revolutionary developments in urban transport over the past century have been used in increasing commuting distances; there is no evidence of a reduction of average commuting time. Similarly a recent study showed no change in the work time of full-time American housewives from the mid-1920s, despite a very considerable increase in the timesavers at their disposal (partly because of increasingly high standards of cleanliness).[12]

These technical innovations improve the productivity of household production time in very much the same way as would institutional reform of work scheduling practices. Our experience with technical change here suggests that a high level of substitution should be expected in the long run (i.e., that while $\sigma_1 - \sigma_2$ may be close to zero, σ_1 and σ_2 are each substantially greater than zero). Hence the introduction of flexible work schedules might well have little if any positive effect on the long-run demand for leisure time.

Hours Reduction and the Demand for Leisure Time

A reduction in paid work time is the most likely way to increase leisure time. The model predicts that the effect of a reduction in paid working time, with a concomitant reduction in consumption goods, will be equal to the sum of the effects of an increase in time, with no change in goods, and a decrease in goods, with no change in time. Thus if $dX = -wdT$ and $dL = dT - dH$, one can differentiate equation E.5 with respect to H, L, and X, eliminate dH and dX, and solve for the change in leisure time

$$dL/dT = \left\{ \sigma_2 + (\sigma_1 - \sigma_2) \left[\alpha - (1-\alpha)\frac{wH}{X} \right] \right\} \frac{1}{D} \qquad (E.15)$$

This expression can alternatively be written

$$dL/dT = \frac{\overline{dL}}{dT} - (wT/X)\, dL/dX \qquad (E.16)$$

where dL/dX is defined as in equation E.7 (i.e., with $dT = 0$) and where $\overline{dL}/dT$ is the change predicted when $dL = dT - dH$ and $dX = 0$. (It can be shown that $\overline{dL}/dT$ equals s/T times the right side of equation E.13.)

These equations yield the somewhat surprising result that leisure need not be increased by a reduction in hours of paid employment if the elasticity of leisure time with respect to goods is positive and large, and the elasticity of leisure time with respect to a change in paid work time (goods held constant) is relatively small. Indeed in this model even a quite sharp reduction in paid working hours—for example, a reduction of the standard workweek from 40 to 30 hours, imposed by government fiat as a worksharing policy—could conceivably lead to a decrease in leisure time. This is the case envisaged by some social prophets, in which a sharp reduction in working hours accompanied by a concomitant reduction in income yields a return to a somewhat simpler life style, where do-it-yourself activities gain relative to market purchases.[13]

In terms of our model, this would be a probable result if it were much more difficult to substitute L for P in producing A than to substitute H for X in producing P, that is, if σ_2 were much less than σ_1. In practice, though, a decrease in leisure time is a rather unlikely result of hours reduction. It is true that this scenario would be consistent with theoretically plausible values of the substitution elasticities; for example, if $\sigma_1 = 1.5$ and $\sigma_2 = .5$, this scenario can easily be generated with a suitable choice of the other parameters. But if we accept the empirical argument on pp. 167-168 that σ_1 and σ_2 are roughly equal, then dL/dX will be close to zero. If σ_1 is just equal to σ_2, equation E.15 simplified to $\dfrac{T}{L}\dfrac{dL}{dT} = E_{L,T} = 1$: in other words the gain from reduction in paid work time would then be shared proportionately between leisure and household production time.

A less complicated case for expecting leisure to increase with gains in time off can be made when working times are reduced gradually through the market, X and T are chosen so as to maximize A and hence utility. Note that in equation E.15 the expression in squared brackets can be written as $(H/P)(P_H - P_X w)$. But it can be shown that $P_H = P_X w$ is a condition for choosing T and X so as to maximize A. Hence one can write $dL/dT = \sigma_2/D$ which is negative, regardless of the sign of $\sigma_1 - \sigma_2$.

In the longer run, if hours continued to decline, this simplication would no longer be valid as we moved further from the original optimum conditions. However, if a future long-term decline in hours followed the same pattern displayed in the late nineteenth and early twentieth centuries, the drop in hours would not be so sharp as to reduce consumption; in the earlier period, productivity gains were shared between increases in time off from work and additional consumer goods. But even if all future productivity gains were taken as a reduction in paid work time (so that the level of consumption X were constant), this model would still predict an increase in leisure time (the result obtained when T is increased with X held constant).

Extensions and Conclusions

The model presented on p. 166 can be modified in several ways; for example, by allowing paid work and household production to have utility or by permitting the size of the labor force to be an inverse function of the length of the standard workweek. However, experiments with these and similar extensions did not change the basic conclusions derived from the simpler model.[14]

On the basis of earlier experience, it would seem that both the long-run elasticity of substitution of household production time for consumer goods and the elasticity of substitution of household production output for consumption time are each substantially different from zero, and may be roughly similar in magnitude. This would argue that (1) a continuation of the post-World War II situation, in which wages rose while hours of paid work changed little, would not yield an increase in leisure time; (2) the introduction of flexible-hours schemes might well increase leisure in the short run, but the long-run effect is more likely to be an upgrading in material living standards, through gains in household production output, than a substantial increase in leisure; and (3) a resumption of the historical tendency to reduce paid working time would be likely to increase leisure time.

Notes

1. See Schelling. More recently the formation of the Committee for Alternative Work Schedules and the broad participation in the two annual meetings of that organization; the congressional hearings over the past several years on bills to encourage or control the spread of alternative work schedules; and the commissioning by the National Science Foundation, the General Electric Foundation, and others of studies of the likely long-term effects of alternative work schedules on a variety of social impact areas, all attest to the social concern about the new schedules.

2. Though not their number.

3. On the operation of flexitime, see Owen (1977), and Racke. For general treatments of the importance of the scheduling of time, see Oi, and Hanoch.

4. See Becker, Gronau, Michael and Becker, and Mincer (1963).

5. Gronau has recently analyzed the effects of income on leisure, using cross-sectional data. He used a very simple household production function, $P = X + f(H), f' > 0, f'' < 0$. The implied assumption that $P_{XX} = P_{XH} = 0$ probably does less violation to real world conditions in cross-sectional analysis than in the analysis of long-term change over time. Gronau mentions that individuals can use additional income to hire maids to replace their own labor. In addition, well-paid individuals can purchase labor-intensive services, such as restaurant meals, to substitute the efforts of others for their own more valuable time. However, in the long run this relative price effect does not occur since the wages of maids, waiters, and so on tend to rise at least as rapidly as the average.

6. Linder puts more emphasis on necessary services and repairs, less on the positive transformation of purchased goods into satisfying consumption experiences, than the presentation here.

7. D equals $\dfrac{-H\sigma_1\sigma_2}{A_L}$ times the left side of equation E.6.

8. There has been a shift from housewife to employee status for many females, with a consequent reduction in household production time and increase in market work time for this group. However, this has not yielded a net increase in leisure time.

9. See note 3 for references on the flexitime system.

10. Workers often report that they feel they have more time off under flexitime, though their hours of paid work are unchanged. See the references cited in note 3.

11. The analysis here can be compared to a model of a two-sector economy. There are two exogenously determined inputs: labor and materials. All materials are used in the first sector, together with a portion of the labor supply. The output of the first sector is used in the second sector, together with the remaining labor supply to produce final output. Labor is allocated among the two sectors so as to maximize output. Flexitime can then be introduced as a labor-augmenting technical change, which raises the productivity of an hour of work. If flexitime directly improves labor productivity in both sectors, labor will be shifted from the second to the first sector if it is easier to substitute labor for other inputs in the first sector and relatively difficult to make this substitution in the second sector. But if the labor-augmenting technical change is confined to the first sector, a shift of labor from the second to the first sector will occur insofar as there are possibilities for substituting labor for other resources in the first sector and for substituting the output of the first sector for labor in the second sector.

12. See Vanek for an analysis of changes over time in the work effort of American housewives. See Lansing and Hendricks for empirical analyses of the relationship between commuter speed and time. (They conclude that at least half of the potential gain from increased speed is used to increase commuter distance.)

13. In this scenario the typical worker is expected to live further from his work, though using a less expensive if slower mode of transportation (such as a bus). Distance from the city center is supposed to offer the opportunity of purchasing cheaper land, yielding such options for do-it-yourself endeavors as repairing and improving one's home or even raising a portion of the family's food supply.

14. Possible labor force participation changes as a result of a reduction in working hours would be most likely to refute this conclusion. However, it is

unlikely that a reduction in standard hours would yield a sufficient increase in participation to actually increase total work time. The already high levels of labor force participation and the existence of a well-developed market for voluntary part-time workers (now one out of seven of all workers) for those who wish to work less than standard hours argue against that conclusion.

Appendix F
The Determination of
Working Conditions

The model presented in appendix E assumes that market work and household production times are regarded simply as means for producing consumption activities. But these work activities also yield utility (or disutility). Moreover, an important aspect of modern economic life is the diversion of resources from final consumption, in the interest of making household production and market employment more pleasant. Partly because of these resource outlays but also partly as a result of technical changes in work and reductions in the number of hours of work from their nineteenth century levels, work time has become much less painful; indeed for some workers it is almost as pleasant as consumption time.

The analysis of these phenomena requires that we expand the model developed in appendix E. Let

$$U = U(A_1, A_2, A_3) \qquad (F.1)$$

where A_1 is consumption activity (identical with A in the model discussed in appendix E), A_2 is a pleasant environment for household production, and A_3 is a pleasant environment for market employment.

Then (continuing to use the notation developed in appendix E) let

$$A_1 = A_1(P, LS_L) \qquad (F.2)$$

$$A_2 = A_2(H, ZS_Z) \qquad (F.3)$$

$$A_3 = A_3(M, w^* S_{w^*}) \qquad (F.4)$$

$$P = P(HS_H, Y) \qquad (F.5)$$

$$(w - w^*)M = Y + Z \qquad (F.6)$$

$$M + H + L = K \qquad (F.7)$$

where equations F.2, F.5, and F.7 are similar to equations in appendix E; equation F.4 states that the quality of working time depends upon the duration of working time and both the amount of resources employed to improve this quality (w^*) and the skill or technology with which they are employed S_{w^*}. Equation F.3 makes a similar statement about the quality of household production time. Equation F.6 modifies the earnings budget constraint to include outlays for improving conditions at home (Z) and on the job (w*M).

If we make the usual assumptions about the continuity and differentiability of these functions, maximize U wrt the allocation of time and money, calculate the first-order conditions, and rewrite, we obtain[1]

$$U_{A_1}A_{1_L} = U_{A_1}A_{1_P}P_H + U_{A_2}A_{2_H} = U_{A_1}A_{1_P}P_Y(w-w^*) + U_{A_3}A_{3_M} \quad \text{(F.8)}$$

$$U_{A_1}A_{1_P}P_Y = U_{A_2}A_{2_Z} = \frac{U_{A_3}A_{3_{w^*M}}}{M} \quad \text{(F.9)}$$

continuing to use subscripts to denote partial differentiation.

Equations F.8 state that the marginal utility obtained from time spent in each of its three uses (L,H,M) is equal. Note that $U_{A_2}A_{2_H}$ and $U_{A_3}A_{3_M}$ have now been added to the middle and right-hand expressions as a result of introducing the utility of work experience. But note also that these terms will be less than $U_{A_1}A_{1_L}$ if the equalities are satisfied and if $U_{A_1}A_{1_P}P_H$ and $U_{A_1}A_{1_P}P_Y(w-w^*)$ are positive. In other words if, on the margin, work time is productive of consumer goods, we would not expect it to be as pleasant as consumption time, which is not. (Otherwise the equality would not be satisfied and the individual would extend his work hours, presumably until work became less pleasant and marginal consumption gains less attractive, and the equality was restored.)

Equations F.9 state that an additional dollar of earnings spent on improving the quality of the three types of experience, A_1, A_2, or A_3, should yield the same increment in utility. In other words no advantage can then be obtained by transferring resources from consumption to improved working conditions or vice versa.

In principle, the effects of changes in exogenous variables can now be worked out. The very considerable improvement in working conditions in recent decades has occurred in the context of three developments: increases in w, the market wage; improvements in technology, reducing the cost of providing good working conditions (increases in S_{w^*} and S_Z in this model); and a cessation of the long-term downward movement in hours of work M.

However, calculation of the effects of these three changes on working conditions in this format is extremely cumbersome. An interesting simplification is possible, though, if we conclude from the empirical discussion in appendix E that it would not be too unreasonable to assume that the elasticities of substitution between L and P in A_1 and between H and Y in P (σ_2 and σ_1 in that appendix, respectively) are approximately unity. If we assume that the utility function relating A_1, A_2, and A_3 is also Cobb-Douglas but make no such assumption about the working conditions equations themselves, we obtain

$$U = A_1^h A_2^i A_3^{1-h-i} \quad \text{(F.10)}$$

$$A_1 = L^{1-b}P^b \tag{F.11}$$

$$A_2 = A_2(H,ZS_Z) \tag{F.12}$$

$$A_3 = A_3(M,w^*S_{w*}) \tag{F.13}$$

$$P = H^{1-e}Y^e \tag{F.14}$$

$$(w-w^*)M = Y + Z \tag{F.15}$$

$$M + H + L = K \tag{F.16}$$

in place of equations F.1 through F.7. Again maximizing U, calculating first-order conditions, and rewriting

$$w^*/w = \frac{(1-h-i)E_3}{hbe + iE_2 + (1-h-i)E_3} \tag{F.17}$$

$$Z/wM = \frac{iE_2}{hbe + iE_2 + (1-h-i)E_3} \tag{F.18}$$

$$Y/wM = \frac{hbe}{hbe + iE_2 + (1-h-i)E_3} \tag{F.19}$$

$$Y : Z : w^*M = hbe : iE_2 : (1-h-i)E_3 \tag{F.20}$$

where E_2 is the elasticity of A_2 wrt ZS_Z and E_3 is the elasticity of A_3 wrt w^*S_{w*}.

If the A_2 and A_3 functions are also of the Cobb-Douglas type, E_2 and E_3 are constants as are the right sides of equations F.17, F.18, and F.19. In that case, as the market wage increases, equiproportionate increases must take place in Y, A, and w^*M. Moreover, in this variant, an improvement in the technology of providing better working conditions results in a gain in conditions just proportionate to the gain in technology there.

However, there is no good reason for assuming Cobb-Douglas forms for A_2 and A_3. On the contrary, it is equally plausible to consider some systematic departures from the unitary elasticity of substitution hypothesis. For example, if the market employment working conditions function is not Cobb-Douglas, E_3 will vary with w^*S_{w*}. If A_3 is a linear homogeneous function of w^*S_{w*} and $1/M$, and the other functions continue to be treated as Cobb-Douglas, then rewriting equation F.17 as

$$w^*/w = f(E_3) \tag{F.21}$$

it can be shown that (since E_3 is a function of $w^*S_{w^*}$)

$$(w/w^*)\partial w^*/\partial w = \frac{1}{1 - \rho\eta} \qquad (F.22)$$

where $\rho = E_{f,E_3}$ and $\eta = E_{E_3,w^*}$. It can also be shown (using equation F.17) that[2] $E_{f,E_3} = \dfrac{w-w^*}{w}$ and that $E_{E_3,w^*} = (1-E_3)\dfrac{(\sigma-1)}{\sigma}$, where σ is the elasticity of substitution between $1/M$ and $w^*S_{w^*}$ in producing A_3 (using the definition of σ).
Making these substitutions and rewriting equation F.22 as

$$(w/w^*)\partial w^*\partial w = \frac{1}{1 - \left(1 - \dfrac{w^*}{w}\right)(1-E_3)\left(1 - \dfrac{1}{\sigma}\right)} \qquad (F.23)$$

it follows that, since w^*/w, E_3, and $1/\sigma$ are each $\leqslant 1$, $(w/w^*)\partial w^*/\partial w \geqslant 0$. In other words that improvements in working conditions would be an expected result of an increase in wage rates.

The extent to which expenditures to improve working conditions will keep pace with increases in the wage rate, and hence in the quality of consumption time, will depend here upon the elasticity of substitution σ. It follows from equations F.22 and F.23 that

$$\frac{w}{(w^*/w)} \frac{\partial(w^*/w)}{w} = \frac{\rho\eta}{1 - \rho\eta} = \frac{1}{-1 + \dfrac{1}{\left(1 - \dfrac{w^*}{w}\right)(1-E_3)\left(1 - \dfrac{1}{\sigma}\right)}} \qquad (F.24)$$

Equation F.24 indicates that working conditions will improve relative to the quality of consumption time if $\sigma > 1$.[3]

A similar algebraic argument (against using equation F.21 yields the result that

$$\partial(w^*S_{w^*})/\partial S_{w^*} = \frac{1}{1 - \rho\eta} = \frac{1}{1 - \left(1 - \dfrac{w^*}{w}\right)(1-E_3)\left(1 - \dfrac{1}{\sigma}\right)} \qquad (F.25)$$

$$\partial w^*/\partial S_{w^*} = \frac{\rho\eta}{1 - \rho\eta} = \frac{1}{-1 + \dfrac{1}{\left(1 - \dfrac{w^*}{w}\right)(1-E_3)\left(1 - \dfrac{1}{\sigma}\right)}} \qquad (F.26)$$

that is, that a gain in the technical processes involved in providing better working conditions will improve these conditions (F.25) but that unless $\sigma \geqslant 1$, technical change will lead to a less than proportionate gain in conditions, with some reduction taking place in expenditures for this purpose (w^*).

Finally it can also be shown that, since A_3 is assumed to be linear homogeneous in $1/M$, it follows (using equation F.21 and the fact that under the linear homogeneity assumption, the elasticity of E_3 wrt $1/M$ equals the elasticity of E_3 wrt w^*)[4] that

$$\frac{M}{w^*/w}\frac{\partial w^*/w}{\partial M} = \frac{\rho\eta}{1-\rho\eta} = \frac{1}{-1 + \dfrac{1}{\left(1-\dfrac{w^*}{w}\right)(1-E_3)\left(1-\dfrac{1}{\sigma}\right)}} \qquad (F.27)$$

Equation F.27 indicates that if $\sigma > 1$, one would predict that as hours are reduced, pressure to improve working conditions are curtailed somewhat. In that case, the leveling off of hours in recent years would have tended, other things being equal, to lead to an improvement in working conditions. Or putting the argument in a more realistic context, one would predict that if $\sigma > 1$, then in a period in which wage increases were not accompanied by hours reduction (as in the past 30 years) we would see a greater effort to improve working conditions, other things being equal, than in a period in which wage increases were accompanied by substantial reductions in hours (as in the last half of the nineteenth and the first half of the twentieth century).

Notes

1. Since w^* is not a function of S_{w^*} under these assumptions.
2. Holding M constant. See note 4.
3. The right side of equation F.24 is positive if $0 < (1-1/\sigma)\left(1-\dfrac{w^*}{w}\right)(1-E_3)$ < 1. It was argued that the expression within the inequalities is less than unity. It will also be greater than zero if $(1-1/\sigma) > 0$, that is, if $\sigma > 1$.
4. Equations F.9 and F.17, giving first-order conditions for an optimal allocation of goods between the improvement of consumption and working conditions, hold whether hours worked in the market are set so as to maximize utility (as in equation F.8) or are determined by union negotiation, legislation, or other factors. To take full advantage of this flexibility, changes in M and in $w^*S_{w^*}$ are both discussed independently. However if hours are chosen so as to maximize utility, their level is of course determined within the system of equations

$$\left[M/T = \frac{(1-h-i)E_{A_2,M} + ebh + iE_{A_2,ZS_Z}}{h + (1-h-i)E_{A_3,M} + iE_{A_2,H} + iE_{A_2,ZS_Z}}\right]$$

Appendix G
Employer Demand for
Part-time Workers

A Model of Employer Demand

Introduction

Other things being equal, employers will tend to prefer part-time workers over full-timers if their hourly wages, adjusted for quality differences, are lower. But other things are generally not equal: training, supervisory, and communications and coordination costs will typically be higher for part-timers. Moreover, problems particular to different sectors of the economy provide other advantages and disadvantages to the use of part-timers. In some sectors, including service and trade, part-timers help the employer to deal more efficiently with uneven patterns of demand over the workweek (if only full-timers are used in these functions, they may be idle part of the time). In other sectors, characterized by a high capital/labor ratio and by demands that are regular within a weekly period, part-time labor is at a considerable disadvantage unless it can be recruited to work at sequential shifts. (Mining, manufacturing, and railroads provide principal examples of this type of employment.)

Direct and Indirect Costs

These considerations can be used in a simple model of employer behavior. Initially the model abstracts from problems particular to certain sectors of the economy (and hence ignores irregular demands for service or excess industrial capacity).
　　Let

$$P = pO(L,C) - J - rC \qquad (G.1)$$

where P is a firm's profit; p is the price of output; O is the firm's output, a function of labor (L) and capital (C); J denotes total labor costs; and r is the rental price of capital. If p and r are parameters to the firm then, holding L and C constant, P is maximized by minimizing J. One can argue that employees impose fixed costs as well as those that vary directly with hours of work. Thus to a first approximation, labor costs per week may be represented as

$$J = w_c(H_c+a)N_c + w_p (H_p+a)N_p \qquad (G.2)$$

181

where w_c and w_p are the costs of hiring a full-time or a part-timer worker, respectively, for an additional hour; H_c and H_p are the weekly hours of full-timers and part-timers; N_c and N_p are the number employed in each category; and a is the fixed or indirect costs imposed by employing another worker, regardless of how few hours he works, expressed in labor units and spread over the number of weeks employed with the company. (For example, training, supervisory, and coordination costs constribute to a, insofar as these costs are a function of the number of persons employed rather than total manhours hired.)

Then labor input $L = H_p N_p + H_c N_c$ so that

$$N_c = \frac{L - H_p N_p}{H_c} \tag{G.3}$$

If w_c and w_p are fixed for the firm (the case if the firm buys labor in competitive markets) then if schedules are fixed at H_p and H_c and if L is held constant as the number of part-timers is increased, it follows from equations G.2 and G.3 that (making the usual assumptions about the differentiability of equation G.2)

$$\frac{\partial J}{\partial N_p} = w_c \left[\left(-1 + \frac{w_p}{w_c} \right) H_p + a \left(\frac{w_p}{w_c} - \frac{H_p}{H_c} \right) \right] \tag{G.4}$$

The first-order condition for an interior minimum here is that $\partial J / \partial N_p = 0$. If a is constant, a boundary solution—of either all part-timers or no part-timers—is likely.

However, a usually varies among jobs; most firms have a variety of positions, some of which (generally the less complicated jobs) impose smaller training and other fixed costs than others. One implication of this model is that employers would rank jobs in terms of the indirect costs required, and begin by assigning the least complicated jobs to part-timers.

Let this ranking yield a distribution $a(i)$ where i is the ith job (with $i = 1$ for the job with the smallest indirect costs) and $a(\ )$ is the indirect cost of that job in labor equivalents.

Let there initially be N^* full-time equivalent jobs. When one of these is converted to part-time jobs (letting $v = H_p / H_c$), $1/v$ part-timers are hired. $N_c = N^* - v N_p$ full-timers are then still needed. On these assumptions if only full-timers are used, labor costs are

$$J = w_c \int_{i=1}^{N^*} a(i) di + w_c N_c H_c \tag{G.5}$$

but if N_p part-timers are used

$$J = w_p H_p N_p + W_c H_c (N^* - \nu N_p) + \frac{w_p}{\nu} \int_{i=1}^{\nu N_p} a(i)di + w_c \int_{\nu N_p}^{N^*} a(i)di \quad (G.6)$$

where the indirect costs of hiring part-timers are given in the third term and the indirect costs of hiring full-timers in the fourth.

It follows that

$$\frac{\partial J}{\partial N_p} = w_c \left[\left(-1 + \frac{w_p}{w_c} \right) H_p + a \left(\frac{w_p}{w_c} - \frac{H_p}{H_c} \right) \right] \quad (G.7)$$

This expression is similar to equation G.4, but a now denotes the indirect cost of hiring the N_pth worker and may vary with N_p. Equation G.7 can be written more compactly as

$$w_c H_p [-(1-s) + a'(s-\nu)] \quad (G.8)$$

where $s = w_p/w_c$ and $a' = a/H_p$. Here the first-order condition for an interior solution for minimizing total labor costs, and hence for maximizing profits, will be

$$a' = \frac{1-s}{s-\nu} \quad (G.9)$$

The s function will vary across industrial-occupation sectors as a function of a number of factors, including the demographic composition of the sectoral labor force (see the development in chapters 7 and 8). The a function will also vary from one sector to another depending upon the level of complexity of jobs and other factors.

Equations G.7 and G.8 suggest that in sectors in which s is higher (holding a and other factors constant), the relative employment of part-timers will be less. Similarly in sectors in which a is higher (holding s and other factors constant), the relative employment of part-timers may also be less since the marginal cost of hiring part-timers here is positively related to s as well as a.

Irregular Demands for Labor in the
Service, Trade, and Other Sectors

Variations in the utilization of part-timers depend upon particular characteristics of the industry or occupation as well as on the relative availability of part-timers and full-timers, and the importance of training and other fixed costs. In much of the economy, the intensity of demand for labor varies over the workweek in a predictable pattern. For this reason, part-timers can be used more efficiently than full-timers in some jobs in these sectors, in the sense that if the latter are substituted for part-timers here, they will only be occupied during part of their work time—in peak periods of demand or for a few hours in the evening or on weekends (see the discussion in chapter 7).

Let the proportion of part-time employees which will just eliminate idleness among full-timers in the firm be

$$g = N_p^* / N_c^* \tag{G.10}$$

If this proportion of part-timers is employed and initially assuming that all part-timers hired are assigned to such jobs, profits

$$P = pO\left[N_c^*(H_c + gH_p), C\right] - J - rC \tag{G.11}$$

Assume further that to maintain output when fewer part-timers are employed, ℓv full-timers must be hired for each part-timer less than N_p^* employed, that is, that

$$N_c - N_c^* = (N_p^* - N_p)\ell v \tag{G.12}$$

This definition implies that if an hour of full-time work in these jobs is as effective as an hour of part-time work, $\ell = 1$. If some idleness of full-timers results when they replace part-timers, $\ell > 1$ in these positions.

If output is held constant in this fashion, profits can again be maximized by minimizing total labor costs. Direct labor costs D here are (using equation G.12)

$$D = N_p H_p w_p + N_c H_c W_c = N_p H_p w_p + \left[N_c^* + (N_p^* - N_p)\ell v\right] H_c w_c \tag{G.13}$$

$$\frac{\partial D}{\partial N_p} = H_p w_p - \ell v H_c w_c = H_p w_c (s-\ell) \tag{G.14}$$

A reduction in the number of part-timers also influences indirect costs; if ℓv full-timers are hired for each part-timer eliminated, indirect labor costs are decreased by $aw_c(\ell v - s)$. Hence

$$\frac{\partial J}{\partial N_p} = H_p w_c \left[s-\ell + a'(s-\ell v)\right] \tag{G.15}$$

the sum of the additions to direct and indirect costs. This result would hold as long as $0 < N_p/N_c \leqslant g$. If an interior solution for maximum P is found within this range, equation G.15 implies

$$a' = \frac{\ell - s}{s - \ell v} \qquad \text{(G.16)}$$

as a first-order condition.

If part-time employment exceeds this level (i.e., if $N_p > gN_c$) so that the extra part-timers are being used in positions in which they have no special advantage, ℓ is equal to unity for these additional part-timers, and equation G.9 can be substituted for G.16.

It is easy to see that if $\ell > 1$, a more generous criterion for hiring part-timers is obtained: equation G.15 indicates that the marginal cost of hiring part-timers is inversely related to ℓ. Hence in those industrial-occupational sectors where g is higher (and hence the average level of ℓ is higher) one might, other things being equal, expect to find more willingness to employ part-timers.

This analysis can readily be combined with the earlier discussion of indirect costs. If a firm has two types of jobs, those in which an uneven distribution of demands creates a need for part-timers and the remainder, while indirect costs continue to vary among jobs within each group, the firm will rank jobs within each in terms of the indirect costs per employee, and assign those with the smaller indirect costs to part-timers within each sector. But the cutoff level of indirect costs a^* in the sectors where $\ell > 1$ will be higher (since the cost-minimizing level of a is a positive function of ℓ; see equation G.16. Hence somewhat higher-level jobs can be assigned to part-timers in these sectors, and employment of part-timers will in consequence probably be greater there. It follows that in those sectors where g is higher we would expect a higher average level of part-time employment (holding a as well as relative wages s constant).

Capacity Utilization in Mining, Manufacturing, and Railroads

In many sectors of the economy, production is for stock, not to provide a service. Here demand is usually known at least a week in advance, and so labor input can be spread evenly over the workweek (thus g is close to zero and the average value of ℓ is near unity). In a number of industries and occupations in these sectors—especially in the mining, manufacturing, and railroad industries—the capital-labor ratio is high, so that management has a strong incentive to schedule work so as to keep capital occupied. Not only are full-timers employed but shiftwork is also used to obtain still greater utilization.

Obviously part-timers are at a distinct disadvantage in this sector, unless they can be used in sequential shifts (so that, e.g., two four-hour shifts of part-timers can man one full-time work station). Otherwise they would only be employed here if they were available much more cheaply.

This situation can be explicated further with a simple modification of the model developed on pp. 181–183. Let

$$P = pO(L, C^*) - J - rC \tag{G.17}$$

where C^* is the flow of capital services actually utilized in production and C is now defined more narrowly as the flow of services paid for.

If there is an A chance that full-timers will be replaced by part-timers working sequentially and a $1 - A$ chance that they will work simultaneously then, if one full-timer is replaced by $1/v$ part-timers, there is an A chance that no additional work stations will be needed and a $1 - A$ chance that $1/v - 1$ additional stations will be required (since $1/v$ work stations would then be required, where one sufficed before). Hence if capital input (C^*) is to be maintained, the expected value of the additional capital service cost imposed by employing another part-timer becomes

$$\frac{\partial C}{\partial N_P} = \frac{A(O) + (1-A)(1/v - 1)}{1/v} \, C' = (1-A)(1-v)C' \tag{G.18}$$

where C' is the additional capital service cost imposed if an additional work station is used.

Equation G.18 implies that (holding L, C^*, and hence O constant)

$$\frac{\partial P}{\partial N_p} = \frac{\partial J}{\partial N_p} - r(1-A)(1-v)C'$$

$$= H_p w_c \left[1 - s - a'(s-v) - \frac{rC'}{H_p w_c}(1-A)(1-v) \right] \tag{G.19}$$

The additional marginal costs of hiring part-timers imposed when it is necessary to provide additional work stations for them (i.e., when A is low) would be expected to limit their employment. Where the marginal cost of an additional work station is high, their use is apt to be ruled out altogether.

This analysis does not imply that part-timers would never be employed in sectors such as manufacturing, mining, and railroads. They can sometimes be employed in a pattern of shifts that does not require additional work stations. They have also been reported as occasionally being used in simple jobs in light manufacturing, in jobs usually held by women, and in times of considerable labor shortage (in England). Light manufacturing generally has a lower capital/

labor ratio than many other industries in this sector; simple jobs usually require smaller direct costs per employee; and a female-dominated occupation in times of shortage might well be one in which there is a large relative wage gap (adjusted for quality) between available full-time and part-time labor. These conditions imply that C', s, and a' are low. Equation G.19 argues that all three of these circumstances would tend to increase the profitability of hiring part-timers.

However, one would more generally expect part-time employment to be minimal in these sectors, in comparison with the level obtained in the remainder of the economy.

Empirical Analysis

Empirically Testable Hypotheses

The model of employer demand developed above implies several empirically testable hypotheses about differences among industry-occupation sectors in the utilization of part-timers.

1. That the employer demand for part-timers will tend to be relatively large where the wages of part-timers relative to full-timers (both adjusted for quality differences) are low. Since investigation of the part-time labor market imposes some fixed costs on the employer, it may also be reasonable to hypothesize that sensitivity to these price differences would be greater where the use of part-timers is above some minimum level and labor costs are high, giving the employer an incentive to search this market.

2. That the proportion of part-timers employed will tend to be lower where indirect labor costs are high. A good case can be made for expecting these indirect costs to be correlated with wage levels, adjusted for differences in education and experience. A primary reason for the wage level in a sector to differ from that predicted by the workers' education and experience is differential investments in employer-specific training. But the model predicts that such training and promotion opportunities will not be available to part-timers (a result confirmed by the available survey evidence). A complementary reason for expecting indirect costs to vary with wage levels is that the latter is often higher in jobs in large, complex organizational settings, where supervisory, coordinating, and communications costs are high. But these costs tend to be higher, when prorated over hours worked, as a body of work is distributed over a larger number of employees. Hence they operate to discourage part-time employment in much the same way as training costs and other fixed or quasi-fixed costs per employee (compare the discussion in chapter 7).

3. Part-timers are not likely to be used in large numbers where there is an even distribution of demands over the workweek and the capital/labor ratio is

high. Thus their use is expected to be minimal in the mining, manufacturing, and railroad industries.

4. In the remaining sectors, part-timers will be employed in greater numbers where there is an irregular distribution of demand over the workweek, for at least some jobs. The time distribution of demand itself is not observable from the usual data sources, since some potential demands go unmet (e.g., when a retail store is closed in the evening). However, the allocation of work time over the week can be measured and sectoral differences in the proportion of workers employed at nonstandard hours used to predict the proportion of part-timers.

Since a large proportion of part-timers are used outside standard hours, a spurious correlation might be introduced between the predictor and predicted variables if total workers employed outside standard hours is used to predict part-time employment; a more conservative alternative would be use the proportion of full-time workers employed at nonstandard hours as a predictor of part-time employment. (This would actually tend to understate the association between nonstandard time demands for labor and part-time employment.)

Data and Variables

Data were available for 200 industry-occupational groupings, the 20 major industries and 10 major occupations in the matched March–May 1973, U.S. Bureau of Labor Statistics Current Population Survey tape. Aggregated data were available for: q, the ratio of part-time to full-time employment; I, an index of indirect costs (the hourly wage level in the sector, adjusted for differences in education and experience); s, the wage (adjusted) of part-timers divided by the wage (also adjusted) of full-timers; T, the proportion of full-time workers employed at nonstandard times (a full-time worker who neither started work between 6:30 A.M. and 9:30 A.M. nor finished between 2:30 P.M. and 5:30 P.M. was classified as working nonstandard hours); and X, a number of variables measuring the demographic composition of the sectoral labor force.

Estimation Procedures

An appropriate empirical employer demand function for part-timers might take the form

$$N_p/N_c = q = f(s,I,T,u) \tag{G.20}$$

where u is a random error. One would expect $q_s, q_I < 0, q_T > 0$.

Estimation in the manufacturing, mining, and railroad industries creates a special problem. The use of the T variable would not be helpful since, it was argued above, work flows are usually more even over the week in this sector, and variations in T would have a different connotation; for example, the use of night shifts to keep manufacturing capacity employed. One way to resolve this problem is to set $T = 0$ in these industries. Alternatively this sector can simply be excluded from the regression altogether.

A second estimation problem is that the measure of indirect costs I may be correlated with the relative wage level s. One alternative (used in the results presented on p. 191) is to develop an instrumental variable to substitute for I ($\hat{I}$ was obtained by regressing I on education, experience, and other factors).[1]

A more serious simultaneity problem arises because s is determined within a system of supply and demand equations, that is, that a supply equation is omitted from the system so that ordinary least-squares estimation will yield inconsistent results. However, it is possible to add this supply equation and then estimate the demand equation, using the two-stage least-squares regression method. It was argued above that the relative supply availability of part-timers in a sector would be a function of the sector's demographic composition. More specifically, one would expect that if a sector is composed largely of women (especially if many are mothers of small children), youths, and others typically more interested in part-time work, part-timers will be more readily available than if most of the sectoral labor force consists of prime-aged males, who more typically prefer full-time work. Hence a vector of such demographic variables X was used to estimate the supply function: X_1, proportion of sector employees over 50 years of age; X_2, proportion under 25 years of age; X_3, proportion of single males; X_4, proportion of single females; X_5, proportion of mothers with children under 15 years of age; and X_6, proportion of married women without children under 15 years of age. The supply equation

$$q = g(s,X,v) \tag{G.21}$$

was used for empirical estimation; v is a random error term.

This method for estimating the supply of part-timers may yield biased results if an increase in the proportion of part-time jobs available will itself change the demographic composition of the sectoral labor force by attracting women, students, and older workers.

On the other hand, the use of the demographic composition of the full-time labor force X' introduces a bias in the opposite direction. To see this, consider the hypothetical case where there is no tendency for demographic factors to influence the creation of part-time jobs, that is, where the latter is determined solely by the employers' need and random factors, but where the likely demographic groups among the sector's employees (e.g., mothers) tend to be given the available part-time jobs in disproportionate numbers. In this case, other things being equal, the proportion of mothers and of similar groups will be less among the full-time work force where the proportion of part-timers in the sector is larger.

Because of these biases, both X and X' were used in alternative predictions.

Results

Equation G.20 was estimated in the form

$$\ln q = a + bI + cT - \sigma \ln s + u \qquad (G.22)$$

This equation form has the advantage that σ can be interpreted directly as the elasticity of substitution between full-time and part-time labor. The argument above would imply that if T and P were held constant, σ would have a high value (if all such sectoral influences are accounted for in the correct equation form, σ would be expected to equal infinity). In the empirical regressions, the instrumental variable $\hat{I}$ was substituted for I.

A test was also made of the hypothesis that management will be more responsive to changes in s where labor costs are high or utilization is above a minimal level. A linear relationship can be posited between σ and $I(-\sigma=d+eI)$ or between σ and P and $T(-\sigma=d+eI+fT)$. This yields the alternative employer demand equations

$$\ln q = a + bI + cT + d(\ln s) + e(\ln s)I + u \qquad (G.23)$$

$$\ln q = a + bI + cT + d(\ln s) + e(\ln s)I + f(\ln s)T + u \qquad (G.24)$$

The results of these several estimations are given in table G-1. (All the results in lines 1–6 of table G-1 were obtained by the two-stage least-squares technique.) These results tend to support the hypotheses of the model. The indirect cost measure $\hat{I}$ has a strongly negative effect on part-time employment in all the demand regressions.

The time distribution measure T has a significantly positive effect on part-time employment, throughout the regressions in table G-1. Moreover, when an estimate of the predicted value of the part-time proportion in all sectors is calculated from the data excluding mining, manufacturing, and railroads (i.e., using the mean values of the data including these sectors and the parameters obtained when they are excluded), the predicted value of part-time employment substantially exceeds the actual. Thus these results support the view that the mining, manufacturing, and railroad industries make much less use of part-timers than does the rest of the economy as well as providing evidence for the hypothesis that, within the remainder of the economy, an irregular distribution of work

Table G-1
Statistical Estimates of the Supply and Demand of Part-time Employees

Demand

	Standard Error	Constant	$\hat{I}$	T	lns	(lns)I	(lns)T	X_1	X_2	X_3	X_4	X_5	X_6
1.	1.24	−6.1162	−11.0430 (−7.02)	+4.0490 (5.44)	−4.3486 (−2.86)								
2.[b]	1.01	−5.6354	−11.1168 (−7.72)	+1.8978 (2.78)	−5.3585 (−3.77)								
3.	1.29	−6.5548	−11.7274 (−6.97)	+4.3604 (5.48)	−5.6545 (−3.27)	−6.1231 (−1.90)							
4.	1.23	−6.3516	−11.5548 (7.15)	+3.3884 (2.60)	−4.5416 (−2.22)	−6.0764 (−1.97)	−8.7129 (−.92)						

Supply

	Standard Error	Constant	$\hat{I}$	T	lns	(lns)I	(lns)T	X_1	X_2	X_3	X_4	X_5	X_6
5.	1.18	−3.4247			+5.4599 (4.04)			−.6480 (−.45)	−.3540 (−.18)	+9.3805 (4.15)	+3.1193 (1.49)	+.4678 (.26)	+4.1050 (1.81)
6.[b]	.92	−3.2775			+4.1229 (3.38)			+1.4467 (1.09)	−.0785 (−.04)	+7.7955 (3.93)	−1.6622 (−.82)	−2.0079 (−1.33)	+9.2968 (4.47)

Prediction

	$\bar{R}^2$	Constant	$\hat{I}$	T				X_1	X_2	X_3	X_4	X_5	X_6
7.	.61	−4.8309	−3.5569 (−3.19)	+3.3380 (5.75)				+3.990 (.37)	+1.2399 (.84)	+2.9835 (1.68)	+3.6738 (2.29)	+1.4836 (1.08)	−.2396 (−.14)
8.[b]	.69	−4.4702	−4.0650 (−4.49)	+.7721 (1.50)				+1.7920 (1.92)	+.9232 (.73)	+3.4921 (2.23)	−1.6456 (−1.13)	−1.8583 (−1.60)	+6.9519 (4.56)
9.	.48	+.2872	+.8335 (4.28)	+.1175 (1.31)				−.2870 (−1.49)	+.0167 (.06)	−.9395 (−2.86)	−.0572 (−.22)	+.2904 (1.22)	−.6046 (−2.17)
								X_1'	X_2'	X_3'	X_4'	X_5'	X_6'
10.	.58	−4.9606	−4.3540 (−3.87)	+3.9115 (6.65)				+.6400 (.66)	−.1792 (−.14)	+3.8874 (2.43)	+3.3570 (2.64)	+3.0309 (2.06)	−1.2814 (−.88)
11.[b]	.63	−4.7002	−4.6146 (−4.72)	+1.3137 (2.34)				+2.0860 (2.39)	+.7764 (.67)	+3.8507 (2.58)	+.4381 (.38)	−.3239 (−.24)	+3.9807 (2.87)

Results in lines 1–6 obtained by the two-stage least-squares regression technique. Results in lines 7–11 obtained by ordinary least squares.
[a]Dependent variable is ln$q$, except in line 9, where it is lnw_p; t ratios in parentheses.
[b]Excluding mining, railroads, and manufacturing.

demands over the workweek (even when measured by the deployment of full-time labor) is positively related to the use of part-timers.

A high degree of responsiveness of employers to changes in the relative price of part-timers, holding I and T constant, is indicated by the estimate of the elasticity of substitution: σ is measured at over 4 (in lines 1, 3, and 4).

A still higher estimate of σ, 5.4, is obtained when manufacturing, mining, and railroads are excluded (line 2). This last result is consistent with the negative (but insignificant) coefficient of $(\ln s)T$ in line 4. The negative coefficients of $(\ln s)I$ in lines 3 and 4 are consistent with the view that management is more responsive to changes in the relative price s of different types of labor when labor costs are high.

Supply Estimation: The corresponding supply equations are also given in lines 5 and 6. The proportion of part-time jobs established by employers is in each case a positive function of s, as expected. Moreover, the set of demographic variables makes an important contribution to the regression, though these variables are highly mutlicollinear, reducing their individual significance. Those coefficients which have relatively high measured t ratios have the expected signs.

Predictions of Part-time Employment and Wages: The exogenous variables employed in the intersectoral model (X, I, and T) predict wages and employment of part-timers fairly well. When the logarithm of the ratio of part-time to full-time employment is regressed on all the independent variables in the system (line 7), an adjusted coefficient of determination $\overline{R}^2$ rises to .61 is obtained. When the manufacturing, mining, and railroad sectors are excluded, $\overline{R}^2$ rises to .69 (line 8). The estimated values of the regression coefficients in these equations generally have the epxected signs: other things being equal, employment of part-timers is relatively high where I is low and where T is high. The supply variables are inter-correlated here, making it difficult to measure their individual contribution; but where they are significant, their coefficients are of the expected sign.

In line 9 the logarithm of the adjusted wage of part-timers ($\ln w_p$) is regressed on the exogenous variables in logarithm form. Here almost one-half of the variance in the dependent variable is explained. As expected, higher values of I and T both act to increase the wage of part-timers. On the other hand, factors that tend to increase the relative supply of part-time job seekers (especially the proportion of young males and the proportion of mothers with children under 15 years of age in the sectoral labor force) tend to depress the wages of part-timers.

Prediction from the Demographic Compositon of Full-time Labor Force: It was argued above that a conservative test of the validity of the supply theory advanced here would be to determine whether the demographic composition of the full-time labor force could be used to predict the proportion of part-timers in a sector. The results of an effort to test this theory is offered in lines 10 and 11. The adjusted coefficients of determination obtained are almost as high as those obtained when the entire labor force is used. An $\bar{R}^2$ of .58 is obtained in line 10 (compared to .61 in the earlier estimation, when the entire labor force was used). Using full-timers yields an $\bar{R}^2$ of .63, when mining, manufacturing, and railroads are excluded (compared to .69 when both part-timers and full-timers are used, and these industries are excluded). Moreover, the values of the individual regression coefficients are in most cases remarkably similar to those obtained when the demographic composition of the entire labor force is used for this prediction.

Conclusions

The preferences of employers and employees tend to influence variations among sectors in the use of part-time employees. Part-time jobs tend to be established where the nature of the work or other circumstances has attracted a labor force that is interested in part-time employment; where the flow of work demands is as well or better served by part-time as by full-time labor; and where indirect costs are low. Employers and employees both tend to be highly responsive to the relative wage of part-time employees.

Notes

1. The results were quite similar to those obtained when I itself is used. See Owen (1977b).

Bibliography

Allenspach, H. 1972. "Flexible Working Time: Its Development and Application in Switzerland." *Occupational Psychology* 46(4): 209–15.

——. 1975. *Flexible Working Hours.* Geneva, Switzerland: International Labor Office.

Barzel, Y. 1973. "The Determination of Daily Hours and Wages." *Quarterly Journal of Economics* 87(May): 220–38.

Barzel, Y., and McDonald, R.J. 1973. "Assets, Subsistence, and the Supply Curve of Labor." *American Economic Review* 73(September): 621–33.

Baum, S., and Young, W. McEwan. 1973. *A Practical Guide to Flexible Working Hours.* London: Kogan Page.

Becker, Gary S. 1965. "A Theory of the Allocation of Time." *Economic Journal* 75(September): 493–517.

Bernard, H., and Ghanadian, M. 1974. "Alternative Work Schedules." Paris: Trade Union Advisory Council of the Organization for Economic Cooperation and Development, mimeo.

Best, F.; Bosserman, P.; and Stern, B. "Income-Free Time Trade Off Preferences of U.S. Workers: A Review of Literature and Indicators." *Leisure Studies,* forthcoming.

Best, F., and Wright, J. 1978. "The Effect of Scheduling on Time-Income Trade-offs." *Social Forces* 57(September): 136–53.

"Betriebsvereinbarung zwischen der Geschäftsleitung und dem Betriebsrat der Firma WOLF-Geräte GmbH, Betzdorf/Sieg." Betzdorf, Germany, 1972.

Bienefeld, M.A. 1972. *Working Hours in British Industry: An Economic History.* London: London School of Economics and Political Science, Weidenfeld and Nicolson.

Bolton, J.H. 1971. *Flexible Working Hours.* Wembley: Anbar.

Bonsall, J.A. 1974. "Flexible Hours and Public Transit in Ottawa." Toronto, Ontario: Presented at the Annual Conference of the Roads and Transportation Association of Canada, mimeo.

Borjas, G.J. 1976. "The Determinants of Hours of Work," mimeo.

Brown, S.C. 1978. "Moolighting Increased Sharply in 1977, Particularly among Women." *Monthly Labor Review* January, p. 28.

Burkhauser, R.V., and Turner, J.A. 1978. "A Time-Series Analysis on Social Security and Its Effect on the Market Work of Men at Younger Ages." *Journal of Political Economy* 86(August): 701–15.

Campbell, A., and Converse, P.E., eds. 1972. *The Human Meaning of Social Change.* New York: Russell Sage Foundation.

Cohen, A.R., and Gadon, H. 1978. *Alternative Work Schedules: Integrating Individual and Organizational Needs.* Reading, Mass.: Addison-Wesley.

DaVanzo, J.; DeTray, D.N.; and Greenberg, D.H. 1975. "The Sensitivity of Male Labor Supply Estimates to Choice of Assumptions." *RAND Paper P 5279*, Santa Monica, August.

de Chalendar, J. 1971. *L'Aménagement du temps*. Paris, Desclée de Brouwer.

Denison, E. 1962. *The Sources of Economic Growth in the United States and the Alternatives before Us*. New York: Committee for Economic Development.

Douglas, P. 1934. *The Theory of Wages*. New York: Macmillan Company.

Easterlin, R.A. 1962. *The Baby Boom in Historical Perspective*. New York: National Bureau of Economic Research.

Economic Report of the President, 1978, Washington, D.C.

Elbing, A.O.; Gadon, H.; and Gordon, J.R.M. 1973. "Time for a Human Time Table." *European Business* no. 39 (Autumn), pp. 46-54.

Elbing, A., and Gordon, J.R.M. 1974. "Self-management in the Emerging Flexible Organization." *Futures* 6(August): 319-28.

Evans, A.A. 1973. *Flexibility in Working Life: Opportunities for Individual Choice*. Paris: Organization for Economic Cooperation and Development.

Evans, M.G. 1975. "A Longitudinal Analysis of the Impact of Flexible Working Hours." *Studies in Personnel Psychology* 6(Spring): 1-11.

Finegan, T.A. 1962. "Hours of Work in the United States." *Journal of Political Economy* 70(October); 452-70.

First National Bank of Boston. 1974. "New Flexible Hours Increase Productivity at First National Bank of Boston," mimeo.

Florence, P.S. 1924. *Economics of Fatigue and Unrest*. New York: Holt.

Ford, H. 1926. "Henry Ford: Why I Favor Five Days' Work with Six Day's Pay" (interview by Samuel Crowther). *World's Work* 25(October): 613-16.

Gilbert, F.L., and Pfouts, R.I. 1958. "A Theory of the Responsiveness of Hours of Work to Changes in the Wage Rate." *Review of Economics and Statistics* 40(May): 116-21.

Golembiewski, R.T.; Hilles, R.; and Kagno, M.J. 1974. "A Longitudinal Study of Flexitime Effects: Some Consequences of an OD Structural Intervention." *Journal of Applied Behavioral Science* 10(4): 503-32.

Gronau, R. 1977. "Leisure, Home Production, and Work—the Theory of the Allocation of Time Revisited." *Journal of Political Economy* 85(December): 1099-123.

Hallaire, J. 1968. *Part-time Employment: Its Extent and Its Problems*. Paris: Organization for Economic Cooperation and Development.

Hanoch, G. 1976. "Hours and Weeks in the Theory of Labor Supply." *RAND Paper R-1787*, Santa Monica, August.

Hedges, J.N. 1975. "How Many Days Make a Workweek?" *Monthly Labor Review* April, pp. 29-36.

——. 1973. "New Patterns for Working Time." *Monthly Labor Review* February, pp. 3-8.

Henle, P. 1962. "Recent Growth of Paid Leisure for U.S. Workers." *Monthly Labor Review* 84: 249-57.

Holley, W.H., Jr.; Armenakis, A.A.; and Feild, H.S., Jr. 1976. "Employee Reactions to a Flexitime Program: A Longitudinal Study." *Human Resource Management* 15(Winter): 21-23.

Jones, E. 1959. "Hours of Work in the United States, 1900-1957." Ph.D. dissertation, University of Chicago, Chicago.

Jones, E. 1978. "Women and Part-week Work." U.S. Department of Labor Grant No. 21-09-76-14.

Kabaj, M. 1968. "Shiftwork and Employment Expansion: Towards an Optimum Pattern." *International Labor Review* 98(September): 245-74.

Kendrick, J.W. 1957. *Productivity Trends in the United States.* New York: National Bureau of Economic Research.

——. 1977. *Understanding Productivity: An Introduction to the Dynamics of Productivity Change.* Baltimore and London: Johns Hopkins University Press.

Khandwalla, P. 1977. *The Design of Organizations.* New York: Harcourt Brace.

Kniesner, T.J. 1976. "The Full-time Workweek in the United States, 1900-1970." *Industrial and Labor Relations Review* 30(October): 3-15.

Knight, F.H. 1921. *Risk, Uncertainty and Profit.* Boston: Houghton Mifflin.

Komarovsky, M.; Lunderg, G.A.; and McInerny, M.A. 1934. *Leisure: A Suburban Study.* New York: Columbia University Press.

Kuznets, S. 1942. *National Income and Its Composition, 1919-38.* New York: National Bureau of Economic Research.

Lansing, J.B., and Hendricks, G. 1967. *Automobile Ownership and Residential Density.* Ann Arbor: University of Michigan, Survey Research Center.

Lauck, W.J., and Sydenstricker, E. 1917. *Conditions of Labor in American Industries: A Summarization of the Results of Recent Investigations.* New York and London: Funk and Wagnalls Company.

Legge, K. 1974. "Flexible Working Hours—Panacea or Placebo?" *Mangement Decision: The European Review of Management Technology* 12(5): 264-80.

Leibenstein, H.M. 1957. "The Theory of Underdevelopment in Backward Economics." *Journal of Political Economy* 65 (April): 91-103.

Leveson, I.F. 1967. "Reductions in Hours of Work as a Source of Productivity Growth." *Journal of Political Economy* 72(April): 199-204.

Lewis, H.G. 1957. "Hours of Work and Hours of Leisure." *Proceedings of Ninth Annual Meeting of Industrial Relations Association.* Cleveland.

——. 1975. "Economics of Time and Labor Supply." *American Economic Review* 65(May): 29-34.

L'horaire libre en 1974; synthèse des travaux du groupe d'études réuni à la demande de M. Gorse, Ministre du Travail et de l'Emploi, et présidé par M. de Chalendar. Paris: La Documentation Française, 1974.

L'horaire variable ou libre: rapport du groupe d'études réuni à la demande du Premier Ministre. Paris: La Documentation Française, 1972.

Linder, S.B. 1970. *The Harried Leisure Class.* New York: Columbia University Press.

Lindsay, C.M. 1971. "On Measuring Human Capital Returns." *Journal of Political Economy* August, pp. 1195-215.

Lloyd, C.R., ed. 1975. *Sex, Discrimination, and the Division of Labor.* New York: Columbia University Press.

Long, C.L. 1958. *The Labor Force under Changing Income and Employment.* Princeton: Princeton University Press.

Maklan, D. 1976. "The Four-day Workweek: Blue-collar Adjustment to a Nonconventional Arrangement of Work and Leisure Time." Ph.D. dissertation, University of Michigan, Ann Arbor.

Manney, J.D. 1975. *Aging in American Society.* Ann Arbor: Institute of Gerontology.

March, J.G., ed. 1965. *Handbook of Organizations.* Chicago: Rand McNally.

Marshall, A. 1920. *Principles of Economics.* London: Macmillan and Co., Ltd.

Martin, V. 1975. *Hours of Work when Workers Can Choose.* Washington, D.C.: Washington's Business and Professional Women's Foundation.

Mazumdar, D. 1959. "The Marginal Productivity Theory of Wages and Disguised Unemployment." *Review of Economic Studies* 26(June): 190-97.

Michael, R.T. 1973. "Education in Non-market Production." *Journal of Political Economy* 81(May/June): 306-27.

Michael, R., and Becker, G.S. 1973. "On the New Theory of Consumer Behavior." *Swedish Journal of Economics* 75(December): 378-96.

Mincer, J. 1962. "On-the-Job Training: Costs, Returns and Some Implications." *Journal of Political Economy* Supplement, October.

——. 1963. "Market Prices, Opportunity Costs and Income Effects," in Carl Christ, ed. *Measurement in Economics.* Stanford: Stanford University Press.

Moes, E., and Bottomley, A. 1968. "Wage Rate Determination with Limited Supplies of Labor in Developing Countries." *Journal of Development Studies* 4(April): 380-85.

Morgenstern, R.D., and Hamovitch, W. 1976. "Labor Supply of Married Women in Part and Full-time occupations." *Industrial and Labor Relations Review* 30(October): 59-67.

Nollen, S.D.; Eddy, B.B.; and Martin, V.H. 1977. "Permanent Part-time Employment: The Manager's Perspective." Report to the Employment and Training Administration, U.S. Department of Labor, under research and development grant No. 21-11-75-16.

Nollen, S.D., and Martin, V.H. 1978a. *Alternative Work Schedules, Part 1: Flexitime.* New York: AMACOM.

——. 1978b. *Alternative Work Schedules, Part 2: Permanent Part-time Employment.* New York: AMACOM.

Northrup, H.R., and Brinberg, H.R. 1950. *Economics of the Workweek.* New York: National Industrial Conference Board.

Oi, W. 1976. "Residential Location and Labor Supply." *Journal of Political Economy* 84(August): S221-S238.

Owen, J.D. 1959. "Reduction in the Workweek, 1900-1957." M.A. essay, New York University, New York.

——. 1964. "The Supply of Labor and the Demand for Recreation." Ph.D. dissertation, Columbia University, New York.

——. 1969. *The Price of Leisure.* Montreal: McGill-Queens University Press, 1970; Rotterdam.

——. 1969. *The Price of Leisure.* Rotterdam: Rotterdam University Press, 1970. Montreal: McGill-Queens University Press, coedition.

——. 1975. Testimony in U.S. House of Representatives, "Alternate Work Schedules and Part-time Career Opportunities in the Federal Government." Hearings before the Subcommittee on Manpower and Civil Service on H.R. 6350, H.R. 9043, H.R. 3925, and S. 792, 94th Cong., 1st sess., Sept. 29, 30, Oct. 7.

——. 1976a. "Economics of Shift Work and Absenteeism," in P.G. Rentos and R.D. Shepard, eds. *Shift Work and Health.* Washington, D.C.: U.S. Department of Health, Education and Welfare.

——. 1976b. "Workweeks and Leisure: An Analysis of Trends, 1948-1975." *Monthly Labor Review* August, pp. 3-8.

——. 1976c. Testimony in U.S. Senate, "Changing Patterns of Work in America, 1976." Hearings before the Subcommittee on Employment, Poverty, and Migratory Labor, on Examination of Alternative Working Hours and Arrangements, 94th Cong., 2d sess., April 7 and 8.

——. 1977a. "Flexitime: Some Problems and Solutions." *Industrial and Labor Relations Review* 30(January): 152-60.

——. 1977b. "An Empirical Analysis of the Voluntary Part-time Labor Market." Report to the Employment and Training Administration, U.S. Department of Labor, under research and development grant No. 21-26-76-13-1.

——. 1977c. Testimony in U.S. House of Representatives, "Part-time Employment and Flexible Work Hours." Hearings before the Subcommittee on Employee Ethics and Utilization, on H.R. 1627, H.R. 2732, and H.R. 2930, 95th Cong., 1st sess., May 24, 26, June 29, July 8, and Oct. 4.

——. 1978. "Why Part-timers Tend to be in Low-wage Jobs." *Monthly Labor Review* June, pp. 11-14.

Owen, J.D.; Haldi, J.; and Vietorisz, T. 1977. "Alternative Work Schedules: A Technology Assessment." Report to the National Science Foundation, under NSF Grant No. IO-40456.

Pigou, A.C. 1929. *The Economics of Welfare.* London: Macmillan and Co., Ltd.

Plowman, D. 1977. "Flexible Working Hours—Some Labour Relations Implications." *Journal of Industrial Relations* 19(September): 307–13. Sydney, Australia.

Poor, R. 1973. *4 Days, 40 Hours: and Other Forms of the Rearranged Workweek.* New York: New American Library.

Price, J.L. 1972. *Handbook of Organizational Measurement.* Lexington, Mass.: D.C. Heath.

Racke, G.M. 1975. "The Effects of Flexible Working Hours." Ph.D. dissertation, University of Lausanne, Switzerland.

Reder, M. 1956. "The Cost of a Shorter Workweek." *IRRA Proceedings.*

Rees, A. 1960. *New Measures of Wage Earner Compensation in Manufacturing 1914–57.* New York: National Bureau of Economic Research.

Robbins, L. 1930. "On the Elasticity of Income in Terms of Effort." *Economica* 10(June): 123–29.

Robinson, C.M.G.F. 1977. "Allocation of Time Across the Day: An Analysis of the Demand and Supply of Shiftworkers." Ph.D. dissertation, University of Chicago, Chicago.

Robinson, J.P. 1977. *Changes in Americans' Use of Time: 1965–1975, A Progress Report.* Cleveland, Ohio: Cleveland State University, Communication Research Center, August.

Robinson, J.P., and Converse, P.E. 1967. *66 Basic Tables of Time Budget Research Data for the U.S.* Ann Arbor: University of Michigan, Survey Research Center.

Rodgers, G.B. 1975. "Nutritionally Based Wage Determination in the Low Income Labor Market." *Oxford Economic Papers* N.S. 27(March): 61–81.

Schein, V.E.; Maurer, E.H.; and Novak, J.F. 1977. "Impact of Flexible Working Hours on Productivity." *Journal of Applied Psychology* 62(4): 463–65.

Schelling, T.C., ed. 1973. "Symposium: Time in Economic Life." *Quarterly Journal of Economics* 87(November): 627–75.

Schulz, J.H. 1976. *The Economics of Aging.* Belmont, Calif.: Wadsworth.

Sen, A.K. 1966. "Peasants and Dualism with and without Surplus Labor." *Journal of Economy* 76(October): 426–49.

Sirageldin, I.; Morgan, J.N.; and Baerwaldt, N. 1966. *Productive Americans: A Study of How Individuals Contribute to Economic Progress.* Ann Arbor: Institute for Social Research, University of Michigan.

Smith, R. 1977. "The Effects of Hours Rigidity on the Labor Market Status of Women." Washington, D.C., mimeo.

Stiglitz, E. 1976. "The Efficiency Wage Hypothesis, Surplus Labor, and the Distribution of Income in L.D.C.'s." *Oxford Economic Papers* N.S. 28(July): 185–207.

Teriet, B. 1977. "Flexiyear Schedules—Only a Matter of Time?" *Monthly Labor Review* December, pp. 62–65.

U.S. Bureau of the Census. 1947. *Current Population Reports,* Series P-50.

——. 1975. *Historical Statistics of the United States.*

——. *Statistical Abstract of the United States,* various issues.

U.S. Bureau of Labor Statistics. 1947. *Hours of Work and Output,* Bulletin no. 917.

——. *Special Labor Force Reports.*

U.S. Civil Service Commission. 1974. *Legal Limitations on Flexible and Compressed Work Schedules for Federal Employees.* GPO.

U.S. Department of Commerce. *Survey of Current Business,* various issues.

——. *The National Income and Product Accounts, 1929–74.*

U.S. Department of Labor. *Employment and Earnings,* various issues.

U.S. House of Representatives. 1975. "Alternate Work Schedules and Part-time Career Opportunities in the Federal Government." Hearings before the Subcommittee on Manpower and Civil Service, on H.R. 6350, H.R. 9043, H.R. 3925, and S. 792, 94th Cong., 1st sess., Sept. 29, 30, Oct. 7.

——. 1977. "Part-time Employment and Flexible Work Hours." Hearings before the Subcommittee on Employee Ethics and Utilization, on H.R. 1627, H.R. 2732, and H.R. 2930, 95th Cong., 1st sess., May 24, 26, June 29, July 8, and Oct. 4.

U.S. Office of Education. 1972. *Digest of Educational Statistics.*

U.S. Senate. 1976. "Changing Patterns of Work in America, 1976." Hearings before the Subcommittee on Employment, Poverty, and Migratory Labor, on Examination of Alternative Working Hours and Arrangements, 94th Cong., 2d sess., Apr. 7 and 8.

U.S. Social Security Administration. 1974. "Report on BDP Flexi-time Study Midpoint Survey." Washington, D.C., mimeo.

Vanek, J. 1973. "Keeping Busy: Time Spent in Housework, United States, 1920–1970." Ph.D. dissertation, University of Michigan, Ann Arbor.

——. 1974. "Time Spent in Housework." *Scientific American,* N.S. 231(November): 116–20.

Vernon, H.M. 1921. *Industrial Fatigue and Efficiency.* London: G. Routledge & Sons, Ltd.

Wade, M. 1973. *Flexible Working Hours in Practice.* Essex, England: Gower.

Walker, K.E., and Woods, M.E. 1976. *Time Use: A Measure of Household Production of Family Goods and Services.* Washington, D.C.: Center for the Family of the American Home Economics Association.

Webber, C.M. 1975. Testimony in "Alternate Work Schedules and Part-time Career Opportunities in the Federal Government." U.S. House of Representatives, Hearings before the Subcommittee on Manpower and Civil Service.

Wellisz, S. 1968. "Dual Economies, Disguised Unemployment and the Unlimited Supply of Labor." *Economica* 35(February): 22–51.

Wheeler, K.E.; Gurman, R.; and Tarnowieski, D. 1972. *The Four-Day Week.* An American Management Association Report, New York.

Wonnacott, P. 1962. "Disguised and Overt Unemployment in Underdeveloped Economies." *Quarterly Journal of Economies* 76(May): 279–97.

Index

About the Author

John D. Owen is professor of economics at Wayne State University. He received the Ph.D. from Columbia University and has taught at the Johns Hopkins University and the Graduate Faculty of the New School for Social Research. Dr. Owen's publications include *The Price of Leisure* and *School Inequality and the Welfare State.*